P9-APO-386

MANAGEMENT SYSTEMS

Working Concepts and Practices

The Irwin Series in Management

Consulting Editor   John F. Mee *Indiana University*

MOORE   *Manufacturing Management*   4th ed.
NIEBEL   *Motion and Time Study*   3d ed.
ROSCOE   *Organization for Production*   3d ed.
JUCIUS   *Personnel Management*   5th ed.
CRUICKSHANK & DAVIS   *Cases in Management*   3d ed.
FILIPETTI   *Industrial Management in Transition*   rev. ed.
SPRIEGEL & MYERS (Editors)   *The Writings of the Gilbreths*
TERRY   *Principles of Management*   4th ed.
VORIS   *Production Control: Text and Cases*   3d ed.
SIMONDS & GRIMALDI   *Safety Management: Accident Cost and Control*   rev. ed.
JONES   *Executive Decision Making*   rev. ed.
NIEBEL & BALDWIN   *Designing for Production*   rev. ed.
PATTON, LITTLEFIELD, & SELF   *Job Evaluation: Text and Cases*   3d ed.
SHULL (Editor)   *Selected Readings in Management*   First Series
SHULL & DELBECQ (Editors)   *Selected Readings in Management: Extensions and Modifications*   Second Series
BRENNAN   *Wage Administration: Plans, Practices, and Principles*   rev. ed.
LAITALA   *Engineering and Organization*
JUCIUS & SCHLENDER   *Elements of Managerial Action*   rev. ed.
HANEY   *Communication: Patterns and Incidents*
JOHNSON   *Personnel and Industrial Relations*
DEPHILLIPS, BERLINER, & CRIBBIN   *Management of Training Programs*
MORRIS   *The Analysis of Management Decisions*   rev. ed.
THAYER   *Administrative Communication*
ROSCOE   *Project Economy*
EELLS & WALTON   *Conceptual Foundations of Business*
HOUSTON   *Manager Development: Principles and Perspectives*
SEIMER   *Cases in Industrial Management*
REED   *Plant Layout: Factors, Principles, and Techniques*
AMMER   *Materials Management*
BROOM   *Production Management*
SCOTT   *Human Relations in Management: A Behavioral Science Approach*
SIEGEL   *Industrial Psychology*
TIMMS   *The Production Function in Business: Fundamentals and Analysis for Management*   rev. ed.
NADLER   *Work Design*
FOX   *The Management Process: An Integrated Functional Approach*
CHAMPION & BRIDGES   *Critical Incidents in Management*
MOORE & KIBBEY   *Manufacturing: Materials and Processes*
MCDONOUGH & GARRETT   *Management Systems: Working Concepts and Practices*
GREENE   *Production Control: Systems and Decisions*
FARMER & RICHMAN   *Comparative Management and Economic Progress*
LING   *The Management of Personnel Relations: History and Origins*
RICHARDS & GREENLAW   *Management Decision Making*

MANAGEMENT SYSTEMS
WORKING CONCEPTS AND PRACTICES

ADRIAN M. McDONOUGH
Professor of Industry
Wharton School of Finance and Commerce
University of Pennsylvania

and

LEONARD J. GARRETT
Director of Computer Research
Temple University

1965

RICHARD D. IRWIN, INC.

HOMEWOOD, ILLINOIS

First Printing, April, 1965
Second Printing, June, 1966
Third Printing, July, 1967

Library of Congress Catalog Card No. 65–17698

PRINTED IN THE UNITED STATES OF AMERICA

ARCHIE

TO ~~WILLIAM~~ B. BUNKER

FOREWORD

TOP MANAGEMENT'S INFORMATION NEEDS*

I have emphasized the factors which you must bear in mind in designing an information system to serve the needs of the top management official, which I presume to represent. I have emphasized the requirement to give me information for planning, controlling, supervising, and reviewing; the requirement for stratifying this information by functions, products, people and geography; the requirement to match the information flow so that it properly segregates the information to match the organizational pattern and structures and, finally, the importance of furnishing to me and my immediate staff complete knowledge about everything that is going on. This would describe an all-seeing "Big Brother" type of network of television cameras that somehow is watching everything that everybody in our worldwide operation is doing individually and, at the same time, integrating all of these operations collectively by any of the myriad of perspectives that I have enumerated. If I have given the impression of an impossible situation, I have succeeded in my endeavor. I do not mean that I feel that it is impossible for the imaginative data processing industry to come up with such equipment. Indeed, I am a little afraid they might! I think the scientific area of information presentation and data processing is in the same dilemma faced by most of the areas of science today and that is the equipment designers and sellers have not been restrained or held responsible for the consequences of their imagination and enthusiasm. Our knowledge of how to make things exceeds our wisdom of what to do with them after they are invented. Our inability to adjust our inter-nation relationships and our military profession to the weaponry of the nuclear physicist, while a conspicuous problem, is no greater than our inability to design management methods and systems which can operate and selectively exploit modern communications and data processing equipments. Management needs to regard this problem as seriously in its area of interest as does the highway engineer the problem of designing his structures to cope with the speed and lethality of the modern motor vehicle. The top manager's curiosity is insatiable, but his needs cannot be met unless data

* From a talk presented to graduate students at the Wharton School of Finance and Commerce, University of Pennsylvania, April 19, 1963.

processors can find some ways of satisfying this curiosity with something less than complete information.

MAJ. GEN. WILLIAM B. BUNKER, U. S. A.
DEPUTY COMMANDING GENERAL
ARMY MATERIEL COMMAND

ACKNOWLEDGMENTS

The development of any management system must reflect the efforts of many people. Similarly, the writing of a book on management systems involves the ideas and work of many individuals. During the period in which this book has been written we have been privileged to meet with and discuss management systems with a large number of educators and managers. In particular, we have been influenced by the ideas of Jay Forrester of M. I. T. and his work in the areas of industrial dynamics and information-oriented organizations. The realistic applications of behavioral approaches in management as developed by Leonard Sayles at Columbia University have also had considerable influence on our thinking.

We would like to thank M. W. Anderson, Manager of Systems, Crucible Steel Company; J. J. Black, Director of Budgets, I. B. M.; J. D. Gallagher, Manager of Systems, Socony-Mobil; and C. J. Thomsen, Senior Vice President of Texas Instruments for their help in expressing the practical problems of management systems. Arthur Thursland, Director of Data Processing Studies for J. B. Joynt, Incorporated was most helpful in the development of our case study materials. The chapter on Output Format and Display reflects some very interesting discussions with Ted Mills and Robert Widener of Information Management Facilities, Incorporated.

Colonel Richard A. Hansen, Chief, Data Systems Office, Army Materiel Command, is given a special note of thanks for the insights he provided in the problems of management of change and for his suggestions as to the combined study of organization responsibilities and management systems. We are pleased to dedicate this book to Major General William B. Bunker, Deputy Commanding General of the Army Materiel Command. We sincerely appreciate his encouragement and his guidance.

We acknowledge particularly the substantial help that Dr. Herbert R. Northrup, Chairman of the Industry Department at the Wharton School of Finance and Commerce gave us in the development and publication of the manuscript. His support included opportunities to test our ideas and funds to facilitate our research. Karl C. Lange and

Kenneth R. Rand, graduate research assistants for the authors, monitored the writing of the manuscript and have contributed many ideas that are expressed in this book. Beatrice McDonough typed the manuscript through the seemingly endless revisions. Her questions and comments made us check our reasoning through each chapter.

TABLE OF CONTENTS

PREFACE

Radical and significant changes are taking place in the concepts and techniques of management systems. There are very few people today who can claim to be experts in all aspects of these developments. For these reasons there is much retraining that is going on in industry and government, as well as that training that is taking place in colleges and universities. Students of management systems, therefore, are not confined to the academic world. In this book we have attempted to present a down-to-earth, relatively non-technical exposition in which certain of the major developments in management systems can be studied. The presentation is not meant to be theoretical or sophisticated. Rather, its main purpose is to give what we believe is a useful set of guideposts for tieing together many of the elements of management systems development.

We have chosen to emphasize a practical framework for a three-pronged attack on the problems of the design of management systems. The approaches of (1) management problem definition, and (2) manpower planning and control, are blended with the approach of (3) systems design and data processing. Systems design is treated as a means for bringing together the best definition of management problems and the best combination of personnel talents and systems techniques for handling these problems.

As environments shift and as any change takes place in one of the areas of *problems, skills,* or *systems,* good management practice calls for review in the other two areas. Only with a balanced approach to these three areas can a management claim that it is in control of its organization. The practicality of this approach is that, on the job, problems, skills, and systems are interacting simultaneously. An approach that considers one without the others can often cause more harm than good. It is for this reason that this book is written with threads of management problem definition, personnel skill requirements, and systems design woven into each chapter.

There are many ways to look at the world in which we live and the organizations in which we work. There is no reason to expect that one view will encompass all that is important in managing an organization. Rather, many views in many time sequences with much overlapping are necessary before one achieves depth and breadth in a particular

xiii

firm's management. This book takes one path through the challenge of management complexities. It concentrates on the problems of information handling in the individual organization. Emphasis is placed on the responsibilities of *managers* as they influence management systems. Although certain parts of this book are written from the point of view of the systems specialist, this is done so that a manager can better understand how his needs may be helped by the systems specialist.

In our society the responsibility for the utilization of land, labor, and capital has been placed in the hands and minds of a group of our citizens who are called "management". Progress in our economy is, to a large degree, governed by the abilities of management in business, in labor unions, and in government to effectively do their jobs. A manager normally produces nothing of a physical nature. Rather, he processes decisions for relating the efforts of others. To do this he stands in the communication "stream" of his particular business.

In the broadest sense, information is the basis for all mental consciousness. This general view is appropriate to either the study of individuals or to groups of any scope and complexity. As organizations have expanded in size and complexity managers have been forced to seek better arrangements that would (1) identify significant problems as quickly as possible; (2) disseminate these problems to appropriate individuals for decisions; and (3) provide the specific information needed for the decisions. Gradually there has evolved a framework for analysis of the formal communications requirements of management. The approach first admits that only a part of the total communications that take place in an organization can be formalized into information systems. This book identifies the varied characteristics of management problems and the related difficulties in attempting to establish formal information systems. Thus the limitations, as well as the opportunities, are developed for the reader.

A particular kind of economics—the economics of information systems—is to be presented to the reader as a balance between the values of the information to be carried by a system and the costs of designing and operating the system. By considering the values produced for management by information systems it becomes possible to connect the systems approach directly to alternative functional views of management organization and operation. For example, management concepts such as "authority", "responsibility", "decentralization", etc., can be enriched in meaning by adding the related communications viewpoint.

We have reached a point in our society where over fifty per cent of our labor force is classified as "white-collar". With increasing efficiency in the technology of production we may forecast that white-collar information gathering and using personnel will make up an even higher percentage of our labor force. The effectiveness of a large part of our economy will thus be influenced by the processing of key information through well thought out formal communications systems. This book is written with this increasing demand for information in mind. *Management Systems,* for example, provides a framework in which the new developments in electronic data processing can be analyzed In the latter part of this book a case example is used to demonstrate computer utilization.

The presentation is organized into fifteen chapters. The early chapters identify the need for a thorough analysis of information needs and describe the scope of interrelationships between organization people and organization systems. These chapters provide a master plan framework for the study of management information systems. This plan is developed using a phased approach for systems development. In particular, these phases are described as they relate to organizing a systems study, to making systems design assignments, and to controlling progress of a systems study.

The last half of the book goes back over the materials which are presented in the first half, this time at a much more specific level. The practical problems of working with statements of information needs and with the design of specific aspects of an information system are analyzed in Chapters 8 to 14. Chapter 15 provides a summary and reviews the techniques described in Chapters 8 through 14. Appendix B contains discussion questions which may be used to review and extend the context of each chapter.

Chapter 4 provides a management game built around the establishment and operation of a management systems department in a manufacturing firm. In this exercise the executive committee of the firm selects key problems and sends them to the management systems department for study. Acting the part of the manager of the department, the reader assigns priorities, hires systems personnel and puts them to work on his selected set of assignments. In simulated time, the systems analysts produce "reports" which further define the problems and allow refining of the priorities among assignments. These assignments cover a rather wide range of management studies and, therefore, show contrasts between the types of approaches that can be used in systems development. Cost and savings reports are produced in the game and the reader can test his skills in a profit and loss framework.

Copies of these reports are placed in the Appendix and are referenced into the game by a scale of achievement which, in turn, is determined by the reader's choice of assignments. There is, therefore, an action and reaction in the game representing the realism of systems development in practice. This game can be played in a few hours. (We use three to four hours in our classes to introduce, play, and recapitulate the game.) The material presented here is not like the traditional case treatment. We believe you will enjoy seeing the management systems concepts and techniques as presented in the framework of this "game".

This management game provides background which is then applied in succeeding chapters of the book. A particular assignment in the area of manpower planning and control is carried through all the phases of systems development down to the programming design for a computer run. Another assignment covers the problems of setting priorities among projects and arranging for feedback and evaluation of results. The case materials provided with this game give opportunity to work with specific examples in the practice of systems development. These specifics include coverage of the concepts and techniques for problem definition, classification and coding, documentation, systems design, and computer programming. We elected to demonstrate these concepts and techniques in some depth for the one area of manpower planning and control rather than to show a variety of applications. The reason for this is that a real perspective of what is involved in a management system can best be illustrated by developing one system. In this way the scope and complexity of systems work is made more understandable and the necessary detail can be shown. For classroom use, we expanded the coverage by assigning outside readings and problems in many of the functional areas including production, engineering, and financial illustrations.

In joining together in this writing we have sought to recognize both the practical needs of education in this field, as well as the problems of management systems on the job. It is for this reason that we have provided specific examples wherever we could bring them into the text. In particular, we suggest that the reader take the time to review the case study in Chapter 4 after he has completed the chapter. We further suggest that this case study be used as the device in which to see the interrelations between each of the problem areas covered in Chapters 4 through 14.

In recent years much progress has been made in the application of quantitative approaches to management problems. Operations research and management science applications are increasing every day. Developments in the behavioral sciences have also been making their contributions, although at an understandably slower rate. This book says that the time is right for joint attention to the behavior of inanimate systems and the behavior of animate people. This is why we have placed our presentation in the context of man-machine systems. The title of the book reflects to this emphasis on the blending of people in organizations and the systems with which they work. The case materials, likewise, were chosen to show these interrelationships.

In particular, we have emphasized the interdependencies among managers and systems specialists. A manager who believes that he can run the company without systems is mistaken. A systems specialist who assumes that his systems can run the company is mistaken. Our emphasis is on the extension and blending of management skills. We propose that such extension and blending is facilitated when a management thinks in terms of its systems, as well as its personnel, as being "skilled". In effect, a good system "knows what to do" when faced with certain circumstances. Skills in this sense have been built into the system. This skill conversion is the vital link between the interests of the manager and the interests of the systems man. With this reasoning by a management it will encourage its systems specialists to spend more time studying manpower skill requirements. And it will also encourage all of its managers to become familiar with the concepts and techniques of management systems development. In this book we have attempted to present a set of working concepts and techniques to aid in the study of such a blending of manpower and systems skills.

Today it is so easy to get lost in either the generalizations or the details of management systems. We have tried to give as concrete a framework as possible for overall studying in this field. Each chapter is written so that its scope can be extended in breadth or depth as a particular reader desires. In our own work, for example, we have used a comprehensive case study of a management information system in a chemical company. We traced this case study through each of the subjects covered in this book. As another example, we were faced with a disparity of knowledge about computer programming background among our students. Our solution was to assign a programmed learning text on this subject. Our purpose was not to teach programming, but rather, to make sure that our students were familiar with the techniques, their advantages, and their present limitations. In both cases this book was used to provide the central theme to which we related the case study and the programmed text material. In this sense, we believe this book can be used with a variety of course outlines as the user wishes to emphasize theory, working concepts, or applications in practice.

Theory provides the probes for exploration into the little known areas of business knowledge. Practice provides guidance for the "how to do it", or technique, aspects of business operations. We believe that a very important area of study is that between the level of theory and the level of technique. Many books have been, and are being, written at both the theory level and the technique and hardware levels of business management. The gap between theory and its application is what we have chosen to call *working concepts.*

Working concepts are ideas that can be used by a manager as he seeks to improve his own planning and control decisions on the job. These concepts are phrased in a language which is less abstract than most theory and in less detail than is usual at the technique level. The presentation is given in a framework in which each concept is related to other concepts. Examples are used to show the significance of these working concepts. It is in this context, and with these criteria, that we have written this book. Departures into theory and technique have been made only where we believed it necessary and useful.

ADRIAN M. McDONOUGH
LEONARD J. GARRETT

PHILADELPHIA, PENNSYLVANIA
March, 1965

Chapter 1

THE SCOPE OF
MANAGEMENT SYSTEMS

With the growing requirements and costs of operating a business, it is especially appropriate that the best concepts and techniques be used for business planning and control. "Best" is a relative term, however, especially when applied to business. Both the art and the science of business are continually in a state of flux. One of the significant areas of change is that related to the study of organization structures as they are influenced by the information needs of the organization.

Until recently it has been normal practice to view organization structure problems as separate, in isolation from the communications problems of the organization. At best, the interdependencies of these two problem areas have been treated in very general terms. An example is the statement to the effect that coordination in an organization requires good communication. Usually such efforts as were made to improve these communications were handled by a separate group concerned with systems or clerical methods.

Now we see opportunities for a simultaneous attack on the problems of how an organization should be structured and how information in that organization should be structured. The basic idea is that any change in organization structure has an impact upon the requirements of the information system, and, conversely, that any change in the content of an information system has an impact on the effectiveness of the organization structure.

Although this idea is easy to state, it is not simple to implement. It is easier to study authority and responsibility in isolation, and it is easier

1

to study simple document flows; it is much more difficult to blend, into one analysis, all the many authorities, responsibilities, skills, information requirements, and data processing methods. Yet this is the challenge faced by the business manager when the structures of organization and information are to be studied for relationships, and these relationships are most critical for business success.

The availability of the computer has solved, and created, many business management problems. Problems requiring simple but voluminous data processing are being placed rapidly on electronic equipment. However, certain problems that were assumed to be simple are now being seen more realistically, and the overall result is that an expanded effort is now being organized under the general heading of "systems." Any combination of pieces that achieves some purpose is a system. If something is organized, we say it is systematic. Thus there is a close tie between the study of "organization" and the study of "systems."

WHAT IS A SYSTEM?

Now let us look at the concept of a system and at some examples of systems applications. We live in a fantastic web of systems. Our day-to-day existence is both supported and restricted by systems. Systems influence our choices of government and our standards of health and welfare; they even determine many of our family and social relationships. The costs of developing and keeping these systems going is astronomical. Yet more and more efforts are being devoted to getting "even better" systems.

Every occupation has its systems. There are systems for getting good things done, but there are also systems for accomplishing evil. Some people fight for their "system." Other people devote all their lives to improving a particular system: medical systems, legal systems, military systems, business systems, and so on.

If one were asked to replace the term The Electronics Age, he might very well substitute The Age of Systems. The fact is that, for a wide variety of reasons, our society—and apparently all others—is seeking progress at an accelerated rate. Newer and better systems are sought as the means to climb to new levels of accomplishments. It was inevitable that people would begin to ask: What is a system? and How do we tell whether a system is good or bad?

A system is a means for accomplishing some purpose or set of purposes. A full description of any system therefore requires the spelling out of (1) the specific expected accomplishments and (2) the specific mechanisms and procedures which are to be used in the process.

An *automobile* is a system with the purpose of transportation. It has specific mechanisms of ignition, combustion engine, driving and driven wheels, and steering.

A *telephone* is a system with the purpose of communication. Its means are a receiver of sound vibrations, a converter to electrical vibrations, a network of wires, and a reconverter for producing sound vibrations at the other end.

An *economic* system is designed with the purpose of providing a nation with a steady economic growth and for distributing the benefits of such growth to the citizens of that nation. Rules, and guidance in the application of these rules, are part of an economic system. Unlike the automobile and the telephone, an economic system does not have physical mechanisms. There are some similarities, however, in that we can think of "mechanisms" in the market and in price setting.

There are forces at work that make it necessary for all fields to take more scientific and better organized approaches to their systems. The field of business management both influences and is influenced by this general acceleration. New systems are being sought by business to improve its planning and organization. The forces are rising costs, foreign competition, customer demands for increased quality and reliability, and the very increased complexity of doing business. These forces determine the purposes for which new business systems ideas must be developed and used.

As new ideas in the physical sciences appear, they are carried into our daily lives by the industries of our country. New fuels, new medicines, and new communications equipment all necessitate requirements for changes in the planning and organization of companies. The shift from the problems of routine, old-product production to the problems and uncertainties of new-product production places entirely new importance on the development of management systems.

It is important at this point to emphasize that the term *management systems* has many meanings today. Let us make our meanings as clear as possible:

1. The first way we use management systems in this book (for example, in the title) is as a label for *all* those activities that contribute to the use of logic in any organization. Management systems, by this broad definition, must include the systematic *thinking* of people at all levels in the organization, as well as the results of this thinking. Management systems, in this sense, offers a philosophy for management progress. This philosophy serves the purpose of keeping the horizon open for management improvements.
2. The second use of *management systems* is when we view the inventory of individual systems in an organization. In this sense it is simply the plural form of the term management system.

3. *A* management system (singular) is a label for one particular area of study and application. The boundaries of this area usually determine the name given to the system. This use in the singular serves the purpose of narrowing and putting into practice the present state of the arts for a particular study area.

The term management information systems also has many meanings today. We use *management information systems* as a direct synonym for *management systems*. The insertion of information between management and systems is used by us to highlight and clarify the relation of management and systems. In this book we develop the idea that a management system informs. Such informing can take place by a change which is registered in a man's mind. He has received information. He is informed. We propose that it is important to think of a medium (a paper form, a punch card, or a computer memory) as also being more informed through the processing of data in a good system. (If "being informed" is appropriate only for humans, we can at least say that the systems medium should hold more information as a result of processing.) This common focus on information of all kinds, we believe, is the important new development in the state of the arts in management. It is for these reasons that we concentrate on the middle word in management *information* systems.

WHAT IS A MANAGEMENT INFORMATION SYSTEM?

From the examples given earlier, we can see that a system can be made from any given set of pieces put together in any set of relationships. A good system must serve a worthwhile purpose and should have reasonable cost compared to its worth. A management information system is a communications process in which data are recorded and revised to support management decisions for planning, operating, and controlling. Designers of a management information system attempt to maximize the use of common data to satisfy the information requirements of many managers.

A management information system accumulates, processes, stores, and transmits data to "relevant" people in the organization, informing them and thereby becoming "information." Until it reaches this last stage in a system, data is only potential information. A good rule to remember is that information informs only when there is a recognized need to know. Information systems are being designed to support management needs-to-know in many critical problem areas of business. The variety and scope of these systems is very broad. They cover systems for planning, operating and controlling, and they include all the traditional functional areas such as marketing, production, and finance. And they cover both external and internal information requirements.

In recent years, especially because of the expense of using the electronic computer, companies have found it necessary to plan and schedule systems design on a much more formal basis. Significant events and activities are identified, target dates are set, and resources are allocated to meet these dates. These activities and events become the critical points upon which management plans and controls the progress of particular systems studies.

While individual systems are getting attention, special arrangements are also being made to study the relationships between systems. Central files are established to collect (in one place) the classifications and codes that go into a variety of systems. Periodically this file is analyzed to seek out any duplication that may exist, or any new combination of data that may give management even better information. This file, in effect, provides a special arrangement for a continuing purification of the information flow within an organization.

WHO IS RESPONSIBLE FOR A MANAGEMENT INFORMATION SYSTEM?

A purification of the information flowing in an organization can involve every job position, high or low. To some degree every employee accumulates, transfers, uses, or stores information in one form or another. To the degree that such activities are formally recognized as part of the work involved in each position this is a responsibility for information about which management should be concerned.

When the movement of information among positions is brought into the picture, responsibilities are no longer on a *one to one* basis in a job position. Rather, they become compound and shared between a number of jobs. This is true when a management system is being used on a day-to-day basis, and it is also true during the time that such a system is being analyzed and designed.

Increasingly, it is becoming standard practice to assemble task forces or project teams to do the actual design of the system. The composition of such teams may change as the various phases are reached. The idea is that the best abilities and experiences are form-fitted to each phase of the systems study. The full impact of this approach is seen in the recent trend toward the use of project managers in industry. To get the feel of this idea, let us assume an operating organization, with all its line and staff levels and departments. Then picture a set of new jobs that have to be done. Instead of assigning these jobs directly to the line and staff departments, we will give them to a project manager, who is given the authority of the president of the firm for this project. The project manager then places demands on the line and staff departments, as required, to expedite his project. Normally, only the most important problems get the project manager treatment, but some organizations, especially in military research and development, utilize project managers for all their jobs. In such cases, all former line departments—such as production—are considered staff departments under the project managers. In such organizations we see extremes of pressures, explicit priority setting, and internal competition for resources. This is a new look in organization and departmentation, and it has a strong influence on systems design efforts.

The significant change reflected here is that companies are now specifying systems design as a prime responsibility of all management. In the past this responsibility was delegated to specialized staff groups. Each organization has to set its own priorities for the particular systems it needs and is willing to pay for. We find an increasing number of companies establishing high-level committees for the specific purpose of setting these priorities.

Recent studies, in both the United States and Europe, indicate that up to 90 percent of the work involved in any white-collar job involves the seeking and obtaining of information. A typical engineering department spends only 10 percent of its time in making engineering decisions; the rest is spent in seeking and obtaining the information that goes into these decisions. Similar proportions of time are involved in accounting, marketing, finance, production, and other management areas.

In the past, white-collar work was viewed as though it were composed of 90 percent functional decisions and only 10 percent information collection. The realization that the reverse proportions are typical has led to even greater emphasis on the development of information systems. A good system will facilitate the obtaining of pertinent and accurate information, and it will provide such information on a timely basis. If we think of 90 percent of man-hours and salaries going into information processing, we can see why management seeks, and will be seeking, improvements in the concepts and techniques of this approach. One breakthrough can yield impressive payoffs.

It is possible, on the other hand, to leap to the conclusion that management information systems are cure-alls and can insure almost automatic operation of a business. This is not in accord with the facts, and for this reason we must look at some of the qualifications of this approach.

Consider the analogy between the "game" of business and the game of football. It would be easy to plan our gridiron defense, if the offense would use only one play; we would finally come up with the one best way to position our players for greatest effectiveness. But in football, as in business, the offense uses a variety of plays. This means that we have three sets of problems:

1. One set is associated with what the offense will do.
2. Having conjectured the offense's move, we must ask: "If this is the case, how should we defend against this particular offense?"
3. Our third set of problems, of course, is associated with the degree of confidence that we feel in our guess. If we really can't tell what the opposition is going to do, we may have to take compromise positions; that is, lay half-way back to cover a pass, but be ready to back up the line if they decide to run the ball.

THE NEED FOR FLEXIBILITY TO ACCOMMODATE CHANGE

A similar situation exists in attempting to develop management information systems. If situations are static, we can design static systems. If we are faced with constantly changing situations, we must necessarily build flexibility into our systems. In essence, this means that our systems can only be as good as our ability to predict, and thereby influence, our future situations. In turn this means that all the problems of forecasting and making adjustments remain with us, and must be considered in designing our system. It also means that an almost perfect combination of job positions and talents for one set of problems can become cumbersome and obsolete with shifts in the business environment and the coming into being of a new set of problems. Change, or lack of change, is especially important in decisions about how far to go in freezing management systems. Radical changes in the environment of the business can make expensive systems obsolete.

Modern systems design is expensive, and, as with any investment, management must predict the rate of return over the useful life of the system. The weakness of the systems approach is that we may be tempted to give everything a full systems treatment, rather than use this approach with moderation and on a very selective basis. Rube Goldberg has shown us, through his cartoons, how systems can be made much too complicated for the result accomplished. Today, under pressure for accomplishment, we must be careful that we do not simply add complication that will fail to produce better results. We must be sure that old systems are not thrown out just because they are old; and, of course, we must not reject new systems just because they are new. The test should be whether we get better results from the new system, and (if the costs are higher) are the better results worth these extra costs.

BEWARE OF THE TOTAL SYSTEM

The present quest for "total systems" should be recognized as a hazardous quest for the ideal. If the use of "total systems" leads to the impression that it is simple to integrate systems—or if it is only a merchandizing slogan—then the term should be discarded. It is better to think of a "system" only as being more complete or more comprehensive than the earlier process. The question: Should certain systems be integrated? is just as important—if not more important—than: How can these systems be integrated? When nature puts certain odd systems together the result is often a freak, and managers must guard against integrated, but freakish, systems.

Because management information systems are not cure-alls, it is especially important that a realistic attitude be maintained by those who authorize and those who design these systems. Despite rapid advances in recent years, systems concepts and techniques leave much room for improvement. There is a great deal of work to be done, and this means that opportunities exist for those who become interested in management information systems.

This book proposes that one of the major opportunities is that of a blending approach which brings together the joint analysis of the organization and information structures. The following chapter describes some characteristics of such a joint analysis.

Chapter 2

THE CHARACTERISTICS OF AN ORGANIZATION/INFORMATION STRUCTURE

More and more we realize the need for bringing together our studies in the areas of organization and information systems. The term Organization/Information Structure is used in this chapter to represent this movement toward joining people and systems for effective management.

The traditional approach to organization has emphasized the relating of the authority and the responsibilities for various job positions. Varying types of authority have been analyzed and principles of authority have been made available to managers as they design organization relationships. The emphasis is on people relationships. Some of the principles of organization that demonstrate the people-orientation of the organization approach are listed below.

- Be sure *adequate provision* is made *for all activities.*
- *Group* (departmentalize) *activities* on some logical basis.
- *Limit* the number of *subordinates* reporting to each executive.
- *Define* the *responsibilities* of each department, division, and subdivision.
- *Delegate authority* to subordinates wherever practicable.
- Make *authority and responsibility equal.*
- Provide for *controls* over those to whom authority is delegated.
- Avoid *dual subordination.*
- Distinguish clearly between *line authority, functional authority,* and *staff relationships.*
- Develop *methods for coordination.*

9

Note how the emphasis in these organization principles is on people-to-people relationships. Such relationships are, of course, extremely important, and they will be highlighted in the following pages. In particular, these relationships between people will be blended with the systems approach to organization. Organization theory and practice have been with us for many years, with a particular set of concepts and vocabulary. The theory and practice of management information systems, however, has been a rather recent development, although it, too, has its particular set of concepts and vocabulary.

KEY RELATIONS BETWEEN ORGANIZATION AND SYSTEMS

To demonstrate that these fields are very closely related, we can consider the relationships among certain key items of vocabulary in each field. These terms often become merged in the working vocabulary used in day-to-day assignments. The first term of each of the following pairs represents a typical organization concept, and the second term represents a related term in systems work (see Figure 2–1).

FIGURE 2–1

RELATED CONCEPTS OF ORGANIZATION AND SYSTEMS

(The inner circle contains the traditional set of management duties; the outer circle contains the related systems terms in a sequence that covers the "life cycle" of the development of a management information system.)

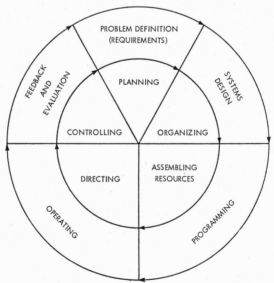

The starting point in this figure is where formal arrangements for problem definition and planning receive management attention. One cycle of the sequence is completed when management asks: How well did we do—and what should we do next? The cycle repeats itself, of course, as long as there is a need to redefine problems and provide adjustments to plans.

1. PLANNING *AND* PROBLEM DEFINITION

These terms represent the recognition of a need for action; they connote the initiating phases in the management process. Planning is the general term used in organizational analysis, and Problem Definition is the term applied to the initial stages of a business system design. The importance of planning, which requires care in identifying the factors that can influence the future of the business, is generally accepted. And only when such factors are spelled out, and given weights of importance, can a management write out its plan of action.

The same sort of thinking applies in management systems. Problem definition requires factor identification and the assigning of priorities to these factors; it is a special form of planning in which the plan of action leads to the development of a management system. Just as all plans are subject to change, so are problem definitions. In both cases, arrangements or allowance for such changes during a cycle must be provided, and especially at the end of a cycle (i.e., in the control or feedback phase shown in Figure 2–1). Chapters 7 and 8 (Setting Systems Priorities and Information Requirements Design) look into some of the specifics involved in the development of problem definition for systems design.

2. ORGANIZING *AND* SYSTEMS DESIGN

While planning and problem definition give us the guidance for *what* is to be accomplished, Organizing and Systems Design refer to *how* we go about accomplishing the objectives. Books on organization stress the importance of the careful identification of activities and the grouping of these activities into departments and other subdivisions. Principles of organization have been developed to guide management in the designing of levels and specialties in an organization structure.

A similar situation exists in the systems design phase of management systems. With a preliminary problem definition available for guidance, systems design takes over the job of providing the general logic for solving the problem. The significance of the "general logic" in the above sentence is that the systems designer should concentrate on refining the initial problem definition. The result should be a gross structure of the management system that defines the data inputs, the appropriate processing of data, and the system's end results. Like the organization chart, the systems design does not show the detailed procedures or instructions which must later be developed to actually carry out the work. Chapter 9 (Systems Design) provides guidance for this phase of systems design.

3. ASSEMBLING RESOURCES AND COMPUTER PROGRAMMING

Assembling Resources refers to those efforts in the management process that are necessary to obtain the men, materials, machines and money required to carry out the plans of the organization. Computer Programming refers to the assembly of the actions performed on data in a data processing system. In particular, Computer Programming assembles:

1. The ideas of men,
2. The characteristics of data,
3. The characteristics of computer hardware,
4. The economies of data processing.

These four factors are the men, the materials, the machines, and the money aspects of data processing. As will be shown in Chapter 10 (Programming Design Background), the programming of computers is accomplished by careful attention to the assembly of these four factors. The flow of men's ideas arrives at the programming stage after careful analysis in the previous stages of problem definition and system design. The assembly of the raw material for a data processing system depends upon careful attention to the original entry of data and to the forms in which they are obtained. Computers, like all machinery, must be rated as to feeds and speeds. The money problems of programming computers can be expressed in the standard context of budgeting and accounting. Though the glamor and publicity associated with the computer have made it appear quite otherwise, the fundamental problems are those which have always been related to the assembly of resources for a production function.

4. DIRECTING AND OPERATING

Directing is the "putting into action" phase in the management process. It is concerned with getting things done once all the preliminary activities of planning, organizing, and assembly of resources have been accomplished. It then remains to see that the work is done according to plan. Directing, therefore, involves the giving of instructions to subordinates for the carrying out of day-to-day job requirements.

The Operating problems in the day-to-day processing of a management information system are quite similar to those of Directing. Once a system has been designed and programmed, it must be placed in the operations schedule of a computer facility. Modern computer equipment requires very explicit instructions, much more than in the past when instructions were given only to people. Instructions to computer operating personnel also are necessary to achieve the proper inputs of data, the appropriate processing steps within the computer production equipment, and the required content and format of the output. A brief analysis of computer facility operating problems is contained in Chapter 12 (Systems Operations).

Life in a computer center is "machine-paced." The expensive equipment must be scheduled in a "tight" manner, so that maximum utilization is obtained. As with all expensive investments in equipment, it usually pays to develop precise procedures for operations.

5. CONTROLLING AND FEEDBACK WITH EVALUATION

The control function has played an important part in the management process. As work progresses under a certain plan, it is necessary that at least periodic checks be made to see if things are going according to the plan. Is policy being followed? Are standards being met? What adjustments should be made? These are typical questions asked in the control phase of the management process cycle.

If we could plan perfectly, and accomplish our objectives perfectly, there would be little need for control. Typically, however, it must be expected that adjustments will have to be made to bring accomplishments in line with the plan—or perhaps to bring the plan in balance with the limited, available resources.

Feedback, with evaluation of results, has a similar purpose in the operations of a management information system. This similarity is so great in some cases that Feedback and Control are the same thing, with feedback representing the communication of actual results for comparison and contrast with the planned results.

In computerized systems, the planned results may be written in the computer. Periodically, actual results may also be placed in the computer and comparisons may be made. If the computer is programmed to note only when the actual results fail to meet the required planned results, we have an example of the "exception principle" at work. More and more use is being made of exception reporting in management information systems, but its use requires careful attention to the relationships of planned results and the array of possible actual results. Exceptions must be identified explicitly, and this can be done only if the plan is made specific at the start of the cycle.

BLENDING THE APPROACHES

As was stated earlier, the purpose of showing these pairs of concepts is to demonstrate the close relationships between the traditional concepts of organization and the more recent concepts of management systems. Now let us go one step farther and see how the new developments in management systems can reinforce and extend the concepts of organization.

THE NEED FOR BLENDING

Organization structure refers to people-to-people relationships, and primarily to the questions:

a) Who reports to whom, from an authority point of view?
b) Who has responsibility for particular problems?

Both are extremely important questions, and clear answers are necessary for the effective operations of a business. However, a limitation is inherent in these questions. Organizations in a constant state of change cannot work with static answers. People can change their "who reports to whom" patterns according to minute-to-minute changes in the complexity of the organization, a reminder that a rigid organization structure is not necessarily a good thing. A business can be so perfectly structured that it loses flexibility and cannot adjust to new situations.

The traditional approach to organization tells management that it must make decisions or choices of emphases while setting up departments or divisions: to organize by product or by service, for example, or by process, function, territory, or customer. The ensuing selection of a particular base for departments provides the opportunity for specialization to take place.

Specialization is cited as a prerequisite for departmentation; and it is also cited as an advantage of departmentation. Specialization, of course, refers to the splitting up of tasks so that pieces with homogeneous characteristics can be sorted into homogeneous departments. The advantages of specialization are well known, but the prices paid for specialization are not. In the past, the disadvantages have been included in the generalization that with specialization one must also do something about coordination and communication between departments.

Too often the result has been very efficient internal operations *in* departments but extremely inefficient operations *between* departments, so that many of the problems have fallen between the blocks on the organization chart. A title for a department can, at best, be only a generalization for what takes place in that department. Therefore departmentation must be more than a simple choice of emphasis on product, territory, or customer.

Whenever one choice is made, arrangements must be made to take care of all the other aspects. For example, organization by product does not eliminate the need for decisions by territory, process, or customer. Thus we have, under any circumstances, the need for a much more comprehensive analysis than that which is typically portrayed in departmentation. In practice, departmentation decisions may be made with only superficial study, but normally a careful analytical study should precede these decisions.

Let us think about an organization chart that is more realistic than those we normally see; and let us discuss both the approach of organization structure and the approach of management information systems. Radio Corporation of America, for example, has an organization chart that covers only the engineering function and identifies more than 3,000 specific job positions. It shows levels and specializations. It shows who reports to whom, and, by reading the titles, you can get some idea of the kinds of decisions made in each position. Despite its detail, this chart is only a generalization for depicting information flow between and among these positions. Who talks to whom? Who asks questions? And who answers these questions? Questions are never asked wholesale, they are asked "retail." Questions are not really asked by departments, they are asked by individuals.

The point to be emphasized is that departmentation, as a management approach, gives us the general structure of organization. It provides a general frame of reference, and as such we should not expect too much from it. It is one thing to describe an organization by departments; it is another thing to get the organization to operate efficiently. Departmentation is indispensable. It is simply that we cannot stop with the general framework, but must add to it the specifics it takes to operate the firm. The systems approach is one way to study these specifics. In this sense, then, the systems approach is a logical extension of the traditional approach to organization structure.

The treatment of systems as a logical extension of the organization structure can—at a minimum—help prevent duplication of efforts in the management process. A major problem today is that systems departments are developing and using new vocabularies that have the same or similar meanings as those used in the rest of the organization. This "battle of jargon" all too often leads to conflicts which serve no useful purpose. Communication is blocked and coordination becomes extremely burdensome. New terminology, that serves a useful purpose, should of course be encouraged. Duplicating terminology should be identified, and it should be stressed that such terms, for all practical purposes, are synonyms.

FIGURE 2–2

A STANDARD ORGANIZATION CHART

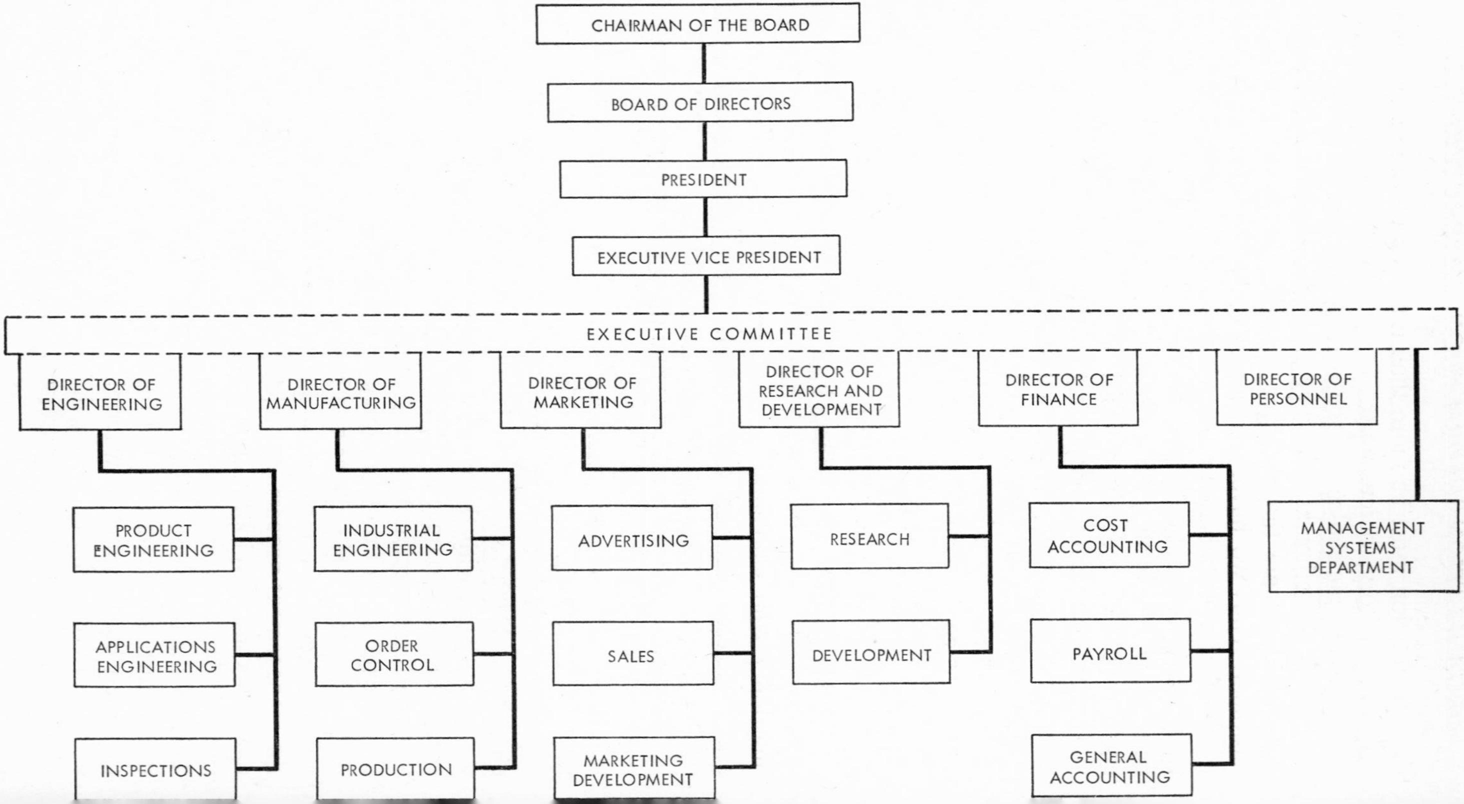

The following contrasts show certain major differences between organization approaches and systems approaches:

a) *Organization* emphasizes the design of organization structure, and then thinks of the communications needed for this structure. (*Systems* emphasizes the design of communication structure, and then thinks of the organization needed to complement this structure.)

b) *Organization* stresses chains of command, authority, and responsibility. (*Systems* stresses channels of communication, information flow, and decisions.)

c) *Organization* provides compartments of authority and responsibility. (*Systems* provides networks between question and answer points.)

THE COMBINED ORGANIZATION/INFORMATION STRUCTURE

A view that would bring the two approaches together should treat a department as an energy source, that is charged with experience and skills. Systems would then be thought of as the wires connecting the decision points in and between the departments. This view has a built-in arrangement for coordination. The boundaries of departments would not and should not be the same as the boundaries of systems. The strength of specialization in the departments would be complemented by the strength of coordination built into the information systems. Coordination points would be identified both as positions in

FIGURE 2–3

A Section of a Management Information System

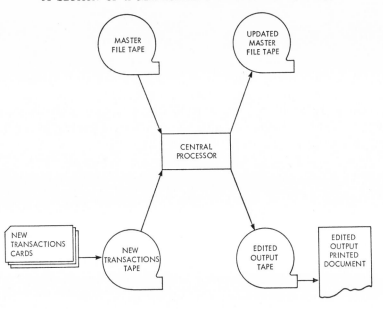

the organization structure and as events in the information structure.

With this dual dimension of structure it would be possible to identify more quickly just when and how changes should be made in either the organization structure or the information structure. The general approach would be to organize around patterns of problems, to watch for changes in types and priorities of problems, and to adjust both organizations and systems.

FIGURE 2–4

An Organization/Information Chart

Chart symbolizes assignments to both men [blocks] and machines [computer tape reels] working in combinations.

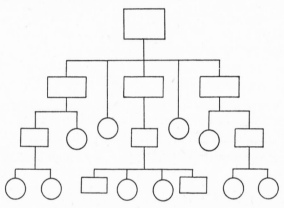

We have been witnessing, in essence, the development of much more flexibility in organization structures during recent years. While it is still useful to think in simple terms of line or staff, this thinking is not sufficient for modern organization design. In the future, we will see that certain organizations, which have been set up in such fashion, can change various parts of their structures on a day-to-day basis, if this is necessary. This will be made possible, to a large degree, by having management information systems that are comprehensive, interacting, and extremely flexible.

1. Systems emphasize *what* and *how* things are done.

2. Organization and departmentation emphasize *who* does these things.

In practice, the *what, how* and *who* must be intimately tied together if success is to be achieved.

Figures 2–2 and 2–3 show two pictures in chart form; the former is an organization and the latter is a system. This book considers both pictures separately, and how these pictures influence one another. This is neither an organization nor a systems book, but rather a book on the interplay between people in an organization and between the systems with which they work. Those who aspire to management positions in today's business world must be able to work with people and with systems relationships, and—most importantly—with compound relationships between people and systems.

Figure 2–4 is a symbolic representation of these compound relationships between organization positions and information systems. The next chapter builds on the notion of a combined organization/information structure by emphasizing the information requirements of organization positions and the "production" of information to satisfy these requirements.

Chapter 3

THE INFORMATION
PRODUCTION PROCESS

The design and management of an information system requires more time and talent than it did a few years ago. New approaches and new equipment have become available in these few years, and most managements seek to take advantage of these new tools.

THE INFORMATION PRODUCTION CYCLE

A thorough analysis of a management information system requires that conceptual problems somehow be brought down to as concrete a representation as possible so that the practicalities of designing a system can be handled. That this is a severe requirement is evidenced in our recent experience with computer-oriented information systems. This book is written to provide a practical framework for managers at all levels (as well as systems specialists) who are given the responsibilities for the design of management information systems. In this book, therefore, we emphasize the idea that production of information is just as important, if not more important, than the production of physical commodities.

THE ELEMENTS OF MASS PRODUCTION

The following is a quotation from a book written more than 30 years ago, during the period when we were making our first breakthroughs in the mass production of physical products. The reason for using this quote in this place is that it gives us some good suggestions for approaching the mass production of information in modern management information systems.

20

ECONOMIC ASPECTS OF STANDARDIZATION
AND SIMPLIFICATION[1]

Industrial standardization consists of singling out specific products and materials; settling upon their performance, properties, and dimensions; and fixing attention upon them both in production and in use to the end that the greatest possible industrial efficiency may be attained. It includes:

1. *Nomenclature* and definitions of technical terms used in specifications and contracts; also technical abbreviations and symbols.

2. *Uniformity in dimensions* necessary to secure interchangeability of parts and supplies, and makes possible the interworking of apparatus. Dimensional standards.

3. *Quality specifications* for materials and equipment; composition, form and structure.

4. *Methods of testing* to determine standards of quality and performance.

5. *Ratings of machinery* and apparatus under specific conditions.

6. *Safety provisions* and rules for the operation of apparatus and machinery in industrial establishments. Safety codes and standards of practice.

7. *Simplification* by the elimination of unnecessary variety in types, sizes, and grades, this selection being usually based upon the relative commercial demand.

Standardization is absolutely essential in any program of mass production. When properly applied, it is one of the major factors in the elimination of waste in industry. Standardization plays an important role in simplifying manufacturing processes and in stabilizing production and employment. With standardization it is more safe for the manufacturer to accumulate stock during periods of slack orders. This he cannot safely do with an unstandardized product. Standardization broadens markets both for the producer and the consumer; it lowers the cost to the public by making mass production possible; it enables buyer and seller to speak the same language and makes it possible to compel competitive sellers to do likewise; it reduces selling costs; it stimulates research and makes for the elimination of antiquated methods and products; it brings about concentration on the essentials, with its consequent suppression of confusing elements intended merely for sales effect; it thus helps to base competition squarely upon efficiency in production and distribution and upon *intrinsic merit of product.*

If we think in terms of the production of information, we can see many similarities in the mass production of physical products. In this

---

[1] With permission. Frank L. Eidmann, *Economic Control of Engineering and Manufacturing* (New York: McGraw-Hill Book Company, Inc., 1931), pp. 261–62 (italics added).

book we will emphasize these similarities and bring out such ideas as the nomenclature, uniformity, and quality specifications of the data that must be processed into the information necessary to run and improve the operations of the business.

QUESTIONS AND ANSWERS AS RAW MATERIALS

To consider information as a "product" is a somewhat novel idea that has only recently been put to use. Production, as a term, has in the past been reserved for the processing of physical products, but now we see large amounts of resources applied to the processing of the questions and answers that go to make up a management information system. Figure 3–1 shows the major areas involved in the information production process. First we will look at this diagram from a broad view, and later in the book get into its specifics.

FIGURE 3–1

SCHEMATIC OF THE INFORMATION PRODUCTION PROCESS

(Numbers indicate chapters covering these topics.)

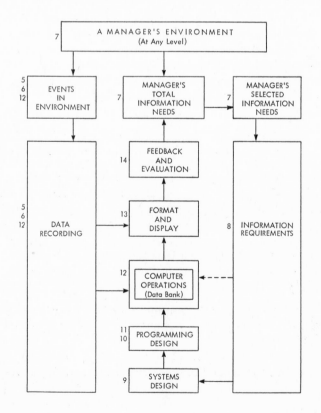

The information production process shows two types of "raw material" inputs: (1) the manager's selected information needs[2] and (2) events in the environment that can be described as data and recorded for entry into a data processing system. Information needs and data are brought together in the center of the schematic, where the computer does the processing. The result is the end product, or the output as delivered to the customer. The production cycle can continue as long as the customer is satisfied or as long as management allows the output to be produced for "stock." In the latter case, information is produced not for immediate sale or consumption but for possible future use. As with hard production, information production may lead to excessive "inventory." The question, "Who needs it?" is important in both cases.

CUSTOMER NEEDS

Attempting to satisfy a customer for hard goods, it is typical for a manufacturer to study the environment of that customer. The customer's needs are spelled out and an attempt is made to "formfit" the product to these needs. The same viewpoint should be taken in analyzing the environment of customers for information. "Who needs it?" and "What do they need?" can be answered only when this market research is adequately done.

Designers of management information systems can very often create a "product" before a customer realizes he has a need for it. The analogy to hard production is also appropriate here, and the designer cannot assume automatic acceptance of his product. In practice, the customer may take the initiative and state a need, which the designer then seeks to satisfy. Alternatively, the designer may, through his research, offer an information product which the customer may try to put to use.

Few, if any, manufacturers satisfy all the needs of all their customers. Similarly, the information producers must concentrate on the prime needs of prime customers. The Figure 3–1 diagram starts with the recognition that it is from the job environment of a manager that questions arise, and that it is the aggregate of these questions which makes up a particular manager's total information needs. It is inefficient, however (if not impossible), to try to satisfy any manager's *total* information requirements through the design of systems. Of the total requirements, only a selected portion can be supplied by management information systems. The block, Manager's Selected Information

---

[2] These information needs are considered as "raw" and in need of analysis because they can usually be refined in the development of a management information system.

Needs, has a particular significance. It represents the need for formal analysis of a manager's information priorities. It is a reminder that these needs are not easy to state, and yet the success of information systems can be measured only against some statement of these needs.

A manufacturer has a similar problem. His customers are in the process of trying to satisfy their customers. At each gap between the levels of suppliers and customers "fog" appears, and no absolutely clear view of requirements is available. This is particularly so when the manufacturer attempts to produce so-called standardized products in a simplified product line. Customers usually want custom-built products at standard product costs.

Today we see many information producers in this same situation. Much can be learned from the experiences that manufacturers have had as they have tried to find their place between the extremes of simplification and diversification. Chapter 7 (Setting Systems Priorities) looks into this problem of determining appropriate specifications for the information requirements of information system customers.

Now let us move over to the other side of the diagram and consider where the other raw material—data—comes from. Here we see a difference, compared to physical materials and products. A manufacturer rarely gets his raw materials from a source to which he also sells. In management information systems, however, the same source—the manager's environment—generates both demand for final product and supply of the input materials.

EVENT PROCESSING: SELECTING INPUT DATA

The second type of input materials is data, the data that represent selected events that have taken place in the environment of the manager. It is good practice for the analyst in organization systems to make a mental separation between events and the data that record such events. This separation is shown in the schematic by the Events in Environment and the Data Recording blocks. An event of significance can happen without anyone knowing about it; and many events occur that are of little real interest to anybody. When an event is recorded as data it means that two basic decisions have been made:

1. Someone decided this event was important;
2. Arrangements were made to make sure this event would be recognized and noted when it happened.

This, of course, means the data processing analysis must be rooted in the manager's environment. The important events are, in essence, the elements that describe his environment: its contents and its changes. If data processing is to be meaningful, the tough job of choosing, identifying, and recording events must be given careful analytical attention. The comparative situation in hard production is the care with which physical materials are analyzed, tested, and selected.

The Events in Environment block emphasizes *what* to record; the Data Recording block stresses *how* to record. As developed in later chapters on Classification and Codes (Chapter 5) and Documentation (Chapter 6), how to record is a critical problem in data processing. Many opportunities for improvement exist in this area of management systems.

INFORMATION PRODUCTION METHODS

Now let us look at the center section of the schematic. This shows the development of information production methods and the use of machinery in the process. The flows of information requirements and data are studied as represented by the Systems Design block. Chapter 9 explores this type of work in some detail, so for now let us consider only in general terms what can be accomplished.

Systems design concentrates on building logical arrangements for describing the flow of data through processing and delivery of information to the customer. The most common terms are block diagram, systems logic, and flow charts; and all imply the writing down of selected events, appropriate data recording, processing steps, and sequences. The result is a documented picture that shows the structure of the system in some chosen degree of detail. As we will see, systems designs can be presented in a gross or extremely detailed fashion. Gross pictures are used when the only purpose is to demonstrate and discuss the concept being developed. Detailed portrayals are needed as the purpose shifts to getting the system into operation at the level of practice.

An especially detailed documentation is necessary when the system is carried into operation by the use of a computer. This is a special area of systems design and is shown on the schematic in the box marked Programming (but there is never the complete separation between systems design and programming that this schematic infers). Programming emphasizes the strengths and weaknesses of the computer machinery and the languages used to instruct the machine. Systems designers, at least in the initial stages, should ignore the existence of the machine and should concentrate on the language in which the manager expresses his problems and wants his answers. Somewhere in the process these two languages (of man and machine) must be brought together, and a common translation must be accomplished.

It is here that we see systems designers and programmers giving advice to one another. The systems designer should know what is desired; the programmer should know what is feasible for the equipment. That the art of compromise must be practiced is evident, and it must be practiced by both sides. As we will demonstrate, there are many management problems that cannot or should not be processed through a computer. All too often it is the programmer who tries and fails, and this shows that the area was not yet ready for computer-based processing.

Note on the schematic that we have provided a bypass of the computer that will allow for all sorts of less formal systems. Though we will emphasize systems which can take advantage of the computer, we do not wish to give the impression that this includes all, or even most, of the data needed in an organization. If you question this, or are a computer enthusiast, remember our earlier comment on the chances of developing freakish systems.

THE COMPUTER-BASED DATA BANK

Systems design and programming result in providing instructions to the computer. Data recording provides the source and initial format of data. Instructions and data are brought together in the computer, labeled here as a "data bank." The idea of a data bank is both useful and troublesome. It is useful because it can be compared to banks of raw material in a factory, ready for assembly to suit customers' needs on demand; it is a difficult notion because it is not simple to build a bank of data, which involves much more than filling shelves or stacking boxes in a shop.

The term data bank is being used more all the time so let us look at the term more closely. Specifically, consider a bank of data from the viewpoints of four individuals: the user of output, the provider of input, the operator of the bank, and the systems designer. Each of these sees the bank as having different characteristics.

The *user* looks at the data bank as a supply of facts that he can use to make his plans and to control his area of operations. He wants as much influence as possible over the supply of these facts. He wants these facts in a form that will be most useful to him; and his needs may or may not coincide with the needs of other users.

The *provider* of the data that go into the data bank looks at the bank as a very demanding customer. This customer wants high quality data and demands that very exacting schedules be met. This customer very often changes his mind, with resultant chaos in the data supply lines.

The *operator,* or the man responsible for running the computer facility, looks at the bank as the machine, or process, that he must handle. He is responsible for machine utilization and usually thinks in terms of machine-hours, run-times, down-times, and maintenance schedules. Obsolescence of equipment, and equipment replacement, also enter his view of the data bank. He likes long production runs. Debugging of computer programs and "odd-ball" requests for information interfere with his operations. He likes "standardization."

The *systems designer*, by the nature of his job, must have a viewpoint that includes all three of the above. A data bank, to the systems designer, is a set of compromises made necessary because he cannot figure out how to design a system that will provide all possible information instantaneously and at no cost. A good systems designer views the data bank as something that gradually develops through careful analysis and test. This means that he must carefully blend the views of the user, the data provider, and the operator. The systems designer must be more than a good technician; he must also be a good communicator and mediator.

We believe the notion of the data bank is worthwhile because it helps us think out the variety of requirements that must be considered in designing management information systems. A data bank can be compared to a savings bank, and this brings in the concept of investment. Data, like money deposited in a savings bank, should be worth more when it is withdrawn. This, of course, depends upon the processing within either kind of bank. Savings banks are structured by account numbers. Some accounts are active, some inactive. Data banks must likewise be structured by classifications, with varying levels of "deposits" and "withdrawals." Savings banks should have good portfolios of depositors, and so should data banks. Users of banking facilities have differing interests, and so do those of data banks.

COMPLETING THE CYCLE

The Format and Display block in the schematic particularly brings out the views of differing interests. How do managers want their information served? Do they want it in one main course, or do they want it a la carte? Do they want it well processed, or do they want it raw? All of these choices are possible if expense is no object. Usually, however, there is some more limited "menu" from which managers' choices can be made. Interest in how information is presented has long been active, but recently this interest has become intensified. Increased attention is paid to such problems as forms design and formating reports. Readability of management reports reflects this need that the output of our systems merge with the capacities of human beings to absorb information. These problems are discussed in Chapter 13 (Output Format and Display).

This brings us back to where we started, back to the context of the manager's "total" information needs. The whole information production process must receive its evaluation in this environment. If the environment is complex, only certain parts of this complexity can be handled with the help of systems. The business of being a manager is not a simple matter of working with concrete facts in standardized situations. Management information systems can produce extremely helpful products for managers. Good managers, complemented by good systems, are the primary ingredients of good management. The information production process recognizes and facilitates the contribution of both managers and systems. In the next chapter this approach is applied within the framework of a case study.

TYPES OF INFORMATION PRODUCED

Now let us consider the types of production that can be accomplished in an information production process. In a hard-goods environment we see operations under the headings of extraction, fabrication, and assembly. Similar processes take place in the sequence whereby events are refined into data, data are machined into certain forms, and the final outputs are assembled. Each stage of physical production is influenced by the requirements of the previous stages, as well as by those of the following stages. The characteristics of the raw materials, the capacities and the limitations of processing methods, and the end uses for the products all require careful attention to assure efficient production. Those who would be successful in processing information have just as broad and deep a scope of production. Further, the elements of information production are not nearly as tangible or observable as those in physical production. It is important that the varying types of information production be identified so that separate stages can be analyzed at a specific level.

A management information system is a process for selectively collecting, revising, and distributing data. In general, there are two types of management information systems:

1. *Management operating systems* are used to produce *working papers,* such as purchase invoices, job orders, or pay checks.
2. *Management reporting systems* are used to aid management in the making of *decisions.*

It is worthwhile to keep these two kinds of systems in mind, for each has unique problems in design and application.

MANAGEMENT REPORTING SYSTEMS

Management reporting systems, or systems used to aid management in making decisions, are quite different from working paper systems.

The output of management reporting systems provides inputs into the planning and control mechanisms of management. Here we see most vividly the joining of management talents and management systems. It is also here that we can recognize that the requirements for executive development and information systems are derived from the same needs. These needs must be satisfied by close harmony between talent and technique. We will return to this point later, but now let us concentrate on the elements and the sequence in the production of management reporting systems.

"Report," like many other words, is easy to use but difficult to define. The dictionary states the term very simply: "report" means "to re-tell." The trouble starts when we try to apply this definition to the re-telling that takes place in a business organization. If we are not careful, every bit of conversation, and all correspondence, becomes a "report." The next few pages suggest a manner in which the use of "report" may be limited and then broken down into useful subdivisions. These divisions will aid in separating the parts of a reporting system. Having a clearer view of the parts, we may then ask if a given system of reports is as good as it should be.

The most simple information system is one of direct observation: few reports are written in corner grocery stores. While this statement is obvious, it is also useful in recognizing one of the basic goals of the decentralization of large companies, faster decision making. In the sole-proprietorship, decisions are made on the spot. The advantage is flexibility. As an organization grows, its structure becomes more complex. Duties, spread over many specializations, call for an emphasis on control and coordination. Mistakes become more costly and each decision must be checked for repercussions throughout the general structure. The necessity for establishing specialized departments brings with it the disadvantage of separation of interests, and this slows the flow of information. One of the main chores of the reporting system should be offsetting this necessary, but restrictive, compartmentalization of information. The same reasoning is applied even more importantly to the up-and-down aspects of information flow, and this reasoning is the basis for attempts to have "flattened" organization structures.

A formalized, written reporting system is only one element in an overall communication system. The overall system must include the following considerations:

1. Accumulation of information,
2. Transfer of information,
3. Use of information,
4. Storage of information.

The next section of this chapter proposes a working definition of management reports, using the above list and a process of elimination in its approach, and arrives at a classification of reports that can be used as the basis for a report analysis system. It should be remembered that the classifications which follow are deliberate oversimplifications; that the end sought is a set of "pigeon holes" into which most of a department's reports can be sorted for analysis.

1. Files are locations of recorded information in any form:
    a) Files can be looked at for facts with which to answer specific questions; e.g., the last price paid.
    b) Files can be used for verification in a "protection of position" sense; e.g., in tax review.
    c) Files can also be reviewed for relationships seeking:
        i) Development of managerial standards for control; e.g., burden rate.
        ii) Factor analysis for planning; e.g., trends in prices.
    d) Files can be required by external authority, with no recognizable internal benefits.
2. Files may include information in the following forms:
    a) Reports: Result or situation descriptions;
    b) Letters or Memos: Request, instruct, describe (report);
    c) Procedures or Manuals: Managerial Standards, bases of control;
    d) Records: Raw data just collected.

Turning this list around, the classifications can be set up as follows:

1. Request or question orally, or by memo, letter, or questionnaire.
2. Advise or instruct orally, or by memo, letter, procedure, or manual.
3. *Describe or identify orally, or by written report:*
    a) A thing or a specific fact;
    b) A situation: past, present, and/or future:
        i) "As is": Static, or strict description;
        ii) A result: Measure of change, or strict description before and after change;
        iii) A trend: Review or interpolation;
        iv) A forecast: Anticipation and extrapolation.

These four points are the main elements in the working definition of the term "management report."

It is important in reporting that we bring out the *changes that have taken place* in order to help someone decide what *changes are going to take place*. The above content-description of a report is based upon the fact that ultimately the collected information must be interpreted. In addition, someone must make decisions relative to the problems brought out by the facts. Reports in a system can be classified by the way they fit into the pattern which leads to a decision. In this sense, reports are a semi-finished product awaiting final assembly in the mind of the manager.

The written communication, which is to be classified as a "report," does not just ask a question, nor does it simply give advice or instructions based upon experience; rather it gives the results of a *recent* investigation. An investigation is a selecting process that picks out certain facts. If someone at a higher level decides which are the important facts to be gathered, the gathering itself (with proper supervision) can be considered as an almost mechanical operation. However, if the investigation is "to find the cause of," or includes the responsibility for making recommendations, the degree of thinking becomes important. "Investigation" includes both the mechanical gathering and the thinking involved, and both results can be incorporated into oral or written reports. The first important division of reporting appears when we separate the gathering of facts from the analysis of these facts. Further divisions can then be made to allow more detailed study. A suggested general breakdown of reports is as follows:

1. Basic Reports (factual data summaries),
2. Secondary Reports (contain conclusions), and
3. Complete Reports (contain conclusions and recommendations).

Basic Reports would be but one step removed from the raw records. Reporting starts as soon as the raw records are looked at for the purpose of selecting facts to send to someone else. If the report shows only gathered data, it is a Basic Report. If conclusions are added, it becomes a Secondary Report, and if recommendations are added, it becomes a Complete Report, ready for a decision to be made. Reporting can be done in one step by one person, or in many steps involving the efforts of many people. The main advantage of identifying these three levels of reporting is to show the limits of reporting; that is, on one side a boundary of raw records and working papers and, on the other side, a boundary of decision making, with reporting in between.

Files of raw records and working papers are prerequisites for a reporting system. They should not be confused with reports proper. The following definitions are intended for use in dividing and classifying the various data and documents in industrial communications.

Files: any information *gathered* and *held* for potential use.
Working Papers: the first collection of data for a *particular purpose,* may be a series of sheets building up data. The important consideration is that these papers are used within the section (smallest reporting unit) and do not normally leave the section.

Basic Report: can be a working paper copy, approved as containing the desired information, and can be sent out of the section. The important point is that the information contained in a Basic Report is simply a summary of the raw data. It shows the situation but does not say whether it is good or bad.

Secondary Report: contains inferences (often conclusions) that may be drawn from the original data. It gives the answers to such often preliminary questions as: "What is the inconsistency here?" "What is it that is wrong?" "Where does it indicate that further information should be sought?" "What is likely to happen?" It does more than collect the facts; it interprets.

Complete Report: includes the survey of the facts. It includes conclusions drawn from these facts, and, finally, recommended actions to be taken. The action to be taken is the result sought from the time the problem was sensed and the raw data surveyed. All phases of reporting should lead to recommendations. The phase of decision making on the recommendations follows, and is not part of reporting. If certain decision making is automatic in the system, this should be identified as such and controlled appropriately.

The above classifications will take in a high percentage of the documents in any system. Other documents may be "hybrids" and can be identified as such. Sorting reports into the above classifications makes it possible to start testing the contribution that each makes in the overall reporting system. Weaknesses in the system become easier to spot as the flow of information is inspected chronologically, from raw data, through the reporting stages, to the making of decisions. The diagram in Figure 3–2 shows the information production sequence as it supports the decisions to be made by managers.

Note how the "lower stages of production" lead into each higher stage. If a "stock" is located at any stage, there is no need to go back and do work at a lower stage. Just as in a manufacturing situation, however, money can be tied up in inventory. This means that a decision has to be made as to how much information should be stocked at each level of the processing sequence.

This processing sequence is not confined to reports that are ultimately produced with a computer. All management reports, no matter what the media, require close attention to the raw material, subassembly, and final assembly stages.

MANAGEMENT OPERATING SYSTEMS

Management operating, or working paper, systems have even more similarities to a physical production process. More stages are routinized; more elements are identifiable. Whereas the end result of a management reporting system goes to a manager for decisions, an operating system is designed to build decisions (choices between alternatives) in the system itself. At least we can say that there are more such built-in decisions in an operating system. In such systems, clerical level procedures are more automatic. Each processing step moves a piece of data through to a terminal point. Examples of such terminal points are the pay check, received periodically by an employee; the payment made to a vendor; or an entry showing a job has been completed. Much of the mass of modern data handling is at this level of processing.

FIGURE 3–2 *M Reporting Sy*

THE REPORT PRODUCTION PROCESS

(From Raw Materials to Complete Reports)

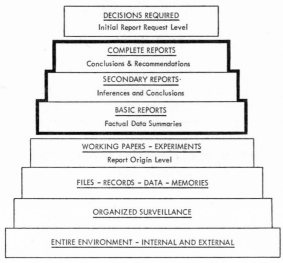

Operating, or "working paper," systems represent situations where talent has been applied and transferred to the system. Built-in rules now are used in the system and, except for periodic reviews, the higher talent level is not needed to do the job. In a sense, the skills have been "tape recorded" in a system and can be "played back" whenever they are needed.

Management literature is now widely available in the areas of operating systems, giving specific presciptions for given operating problems. We have minimized our attention to management operating systems at this point of the book. In later chapters we present a comprehensive example of an operating system in the functional area of manpower planning and control. This example shows the typical types of problems encountered in the design of a specific system at the operating level. As noted in the preface, our purpose is not to show how to design a specific system. Our intent, rather, is to present the factors that should be included in developing management systems regardless of the particular type.

We should take a minute to note how Management Reporting Systems and Management Operating Systems interact over a period of time. Reporting emphasizes the manager's talents in making decisions, and operating stresses the use of techniques to achieve routine decisions in a system. Talents are recorded in the minds of people, and techniques developed by talented people can be recorded on paper. Thus we see that one of the challenges of talented people is the need to provide improved techniques. Such techniques are then used to make easier the handling of a business' recurring problems.

In simplest terms, a good technique records the use of good talent. The talent is built into the technique, applied as a system, and can be used over and over again. We have seen the same phenomena at work in the past as certain talents of craftsmen were analyzed and built into production processes. Progress in management information systems can be represented as talents are able to convert judgment decisions into routine procedures.

There are many ways of classifying management information systems. Here we have made a simple, initial split between reporting and operating systems. This viewpoint is useful for it acts to remind us that systems development can lead to machine-based data processing only as we are able to understand man-based data processing. The information production process requires that one analysis blend both men and machines. As time goes on and progress is made, some work will move down from a reporting to an operating level. That which previously required much attention by managers will be delegated, and with a degree of confidence, to the operating system. As we will see later, management reporting systems often draw on the data generated initially in the operating systems. This is an example of the multiple use of basic data. In manufacturing we see a similar phenomenon as many end products are made from relatively few parts.

In the following case study you can see examples of the various types of information production and the stages in the processes of a management information system. Some "products" will be at the reporting, or decision, level. Other products will serve the needs of operating systems. In both cases the output must satisfy customer needs. Productivity for information products, as well as for physical products, must ultimately be tested in the marketplace. In the next chapter you can run your own information production business.

Chapter 4

A CASE STUDY:
THE SMART CORPORATION[1]

As a framework in which to demonstrate the information production process, let us look at a case study of an actual (but disguised) firm. In this case study we consider the priority framework and the manner in which systems studies originate and are processed in the development of a variety of management information systems. The materials in this chapter form the background for extensions of this same case study as examples in later chapters. This gives a realistic framework in which to consider applications of both systems concepts and techniques. As with all case studies, it is impossible to provide *all* the relevant detail; we have, however, by the use of this case in later chapters, provided more than the usual case study coverage. These materials allow the reader to test his skills in solving management systems problems.

For this case study we suggest that the reader take the part of the manager of the Management Systems Department in the SMART corporation.[2] This department has just been formed and you have been selected to manage it. You will have to hire men, select projects, assign men to projects, and develop sound personnel policies for your staff. All this must be done within the limitations of your budget. Details on the budget procedure are given later in the case.

Your basic job as manager is to maximize the value of systems used

---

[1] The SMART game was developed at the request of William Spray, General Chairman of the 11th International Systems Meeting of the Systems and Procedures Association. The format of the game was designed by Adrian McDonough and the staff of the Wharton School's Taylor Management Laboratory.

[2] The acronym stands for Systems Manager's Administrative Rating Test.

35

in the company, and you are exposed to a variety of situations for which systems efforts *may or may not* be justified. Your task is to search for, and select, the best opportunities for company improvements. A general background on the company follows as the context in which specific projects can be evaluated.

SMART CORPORATION BACKGROUND INFORMATION

SMART Corporation is a medium-size firm (annual sales $35 million), located at Fall River, Massachusetts. The corporation is a leading producer of electronic instruments and automatic control systems for indicating, recording, and controlling variables in a wide variety of industrial processes. In addition, the corporation manufactures, on special order, many types of laboratory instruments (20 percent of its business).

The corporation has three plants. Two are modern buildings, on the outskirts of town, while the third is a 50-year-old four-story building in the heart of the city's old industrial area. During the past year the corporation had its highest employment, 1,800, as opposed to 1,700 the previous year. Of this total, over 10 percent had service with the firm of 25 years or more.

The fiscal year, which ended September 30, produced an all-time high in new orders and shipments. New orders received totaled $39,000,000, as opposed to $35,000,000 for the preceding year. Shipments amounted to $35,000,000, compared to $30,000,000 for the preceding year. The log of backorders stands at $13,000,000.

Net profits after taxes have shown a sharp drop, from $1,500,000 in the preceding year to $1,200,000 in the past period. In an effort to counteract this drop, the Executive Committee has instituted several new programs. The new Management Systems Department was one of these additions. To head the department, you, an outsider, were brought in because the Executive Committee felt the department required complete freedom to alter the systems already in use. Certain additional background is shown in Figures 4–1, 4–2 and 4–3.

ASSIGNMENTS TO THE SYSTEMS DEPARTMENT

As shown in Figure 2–2, the Management Systems Department reports directly to the Executive Committee. In the minutes of the meetings of this committee, certain assignments are made to the Management Systems Department. These are usually sent to the manager of the Management Systems Department with the note: "Please give this problem attention as soon as you can work it into your schedule." At other times the note is less gracious: "Do the following fast!" Examples of such assignments follow later in this chapter.

FIGURE 4–1

SMART Corporation, Fall River, Mass.

BALANCE SHEET

ASSETS

		Previous Year Results
Current Assets:		
Cash on hand............................		$ 1,300,000
Accounts receivable......................		5,000,000
Inventories:		
Finished product....................	$2,500,000	
Work in process.....................	3,300,000	
Stores..............................	5,900,000	
Total Inventories................		11,700,000
Total Current Assets.....................		$18,000,000
Fixed Assets:		
Land.................................	$ 500,000	
Buildings............................	7,000,000	
Machine and equipment..................	4,000,000	
Total Fixed Assets......................		$11,500,000
Less depreciation....................		3,500,000
Fixed Assets Less Depreciation............		$ 8,000,000
TOTAL ASSETS LESS DEPRECIATION....		$26,000,000

LIABILITIES

		Previous Year Results
Current Liabilities:		
Notes payable (short-term)................		$ 750,000
Accounts payable........................		3,500,000
Withheld accounts		
Taxes..............................	$2,000,000	
Salaries............................	1,200,000	
Total Withheld Accounts.........		3,200,000
Total Current Liabilities...................		$ 7,450,000
Long-Term Liabilities:		
Bonds payable...........................		4,000,000
Reserve for pensions.....................		350,000
Stockholders' Equity:		
Capital Stock...........................		6,700,000
Retained Earnings.......................		7,500,000
TOTAL LIABILITIES.....................		$26,000,000

As you read through these assignments, decide in general terms which are most important. There are ten assignments. With only the present amount of background available, what order or priority would you assign to each as a systems project? As a new employee managing a new department, you can work only with what you see of the situation. As time goes on you will be able to refine your priorities. As a

FIGURE 4–2

SMART TRENDS

EARNINGS
YEARS IN PAST

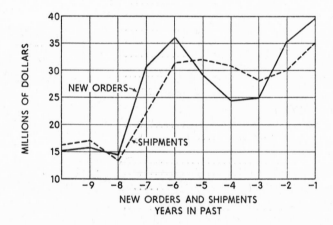

NEW ORDERS AND SHIPMENTS
YEARS IN PAST

matter of fact you will, once you have set priorities, put your systems analysts to work getting more information in the study areas, and you can then refine your priorities in keeping with the additional perspective obtained through their reports. Beyond this, you will have to apply your best intuition.

In the assignments which follow you will note that some suggested projects are quite broad and some quite narrow. Some represent situations where short-run returns are possible, and others necessitate a long-range viewpoint, that is, a willingness to invest now and realize returns quite a bit later.

This variety was deliberately chosen to demonstrate that the study of management systems can span every aspect of a business. The

FIGURE 4–3

SMART CORPORATION INCOME STATEMENT FOR THE YEAR ENDING
SEPTEMBER 30

Net sales...............................		$35,000,000
Cost of merchandise sold..................		28,856,000
Gross margin...........................		$ 6,144,000
Less operating expenses:		
Wages, salaries, and commissions........	$2,100,000	
Depreciation.........................	1,500,000	
Other operating expenses..............	40,000	
Total Operating Expenses...........		3,640,000
Operating income........................		$ 2,504,000
Other income and expense:		
Other income........................	11,400	
Other expense.......................	(15,400)	
Net Other Expense................		4,000
Net income before income taxes............		$ 2,500,000
Provision for federal income taxes...........		1,300,000
Net Income....................		$ 1,200,000

abilities to seek out, to describe, and to apply weights of significance are the essential talents of the systems analyst. The examples demonstrate situations in which these talents may be applied. Each of these ten assignments represents initial guidance from the Executive Committee.

Because this is a new position for you, it is going to take some time before these study areas can be seen in any degree of breadth and depth. This lack of perspective, however, is not due only to your newness on the job; the problems themselves are new. If these situations were all clear, and easy to describe, there would be no need for you or for a systems department. Because management has decided that these areas are worth investigating, they have initiated these assignments. They have not, however, placed any significant rankings on these problems. You must do this in order to know which types of analysts, and how many, to assign to the proper projects. Before you do this, it is well to look at the resources you have available for work on such projects.

BUDGET AND ACCOUNTING FRAMEWORK

To get the department started, the company has set up a salary budget of $100,000. This figure is exclusive of your salary. You therefore have the total amount for the hiring of personnel for your department. Secretarial and clerical help are assigned to you, but are not (for the present) charged against your budget. This budget is for a six-month period. Near the end of this six-month period the Executive Committee will review your results and consider funds for the following six months. Obviously, they are keeping pressure on you to obtain results.

You have been told, tentatively, that a budget formula will be applied to your department. This will not take effect until results are recorded for your department at the end of the second six-month period. At that time the formula may be used to set your budget for the third six-month period, and for each period thereafter. The formula to be used is: budget for next six months (B_{p_2}) = budget for the previous six months (B_{p_1}), plus 10 percent of the difference between savings from systems studies last period (S_{p_1}) and *twice* the costs of your salaries last period $(2C_{p_1})$:

$$B_{p_2} = B_{p_1} + \frac{(S_{p_1} - 2C_{p_1})}{10}.$$

A systems department works on projects that result in savings *in the other departments* of the company. The savings referred to in the budget formula are *net savings* in these departments: the total benefits of the new system in these departments are expressed in dollars and the expenses of installing the system in these departments are then deducted to give net savings resulting from the project. These net savings are net only as far as the departments are concerned. The salaries you pay to your analysts still have to be justified.

The formula measures the systems department performance by subtracting the project's salary costs from the net savings in the departments. As is typical, the systems department is required to do better than just break even. Under this budget arrangement you must get savings that are twice your salary costs merely to *keep* the same budget. Above or below this point, you get a higher or lower budget for the next period.

You of course are happy that this formula will not be used until you get your feet on the ground. With a good start, you believe that this formula will provide growth for your staff as the work load increases. Meanwhile you have ten projects and $100,000. To make money you have to spend money, in this case for hiring personnel.

SYSTEMS PERSONNEL CLASSES AND SALARIES

You have worked out an agreement with the Personnel Department on grades and salaries for the systems analysts that you must hire. For the present, your needs are for people who can dig in and come up with refined problem definitions. Computer programming has also been assigned as your responsibility. The little programming that is presently necessary is being done by outside contract, and you plan to continue this until there is greater need for in-house programmers.

Three grades of systems personnel appear to satisfy your present needs. These have been given position titles of Group Leader, Senior Systems Analyst, and Junior Systems Analyst. The average charge for each of these grades, and the initial costs of hiring, are as follows:

	Budget Charge*	Hiring Cost†
Group leader	$15,000	$5,000
Senior analyst	12,000	3,000
Junior analyst	8,000	2,000

* The budget charge is for six months and includes an overhead factor prorated to each employee based upon salary.

† The hiring costs are one-time expenses and were set by the Personnel Department. You have already complained about these figures.

Junior analysts are used primarily to gather facts and to present these as basic reports. Seniors have more experience and are expected not only to be able to gather facts but also to be able to draw conclusions from these facts. Group leaders represent trained systems analysts, with experience in a variety of management areas, and with the abilities necessary to provide recommendations to management. For purposes of this case, assume that all personnel within a grade are equally talented. Talents vary between grade levels. It serves no purpose to consider individual differences in this case study. (You would have to consider too much detail to make this worthwhile in playing the game.)

After the department has been in operation for some time, you will have to think about promotions for Seniors and Juniors. If you wait too long you may have some "quits" right in the middle of certain studies, and this means that your possible savings for that period will be lost.

This background and operational information has been provided in order to allow an analysis that is reasonably realistic. You now have:

1. Ten unevaluated possible studies;
2. A $100,000 budget for six months;
3. Costs for three levels of systems skills.

One other fact is important, and that is the way you look at the achievements of your analysts. In practice, success is a reflection of three things: (1) the talents of your personnel; (2) the opportunities that actually exist in possible projects; (3) your skill in recognizing project opportunities. In this game we have emphasized the last two factors. Personnel achievement is handled in a simplified fashion. As noted above, we ignore individual performance differences within a skill grade, but we recognize differences in the contributions of group leaders and senior and junior analysts. We use a point system. Any group leader produces 100 achievement points if you use him on any project for a period. A senior produces 75 points and a junior 50 points. You will have to keep track of these points as measures of the total resources that you have assigned to each project. This is explained in the following description of the sequence of play.

SEQUENCE OF PLAY

INSTRUCTIONS FOR USE OF FIGURE 4–4[3]

1. For each play read over all background materials and (after first play) read any report pages received from your analysts (as determined by use of Figure 4–5, described below).

2. Decide which projects offer the most potential for net savings. Rank these projects and then assign types and numbers of analysts.

3. Record your selected number of analysts on the Study Cost Worksheet (Figure 4–4) by type and by project.

4. Add the analysts of each type and multiply by the salary charge. Record this total at the right of the worksheet.

5. Record the number of new "hires" by type of analyst.

6. Add the new analysts of each type and multiply by the hiring charge. Record at right of the worksheet.

7. Add and record the total study cost for this period.

8. On scrap paper, calculate salary and hiring charges for each project, and record this at the top of the worksheet.

9. Convert the number of analysts you have placed on each project into achievement points; that is, multiply by the following factors:

Group leader: 100 points
Senior analyst: 75 points
Junior analyst: 50 points

10. Record the achievement points (if any) accumulated from previous plays.

11. Add and record the achievement points earned this period.

12. Add and record the total achievement points for each project to date.

---

[3] Extra forms will be found at the end of this chapter.

FIGURE 4–4

STUDY COST WORKSHEET

(Fill Out One for Each Period)

Actual Study Costs by Project This Period   Period No.___

Fill in number of analysts for each selected project	Project Number										Total Dollars
	1	2	3	4	5	6	7	8	9	10	
Group leaders											x $15,000 =
Achievement points*											
Senior analysts											x $12,000 =
Achievement points											
Junior analysts											x $ 8,000 =
Achievement points											
Achievement points previous period											
Achievement points this period											
Total achievement points to date											
Page reference											

(Fill in below only for new hires)

Group leaders recruited											x $ 5,000 =
Senior analysts recruited											x $ 3,000 =
Junior analysts recruited											x $ 2,000 =

$ _____

Total Study
Costs This
Period. Stay
within Budget.

---

* *Achievement Points*:
  Group Leader: 100
  Senior Analyst: 75
  Junior Analyst: 50
  Deduct 20 points if you transfer anyone between projects.

FIGURE 4–5

TABLE LOOK-UP FOR RELATING ACHIEVEMENT POINTS TO
WRITTEN REPORTS

Project No.	1	2	3	4	5	6	7	8	9	10
Achievement Point Scale:	Page listings for Project Reports available in Appendix A*									
1–100	213	223	233	243	253	263	273	283	293	303
101–200	214	224	234	244	254	264	274	284	294	304
201–300	215	225	235	245	255	265	275	285	295	305
301–400	216	226	236	246	256	267	276	286	296	306
401–500	217	227	237	247	257	267	277	287	297	307
501–600	218	228	238	248	258	269	278	288	298	308
601–700	219	229	239	249	259	269	279	289	299	309
701–800	220	230	240	250	260	270	280	290	300	310
801–900	221	231	241	251	261	271	281	291	301	311
901–1000	222	232	242	252	262	272	282	292	302	312

* *Multiple page numbers* are shown on some pages in Appendix A to indicate that no more information has been obtained on this project.

INSTRUCTIONS FOR USE OF FIGURES 4–5 AND 4–6

1. Figure 4–5 shows an achievement point scale cross-referenced to page numbers in this book. On these pages you will find reproductions of the project reports. Take the total achievements points to date for each project from the Study Cost Worksheet (Figure 4–4) and move down column A on the Table Look-Up (Figure 4–5) until you run out of points. Trace across horizontally to find the page you are eligible to read for the particular project. For example, two Seniors on Project 1 would give a total of 150 points. Read across from 101–200 on the Achievement Point Scale, and under Project 1 you find page 214. The material on 214 represents the most recent written results produced by your analysts on Project 1. You should not read beyond this page as this would bias your play. Write this page reference number (for each project worked on) on the Study Cost Worksheet.

2. Now go to these pages and read the new facts concerning the project. You are eligible to read all pages "produced to date" on the project.

3. At the bottom of each report page, three figures are provided by your analysts. The first two figures represent the analyst's best estimate of (1) what it will cost to continue the particular project to completion, and (2) what savings could be obtained in the departments studied after completion of the project. Note that these two estimates are no more than the analyst's expression, in dollars, of what he has written out on the page. He is required to make these numerical estimates, and therefore he does. This means that you must temper your confidence in these figures by careful reading of the written materials that represent the analyst's best statement of the project to date.

The third figure is less of an estimate. It is the amount of net savings that has already been obtained (in the department studied) as a result of a project. The analyst has a standard procedure for making this calculation. Note also that the Actual (Net) Savings to Date, shown at the bottom of each report sheet, are cumulative; that is, they can include savings that you might have made in previous periods. Do not double-count by adding the last period's Actual Savings to Date; these are already included.

4. Take the three figures in dollars, at the bottom of the last report page (for which you are eligible), and transfer these figures onto the Project Accounting Form (Figure 4-6). Do this for each project. Also, fill in the column for Actual Cost to Date from your Cost Worksheet. (Include any actual costs accumulated from the previous period.) These four figures give you an accounting picture of the status of each project studied.

These accounting figures, plus the reports, are used by you as you make the decisions regarding the quantity and quality of analysts you will assign to projects in the next period. The idea is to spread your group leaders, and senior and junior analysts, over the projects you select so that they will return you the highest savings over costs.

5. The rule, of course, is not to peek ahead of what your analysts could have written. The reports, for simplification purposes, are set up so that they appear to be written over a period of time. Of course you can compress the time of any project by putting more analysts on the job.

We have provided for three plays, covering simulated time periods of six months each. At the end of three plays you will have spent some $300,000. Your performance can be measured by the amount of savings you are able to produce, over and above the $300,000 you spent. Calculate your net gain or loss on the bottom of the Project Accounting Form.

6. Use the budget formula on page 40 to determine your budget for the second and third periods.

FIGURE 4–6

SMART CORPORATION SYSTEMS DEPARTMENT MANAGEMENT
PROJECT ACCOUNTING
ESTIMATED AND ACTUAL DATA
ON COSTS AND SAVINGS

Period 1

		(These Figures Are from Report Pages)		
Project	Actual Study Cost to Date by Project (From Cost Worksheet)	Estimated Cost at End of Study	Estimated Savings at End of Study	Actual Savings to Date (Cumulative)
1				
2				
3				
4				
5				
6				
7				
8				
9				
10				

Total Actual Savings to Date: $______

Period 2

	(Add Study Cost to Date from Previous Period)			
1				
2				
3				
4				
5				
6				
7				
8				
9				
10				

Total Actual Savings to Date: $______
Minus Savings to Date Last Period: –$______
Total Actual Savings This Period: $______

FIGURE 4–6 (Cont.)

Period 3
(Add Study Cost to
Date from Previous
Period)

1				
2				
3				
4				
5				
6				
7				
8				
9				
10				

$\underline{}$
Total Salaries*

Total Actual Savings to Date*: $ \underline{}$
Minus Savings to Date Last Period: $-$$ \underline{}$
Total Actual Savings This Period: $ \underline{}$

* To calculate overall gain or loss at end of Game, compare your Total Actual
Savings to Date with the Total Cost of Salaries to Date:

$ \underline{}$ $-$ $ \underline{}$ $=$ $ \underline{}$
Gain or Loss

THE TEN ASSIGNMENTS FROM THE EXECUTIVE COMMITTEE

SUBJECT: *Attention to Product Line Analysis Problem, Code 1–0.*

Although we seem to have large inventories, we are continually out-of-stock on many lines. Customers are not served and money is tied up in slowly moving inventories. The basic question is: How well are we doing in keeping our product line in balance with market demands and trends? Are we watching for opportunities to improve our profit position through both simplification and diversification of product offerings?

SUBJECT: *Attention to Shipping and Receiving, Code 2–0.*

There have been several complaints about the apparent lack of efficiency of these functions at Plant No. 1. These complaints range from "It takes half a day to find out anything" to "They are the most independent bunch of people in this whole company." Obviously, these two functions can seriously influence vendor and customer relations. Further, they are creating an undesirable degree of friction within the Company.

SUBJECT: *Attention to Purchasing Department Study, Code 3–0.*
1. Recently several key orders have been delayed because raw materials were not received in time.
2. There is no assigned responsibility for coordinating market price fluctuation and purchasing policy.
3. Presently there is little, if any, "coordinated" purchasing by the several company plants.

SUBJECT: *Attention to Inventory Control Problems, Code 4–0.*
In keeping with the current Management Improvement Program, it appears advisable to investigate the effectiveness of our Inventory Control activities. Certain trouble spots are apparent:
1. Despite our efforts to forecast future inventory balances we often come up with results very out-of-line.
2. Year-end physical inventories have likewise had wide deviations from perpetual inventory records.
3. Various departments have made gross departures from the general inventory policy of the Company.
4. Engineering and Experimental stock rooms have expanded without apparent control.
5. No recent check has been made on non-moving items held in stock.

SUBJECT: *Attention to Typing Pool, Code 5–0.*
The head of Finance has recently returned from a workshop at the Amalgamated Management Association. At this meeting the savings resulting from typing or stenographic pools were presented in great detail. It is his impression, based on the material presented, that our clerical operation is of sufficient size to warrant such a pool.

SUBJECT: *Attention to Policy Formulation and Compliance Problems, Code 6–0.*
The results of the recent attitude survey would appear to justify a new look at the manner in which policies are formalized and at the arrangements for checking to see that the policies are being followed. Excerpts from the findings follow:
1. "Too little opportunity to express views. Policy set at top without seeing impact down the line."
2. "Many policies are inconsistent."
3. "Policy appears only when I have done something wrong."
4. "Policy manual classification system is poor."
5. "Policy manual never up-to-date."
6. "Systems changes are often ineffective because related policy has not been spelled out."

SUBJECT: *Attention to Automatic Factory, Code 7–0.*
The developments in recent years of electronic digital computers and control systems for machine tools indicate the possibility of combining these equipments in an integrated "automatic" manufacturing process. We think our company should at least be thinking about these possibilities.

Because of the "total system" aspects of this kind of a survey we feel that the Systems Department should perform an exploratory study, collecting and coordinating the views of all departments that might be concerned.

SUBJECT: *Attention to Development of an Executive Information Display Center, Code 8–0.*

In keeping with the Company's policy of progress, it seems advisable to study the new developments in visual displays of management information using the computer.

Please determine the feasibility of setting up a room in which key information can be presented to Company executives.

SUBJECT: *Attention to Clerical Work Measurement, Code 9–0.*

1. A management consulting firm has offered to install a system of clerical work measurement. They predict an estimated savings of 20 percent in labor cost.
2. Please evaluate this offer immediately, giving us answers to these questions:
    a) Is this prediction realistic?
    b) Can we accomplish similar results using Company personnel?
    c) Should we enter into further negotiations with this firm?

SUBJECT: *Attention to Self-service Stockroom Problem, Code 10–0.*

It has been brought to our attention that some companies have inaugurated self-service stockroom facilities and systems to provide service and to control expenditures on engineering and experimental material inventories. The Executive Committee would like more information on this development.

Now that you have seen examples of the types of problems that may be assigned to a systems department, let us go one step further and have you organize and staff your department to work on these problems.

Assignments Received

Code	Subject
1–0	Product Line Analysis Problem
2–0	Shipping and Receiving
3–0	Purchasing Department Study
4–0	Inventory Control Problems
5–0	Typing Pool Study
6–0	Policy Formulation and Compliance
7–0	Automatic Factory Study
8–0	Executive Information Display System
9–0	Clerical Work Measurement
10–0	Self-service Stock Room Study

You can work on all ten projects, or on any number up to ten. You can hire any number of analysts, in any of the grades, as long as your total study costs do not exceed $100,000. Figure 4–4 is a study cost worksheet. It is used to record the types of analysts you assign by project and the related costs. It also provides a check to see that you do not exceed your budget. However, you should spend as close to the total of your budget as possible because the budget does not carry over from period to period.

After analyzing the assignment descriptions, make your decisions and record them on a copy of the study cost worksheet. In an actual situation this would mean that you have hired certain skills and have put them to work on certain priority problems. You now wait for results.

We are going to do some condensing of time and assume that six months have passed. During these six months your analysts have been working on the projects to which you assigned them.[4] At the end of this period each project worked on is written up as a progress report. These reports are available to you to help you make new assignments to your personnel.

Three forms (two extra copies of the worksheet are at end of this chapter) are used to collect all the data necessary for this game. Costs, achievement points, and savings are the ingredients for both estimated and actual results. Note how these forms provide a system for progress planning and control. As the manager of the department, you of course are seeking savings. The actual savings at a point in time, however, are only one part of the system's contribution, for you now have estimates of what savings are possible and what it will cost to do the necessary studies. Behind each of these estimates you have the documentation provided by the analysts' reports. As a matter of fact, the dollar estimates are derived from these reports and can be no better than the reasoning presented in them. You should read the reports with this in mind.

RECAPITULATION OF THE SMART CASE STUDY

A management game is a case study that "plays back" at you; as you make certain decisions, the game reacts and confronts you with changed situations. A game is more of a moving picture than a standard case study. It is still a case study, however, and has the advantage of looking at practical difficulties in a variety of situations.

---

[4] This is a simplification for case study purposes. In practice, assignments would probably change more often than once in six months.

We know, having used this game in education and industry, that some will question the reality of the problems and the approaches to them. The answer to this is that reality is much more complicated than we have shown here. We have compressed and skeletonized many factors and much detail in order to present a framework in which management systems can be conceptualized and in which the student can exercise his judgment at a simulated level of practice. This case study was originally developed and played as a management game for systems professionals. It is used here primarily to demonstrate the environment in which management problems develop—and from which the need for management systems studies is derived. Systems studies originate in vague, uncertain terms. It takes both good intuition and good technique to make meaningful progress in clarifying the problem characteristics, especially those characteristics which demonstrate the worthwhileness of making and continuing such a study.

The information production process, like the physical production process, depends on the description of the market which is to be served and the steps that must be taken to produce marketable results. In this case study, the market for information and certain preliminary techniques for producing results have been described. This framework is further developed as this case is extended in the following chapters. The notion of gradual extension into specifics is typical in systems development, and we have incorporated this same approach into the design of the later chapters.

EXTRA COPY OF STUDY COST WORKSHEET

(Fill Out One for Each Period)

Actual Study Costs by Project This Period   Period No.__

Fill in number of analysts for each selected project	Project Number										Total Dollars
	1	2	3	4	5	6	7	8	9	10	
Group leaders											x $15,000 =
Achievement points*											
Senior analysts											x $12,000 =
Achievement points											
Junior analysts											x $ 8,000 =
Achievement points											
Achievement points previous period											
Achievement points this period											
Total achievement points to date											
Page reference											

(Fill in below only for new hires)

Group leaders recruited											x $ 5,000 =
Senior analysts recruited											x $ 3,000 =
Junior analysts recruited											x $ 2,000 =

$_____

Total Study
Costs This
Period. Stay
within Budget.

---

* *Achievement Points*:
   Group Leader: 100
   Senior Analyst: 75
   Junior Analyst: 50
   Deduct 20 points if you transfer anyone between projects.

(Fill Out One for Each Period)

Actual Study Costs by Project This Period   Period No.__

Fill in number of analysts for each selected project	Project Number										Total Dollars
	1	2	3	4	5	6	7	8	9	10	
Group leaders											x $15,000 =
Achievement points*											
Senior analysts											x $12,000 =
Achievement points											
Junior analysts											x $ 8,000 =
Achievement points											
Achievement points previous period											
Achievement points this period											
Total achievement points to date											
Page reference											

(Fill in below only for new hires)

Group leaders recruited											x $ 5,000 =
Senior analysts recruited											x $ 3,000 =
Junior analysts recruited											x $ 2,000 =

$ _____

Total Study
Costs This
Period. Stay
within Budget.

---

* *Achievement Points*:
    Group Leader: 100
    Senior Analyst: 75
    Junior Analyst: 50
    Deduct 20 points if you transfer anyone between projects.

Chapter 5

CLASSIFICATION AND
CODING APPROACHES

In every field of endeavor constant attention is given to better means of describing problems and their methods of solution. These descriptive means include all types of representation. Representation is necessary in all fields for it is rarely possible to work only with the real world, and substitutes must be found. These are the symbols with which we build descriptions of both simple and complex phenomena.

The real world of business is no exception. A wide variety of symbols has been, and is being, invented to carry the burden of description and analysis of business activities. This chapter will consider business problem identification and business problem solving symbols under the headings Classification and Coding. First, however, let us look at the more general but very important subject of the manager's need for a working vocabulary.

THE MANAGER'S WORKING VOCABULARY

A manager must be able to understand and speak the language peculiar to his business. He must also be able to discuss management problems with people outside his business. Only gradually, with training and experience, does a manager develop the vocabulary with which he thinks and communicates. His success, to a large degree, depends on his vocabulary and the effectiveness with which he puts this vocabulary to work.

It is appropriate to think in terms of a basic management vocabulary and a variety of specialized vocabularies. The basic vocabulary contains the terms that are used in every type of business. Examples are budgets, sales, purchasing, organization, and financing. This type of terminology applies to any enterprise.

Specialized vocabularies generally develop from two directions. Each *function* of organization has its own special jargon to describe its types of problems. Accounting provides good examples of such a specialized vocabulary, as does the personnel function. The second type of specialized vocabulary comes from the *type of business* involved. A manufacturing enterprise develops terminology unique to its products and markets. This is also the case with such organizations as retailers, insurance companies, or banks. Each has its set of peculiar terms for its managers to learn and to use. The student and the practitioner—both looking for a successful career in management—should pay close attention to their particular needs for working vocabulary. Education and training can do much to add to basic and functional vocabularies, but only on-the-job experience can provide the special vocabulary of a particular firm.

The reasons for stressing vocabulary at this point are important. Vocabularies are the raw materials with which problems and solutions are expressed and communicated. The systems designer, for example, must not assume there is only one language for solving problems, *his* language. As his assignments move him to problems at a variety of levels and specialties, he must know or learn the "local" languages. All too often, terminology is brushed aside with the assertion "Oh, that's just a matter of semantics." This is hazardous reasoning, for the meanings of words are the very essence of thought and action in management situations. And this is particularly true in the development of management information systems.

In the remainder of this chapter, two aspects of management vocabulary are given specific attention: Classification and Coding. These two factors were selected because of the vital part they play in the design of a business system.

CLASSIFICATION DEFINED

What is a classification? The nature and importance of classification in business is demonstrated in the following quotation.

Classification is the beginning of the organizing of facts and information. Classification of *the activities* of any given industry is necessary for good operation. Unless they are subdivided, it will be difficult if not impossible to establish comparisons or find costs, and thus ascertain which sections are being run at a profit and which at a loss. Unless such knowledge is available, the management has no way of properly directing business. . . . The *economy* of classifications and symbols cannot be too highly stressed. These standardized representations, groupings, and arrangements have a common purpose, namely, to save mental effort, time, and expense, and to prevent troublesome and costly mistakes. They permit concentration on the subject matter of information, reports, and orders with a minimum of attention to the way these papers are expressed. They aid in recording, transmitting, and comprehending ideas and intakes, misunderstandings, and wrong actions. They concern all aspects of industrial operation, for classifications, forms, and symbols are practically useful in every activity.[1]

It is useful to separate those who develop classifications and those who only use classifications. Those who use classifications are normally not expected to be completely familiar with how such classifications were developed. To a degree, it is an advantage for most users to accept pre-built classifications and apply them without question. This, of course, holds only when the developers of classifications make improvements to classifications as opportunities are seen.

Classifications are the building blocks of representations. These blocks can be big or small, gross or detailed, and it is the critical job of the developer to match needs with an appropriate coverage of classifications. Let us consider a typical case of need for classification. Every business has an accounting system, and each accounting system includes a chart of accounts. An example of such a chart is shown in Figure 5–1. Each line on this chart is a class of costs. The overall list is a system of classification, a picture of the parts making up the whole. An overall classification of a business' primary areas of costs provides the framework for an overall cost control program. The detailed cost classes give specific areas in which costs can be recorded and improvements sought.

In the example shown, note that each class can be questioned. First, should the class be included? Is this cost area important enough to justify the effort involved in keeping track of these costs? Secondly, if we decide the area is important, should we show only one class, or should this class be broken into subclasses to allow more specific investigation of possibilities for cost reduction? In an actual situation, answers to these questions will determine just how many and how detailed the classes will be in the chart of accounts classification.

Similar questions apply to the development of any classification system. A classification is a grouping of items of similar characteristics into classes or groups. This is not, however, a sufficient definition for it ignores the need for identifying what we mean by similar characteristics. Further, it ignores the needs to treat differences as well as similarities. Let us look at this point more closely.

---

[1] With permission. L. P. Alford and John R. Bangs (eds.), *Production Handbook,* (New York: The Ronald Press Company, 1956), p. 1337 ff.

An overall classification development requires consideration of both differences and similarities. Similarities are sought so that they can be brought together in one place and worked on with a relatively uniform approach. Differences are sought in order to recognize when different treatment must be applied to the classes. A class, therefore, represents a grouping within which the subclasses fit together in relative harmony. These subclasses have meaning in the sense that they

FIGURE 5–1

SMALL CORPORATION'S CLASSIFICATION OF GENERAL LEDGER ACCOUNTS

Classification Plan, Major Classes
- 100   Assets
- 200   Liabilities and Net Worth
- 300   Sales and Costs of Sales
- 400   Administrative Expense
- 500   Manufacturing Expense
- 600   Direct Labor
- 700   Selling Expenses
- 800   Shipping Expenses
- 900   Miscellaneous

Classification Plan, Second Level: Manufacturing Expense (Example)
- 510   Indirect Labor
- 520   Payroll Taxes, Insurance, and Reserve
- 530   Operating
- 540   Maintenance Supplies
- 550   Purchasing Services
- 560   Fixed Charges

Classification Plan, Third Level: Operating Supplies (Example)
- 531   Belting
- 532   Gloves
- 533   Uniforms
- 534   Cleaning Materials
- 535   Safety Glasses

---

form the class as a whole. Contrasts of classes, however, emphasize the need to identify differences and the significance of these differences.

This running back and forth between similarities and differences plays an important part in the development of a useful classification system. The fundamental idea is that classifications are built to facilitate decisions. Decisions involve both the making of comparisons for similarities and of contrasts for differences. In a good classification system, certain significant comparisons and contrasts are already built in.

Because classifications touch every part of a business, great care should be used in their design. It is very easy to develop classifications which are overstructured, too detailed, and too complicated. From a data-processing point of view, the more detailed the classes the higher the volume and cost of processing. We will demonstrate some types of classifications, in the order of increasing complexity, after a word on the "see-saw" rule of classification.

The rule is: *As the costs of classification go up, the costs of using the classification go down.* The reverse is also true: *As the costs of classification go down, the costs of using the classifications go up.* This rule is related to the earlier statement that a good classification system has already built in significant comparisons and contrasts. The investment in such "building-in" is recovered when a user of the classification has less work to do.

An example is a classification system for storing books in a business library. Let us assume a simple, low-cost classification system for putting books on the shelves. Three separate parts of the library are labeled: (1) Procurement (2) Production, and (3) Distribution. Each time a book is obtained by the library it is inspected, identified as one of the three classes, and placed on any available shelf in one of the three sections of the library. (Of course, this is an exaggeration, but it makes the point.) It is relatively simple for the librarian to do her work, but it is also very difficult and time consuming for anyone to locate a book. The cost of classification is low; the cost of use is high.

The reverse situation exists when the library uses a large number of specific classes. This, of course, requires that each new book be inspected in great detail and its various classes of material identified. It also leads to the cross-referencing of materials for user guidance. With such a classification system the user can locate more specific materials in less time. The cost of classification then is high, and the cost of use is low.

Because classifications can be simple or complicated, it is necessary that the systems developer become familiar with the types of classifications. Note that the following headings represent a classification, and include five classes from simple to complex.

Random Classifications. This is a starting point for classification, for it is, in effect, no classification. If we were filing under this system, the most we could say is "It is somewhere in the filing cabinet." No relationship has been established; there is no sequential pattern. On the average we would have to look at half of the items in the file before we could find what we were looking for, assuming the item is in the cabinet to start with. This is the bench mark from which we can measure improvements in classification systems design.

One-dimensional Classification.   Under this approach we classify all elements with respect to the single factor that we have chosen as the significant indicator. Examples are: age, payroll number, name, social security number, address, and so forth. In this case a file would have just one way of entry: by the selected factor in serial order. There are no relations except serial. A search for factors other than the one used for classification is not helped. If such other factors are wanted we must search item by item, as with the random classification.

List, or Tree, Classification.   With this classification approach more work is necessary in the preparation stage. We do not limit our classification of an item to one dimension as in serial filing. Rather, we can assign an item to satisfy several uses. Within the code number string we provide an arrangement whereby the first number in a list is linked to the next list. This continues as long as successive movements from list to list are required.

Consider the following example of a code number representing a part in inventory: 2847–1942–7210. The first four digits represent the item number. The second four digits identify the subassembly that this part goes into, and the last four digits cite the code for the end product into which the subassembly goes. This is a simple list, for it provides only for a one-to-one progression through the list. More complicated list structures are available to handle situations where one part goes into more than one subassembly. The problem, of course, is to limit the overall size of the serial number and the number of digits required to get to the next position. The advantage is that this type of classification has built-in routes for certain channels of data.

Unit Term Classification.   This system of classification requires a very explicit study of the items to be classified. The use of this system has been primarily in the filing and retrieval of reports and documents. Before these materials are filed they are read carefully and key terms (uniterms) which represent their content are chosen. These terms are (1) written in a special glossary of terms for the field of interest, and (2) written as a header on a single card. Thus every term (factor) has a separate card (or other means of recording), and all the ways of entering the file for retrieval are listed in the glossary.

Every time a new document is studied, its key terms are identified and a number representing that document is written on all the cards that have uniterm headings that match those selected in the document. Figure 5–2 shows four such cards and how they would record the content of certain chapters in this book involving these terms. Note

FIGURE 5–2

UNITERM EXAMPLE

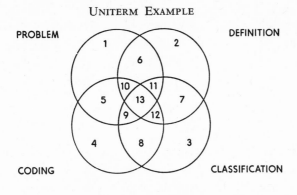

TERM	PROBLEM (a)									
0	1	2	3	4	5	6	7	8	9
		12					17 27		

TERM	DEFINITION (b)									
0	1	2	3	4	5	6	7	8	9
					⑮		17 27		

TERM	CLASSIFICATION (c)									
0	1	2	3	4	5	6	7	8	9
		12			⑮				

TERM	CODING (d)									
0	1	2	3	4	5	6	7	8	9
		12			⑮				

that the retrieval can proceed by asking for materials under any one term or by any combination of terms up to the total of those listed in the glossary. In practice, of course, relatively few terms would be asked for at any one time.

Let us look at Figure 5–2 and trace through a uniterm application. Take four terms used in this book: (*a*) *Problem,* (*b*) *Definition,* (*c*) *Classification,* and (*d*) *Coding.* There are 15 possible combinations (2^x-1) from these four uniterms:

1. Problem
2. Definition
3. Classification
4. Coding
5. Problem Coding
6. Problem Definition
7. Definition Classification
8. Classification Coding
9. Problem Classification Coding
10. Problem Definition Coding
11. Problem Definition Classification
12. Definition Classification Coding
13. Problem Definition Classification Coding
14. (Not numbered on diagram) Problem Classification
15. (Not numbered on diagram) Coding Definitions

Assume that, as you read this book, you set up a uniterm system to identify chapters that refer to any combination of the above terms. As you read the chapters in sequence you might identify the following:

> Chapter 4 refers to uniterms *a, c* and *d;* use chapter code 12.[2]
> Chapter 5 refers to uniterms *b, c* and *d;* use chapter code 15.
> Chapter 7 refers to uniterms *a* and *b;* use chapter code 17.
> Chapter 8 refers to uniterms *a* and *b;* use chapter code 27.

You would then write in the code numbers as shown on the bottom of Figure 5–2. If someone uses these uniterm cards seeking to obtain a reference to a term, he goes directly to that card and notes all code references. He then looks at the titles assigned to these code numbers and goes directly to the source. If he wishes a reference made from a combination of uniterms (e.g., Definition, Classification, Coding), he looks at these three cards and picks out any references that show on all three cards (i.e., reference code 15). Looking up code 15 he would find that it referred him to Chapter 5 of this book, which includes *definitions* for both *classifications* and *codes.*

The uniterm system and related approaches provide a quite efficient means for classification and retrieval of information in specific areas. It has been pointed out that the size of a library catalog, for example, can be reduced by as much as 90 percent. To accomplish this, of course, it is necessary to provide the glossary of terms and the actual list of documents that has been selected for relevancy to the subject area.

"Concept" Classifications.   This is a rather new and advanced approach to classification. It requires a real investment in reading and

---

[2] Uniterm cards filled out for these references are shown in Figure 5–2. The chapter codes are chosen so that the last digit in the code corresponds to the column number (from 0 to 9) in which it is posted. New documents (in this case chapters) are always given a higher number than any number used previously. There is, therefore, no problem of leaving spaces in the columns for preassigned numbers.

identifying the content of any package of information. Again, let us consider a report. The reviewer of the report not only picks key terms but he relates these in such a manner that they represent a generalized context and content of the document.

The document content is put in condensed form by selecting key nouns, adjectives, adverbs, and prepositions. This condensing is done by experts in the particular field of knowledge. An asterisked term is also selected as the most significant of the key terms. This term is, in a sense, the uniterm that will be retrieved. In this case, however, the "uniterm" will come out with a set of other terms that gives a more specific description of the overall concept involved in the document. The asterisked term and the other selected terms are printed out on a space about the size of a 3 by 5-inch card.

The user can go through these cards quite quickly and select those cards representing documents that he would like to see. The talents and time previously invested have facilitated his job. To prepare the context statement the expert must be qualified enough to put himself in the place of the person who will later come to this system and ask for certain literature. He must be able to anticipate not only one dimensional requests but a wide variety of multi-dimensional questions. He therefore commands a good salary. This system, of course, represents the case of high costs in classification and low costs in use.

The foregoing five examples were given here to show a variety of classifications that moves from simple to complex. These examples emphasize classification of literature-type documents, but the same reasoning can be applied to storage of pieces of business data. This is demonstrated in the example at the end of this chapter.

THE SEE-SAW *RULE*

Figure 5–3 is graphic representation of the see-saw rule. It is an adaptation of the economic lot-size rule used in manufacturing. As we develop and use more refined methods for classification, our classification (preparation) costs obviously will increase (curve A–B). Refined methods of classification make it easier for the user to get to stored materials, and therefore the user costs decrease (curve C–D). E–F is a total unit cost curve (sum of vertical distances of the other two curves). The U shape demonstrates the see-saw rule, and the lowest point on the U gives a general notion of how to find the lowest overall cost of a classification system. This, of course, says nothing about the value of what is classified and retrieved, but it gives us guidance in how far to go in refining classifications for given situations from a cost point of view.

FIGURE 5-3

THE "SEE-SAW" RULE

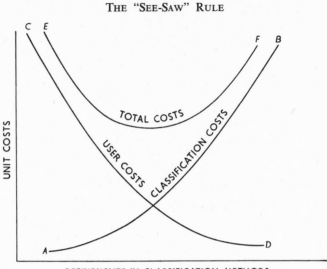

REFINEMENTS IN CLASSIFICATION METHODS

CODING DEFINED

Figure 5–4 is a visual aid to remind us of the need to minimize the amount of detail that is carried in a management information system. "Universe" represents all the detail which is, or can be, involved in a particular management situation. A fact of life is that no one can handle all the details in even a simple situation. Further, even if we

FIGURE 5-4

CLASSES AND CODES AS A SELECTION PROCESS

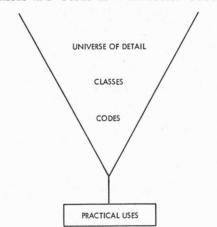

could treat all details, it would not be efficient to do so. Many of the details in a study should be ignored because they either have insignificant effects or they are just too expensive to allow analysis. The problem, of course, is to know which details can be ignored.

The decision to establish a class, or to use an existing class, is the threshold at which we determine that a certain factor cannot be ignored. The identification of a factor as significant is the justification for having a class. There is no sense in paying the expenses for classification if we cannot see meaningful uses for the classes. The recognition that classes should be selected carefully is a major step in the process of minimizing detail in an organization's systems.

THE PURPOSE OF CODES

The next reduction in the level of detail is in the care with which codes are selected and used. *A code is a shorthand expression for a class.* Codes provide abbreviation. In the simplest sense this means that there can be fewer characters (such as letters and numbers) which must be handled in data processing. Even though certain codes may be very long they can have more information compressed into them by the use of shorthand symbols.

It is important to remember that codes are only shortened expressions of classes. This "mirror image" should be kept in mind, for it shows us that codes should retain the characteristics for which we established the classes in the first place.

SOME TYPICAL CODES

Now let us look at a few of the typical codes used in business. Basically codes, like classes, can represent nouns, verbs, and various qualifiers. This amounts to codes for persons, places, things, types of actions, and states of condition. A social security number represents a person. A ZIP Code number designates a place. A part number identifies a thing. Much modern data processing is concerned with keeping records by person, place, or thing; and code numbers help reduce the burden of such processing.

A code can also give instructions. It may tell, by representing a verb, just what action should take place. "Red" is a coded verb in a traffic light. A ZIP Code number represents a place, but used on a letter it means *send to* 19104. As we shall see later (in the chapter on computer programming), a whole set of codes is used to instruct a computer as to the actions that should be performed. By combining codes for nouns and verbs we are able to describe entire procedures in coded form. The code 1A2B3C can represent three actions (numbers) and three things (letters) to which the actions apply:

Verb (Action)	Noun (Thing)
1. Report	A. Results
2. Compare to	B. Standard
3. Make any	C. Corrections necessary

1A2B3C is a very compact way of substituting for all the above words.

As noted above, codes can also show states of condition. AOK is an example of this sort of code application. In many management situations it is important to know how well things are going. Classes of possible conditions can be established and these classes can then be represented by codes. AAA is a code saying that a business is in first-class condition, but DDD says that the sheriff is on the way. A wide variety of codes is used to represent scales of differences in business conditions.

Codes can be built by assembling letters, numbers, and other short symbols. Individual codes often appear as a string of such symbols in which the position—as well as the identity—of the symbol has some significance. In the code 729–142–218–300, for example, the first three digits could represent a date, July 29; the second three digits could indicate a code number for a physical location; the third set of digits might refer to a part number; and the last set could be a quantity. The overall code would say: Send 300 parts No. 218 to location No. 142 by July 29. When many such orders are sent, the compressibility through coding of data becomes quite apparent.

Codes may have significance as a result of their position in a string, and they may also have significance because of the position in which the overall code is placed on the face of a form. In the above example, the code number would be so placed that it came under a heading that meant "Ship to." A wide variety of shorthand messages can be assembled by the use of code symbols, strings, and format position. This introduction to codes demonstrates that there are many methods of reducing the detail in the data that must be processed for business planning and control purposes. We look at certain more specific applications of codes in later chapters; here we are demonstrating why classifications and codes are necessary in systems development.

AN EXAMPLE OF THE PROBLEM CLASSES AND CODES IN MANPOWER PLANNING AND CONTROL

In data processing, as in document search, we may want to find certain combinations of facts. An example is a search for a qualified individual to fit a particular job specification. Such a search puts us right in the middle of the overall problems of manpower planning and control. It is not simply a matter of one man and one job; rather, it involves a search through all jobs and all positions seeking the most effective combinations. Masses of data can be accumulated, transferred, used, and stored in a modern manpower planning and control program. Careful analysis of classes and codes is required to assure that such data processing produces good results at reasonable costs. Let us enter this example through problem definition, phase I.

As a preliminary problem definition, we can assume that the Management Systems Department receives the following assignment:

FROM: The Executive Committee
SUBJECT: *Development of Data Bank for Manpower Planning and Control, Code 11–0.*

Please investigate the possibilities for improvements in the Employee Records Division of our Personnel Department. We are spending over $80,000 a year in salaries alone for this Division. What are we getting for this money? What services are performed by this Department? Is it feasible to develop a computer program that can improve these services?

Assume that the relative priority of this assignment confers immediate attention. Two analysts at the senior level are placed full-time on this investigation. At the end of a short period they have accumulated the following information, as described in their report.

Preliminary Report on Project 11–0:
The findings at this time are primarily descriptive in nature. We have sought to document the present set of requirements for this function as well as the present methods used to satisfy these requirements. In particular, we have identified the classifications and codes used in the processing of requests for candidates to fill open positions. At this time we sense that there is excessive duplication of information kept in a variety of files. We are proceeding to analyze this possibility. We request that arrangements be made to extend this study to include records kept in two other offices, i.e., the Payroll Records kept in the Controller's Office and the Pension Records kept in the Pension Division of the Personnel Office. This extension will be limited to determining how these records relate to those kept in the Employee Records Division.

A brief description of the records presently kept in the Employee Records Department follows:

The records originate with the forms filled out by applicants and their interviewers. Thereafter, each employee's record documents changes in his assignments, changes in his personal data, and any evaluation of his performance. Most of this change data originates in the department to which an employee is assigned. One of the significant problems is that these changes either do not get recorded or they are recorded very late, and often incorrectly. The result is a rather low-quality level in the Employee Records File. A sample of 100 transfers was traced through the system. These transfers took place one month earlier. When the files were in-

Physical Codes

B Epilepsy
  Diabetes
  Fainting
  Head injury
  Balance
  Heights
C Visual defect
D Hearing defect
E Noise sensitive
F Heart condition
  High blood pressure
G Respiratory condition
H Digestive disorders
I Hernia, back condition
J Impairment of extremities
K Dermatitis
X Others
N No disability

Series 0: Change in Rate
00 Advance automatic progress step
01 Merit increase
02 Automatic rate progress
03 Job revaluation
04 General increase

Series 1: Leave of Absence
10 Medical leave
11 Maternity leave
12 Military leave
13 Educational leave
14 Personal leave
15 Union leave
16 Government leave

Series 2: Retirements
20 Retirement, normal
21 Retirement, early

Series 3: Terminations
30 Termination, voluntary
31 Termination, disciplinary
32 Termination, unsatisfactory problem employee
33 Termination, deceased
34 Termination, no show

Series 4: Layoffs
40 Layoff, lack of work
41 Layoff, optional
42 Layoff, inability to perform
43 Layoff, capacity to perform
44 Layoff, emergency

Series 5: Transfer Requested
50 Transfer per grievance
51 Transfer request procedure
52 Transfer per verbal request

Series 6: New Employee: Recall, Return
60 Additional help (new employee)
61 Replacement (new employee)
62 Rehire (new employee)
63 Return or recall to former Division
64 Return or recall to former Senior Group Department or occupation
65 Return from leave of absence
66 Recall from layoff

Series 7: Replace Employee
70 Replace employee, vacation
71 Replace employee, absent
72 Replace employee, jury duty
73 Replace employee, leave of absence
74 Replace employee, miscellaneous

Series 8: Miscellaneous
80 To or from salary
81 To or from unit
82 Clock number change
83 Shift change
84 Start or finish apprenticeship
85 To installation training
86 Per unit transfer list
87 New department created
88 Per shop transfer list
89 Correction to previous status card

Series 9: Other Transfers
90 Promotional transfer
91 Production requirements
92 Additional help required
93 Transfer per 45-day provision
94 Transfer per 4-month provision
95 Lack of work
96 Inability to perform
97 Not suitable for occupation
98 Transfer due to health

SMART Corporation: Employee Record Data Classes and Codes

A. Statistical Data	B. Job Data (Current)
1 Name	1 Occupational code
2 Social security number	2 Job number
3 Address	3 Wage group
4 Telephone number	4 Guaranteed hourly rate
5 Birthdate	5 Base rate
6 Sex	6 Incentive rate
7 Marital status	adjustment
8 Number of exemptions	7 Department number
9 Citizenship	8 Clock number
10 Seniority date	9 Seniority group
11 Last date of hire	10 Superintendent code
12 Accumulated service	11 Shift
13 Vacation credit date	12 Job description
14 Former employee	13 Reason for transfer
15 Shop, main office, or	14 Date effective
supervisory employee	
16 Instrument or	
industries group	C. Job Data (All Past Jobs)
17 Test scores	
18 Inactive status code	1 Occupational code
19 Journeyman code	2 Job number
20 Apprentice code	3 Wage group
21 Educational code	4 Guaranteed hourly rate
22 Physical code	5 Base rate
23 Do not transfer code	6 Incentive rate
24 Bargaining unit code	adjustment
25 Literacy code	7 Department number
26 Automatic rate	8 Seniority group
progression code	9 Superintendent code
27 Military code	10 Shift
28 Seniority group	11 Job description
29 Date started in	12 Reason for transfer
seniority group	13 Date effective
30 Occupational sub code	14 Over-rate
31 Job code	

spected, errors were found on 20 percent of the involved employee's records. These mistakes meant that incorrect wage payments were made. Seniority requirements were not met and eligible employees were bypassed for beneficial transfers and promotions.

Underlying these difficulties are two basic areas where improvements should be made:

1. There are just too many forms used to record change data.
2. The classes and codes are not well thought out. In many instances

there are inconsistencies. In other cases classes and codes do not exist to cover certain important types of changes.

There will be no easy solution to this problem. It makes no sense to attempt to set up a so-called "central record" operation on our computer until the classes and codes have received tho:ough study and until we can identify the relationships among these classes and codes. Attached is a preliminary survey of the classifications and codes which are now being used in processing employee records.[3] Since codes can be designed only after classes and relations are established, we are not attempting at this time to anticipate the types of codes that should be used.

This "report" was placed in this chapter to show how even a most generalized problem statement can lead quickly to an analysis of classifications and codes. As stated above, it is useful to separate those who only use classifications and those who are responsible for developing classifications. Those who work in management systems must get to the practical information requirements of job positions and to the requirements of related systems before they can do good analysis and provide improvements. Others may generalize, but the systems man cannot afford this luxury.

The vocabulary of management is always changing. New concepts and new techniques receive names, and these become possible additions for inclusion in the vocabulary of management. When these names are considered from the point of view of classifications and codes, we see the need for great care in order to prevent duplication and confusion.

The dependence of systems development on clarity in classifications and codes is often overlooked. To repeat, this should not be the case with the professional in the field of management systems. He cannot afford to work with poor materials. He therefore becomes very interested in all situations that influence the classifications and codes of his business. As we will see in the next chapter, these are the raw materials with which systems are built and described in documentation.

---

[3] To the reader: We show these classes and codes here to demonstrate the amount of detail that must be handled in a problem of this sort. This case study on Manpower Planning and Control is further developed as we move through the succeeding chapters of this book. We return to classes and codes in Chapters 8, 9, 10 and 11.

Chapter 6

INTRODUCTION TO
DOCUMENTATION

The documentation of business systems is a very important, and difficult, area of analysis. For this reason it is appropriate that it be given separate and specific attention. Also, in later chapters we will see that documentation plays a part in every phase of a system's development. The background on documentation given in this chapter is therefore introductory in nature, and it will be extended in the following chapters.

The dictionary defines the verb document as: *to teach, to instruct, to furnish evidence of, to equip with exact references.* "Documentation," as used in business, has several meanings, but the one with which we shall be concerned is: *a recorded set of evidence showing the characteristics of some part—or all—of a management system.* The term also includes the overall set of evidence of choices or decisions made throughout the study of a system.

The idea of evidence is worthwhile when we consider the uses for documentation. There is no one use, but rather a set of uses that covers the range of need from general objectives to specific applications. Think of the number and variety of questions that may be asked of a particular management system, and this will give some idea of the scope of possible documentation. Obviously, the rule of selectivity applies; the documentation must fit the anticipated use, and we can, to a certain degree, predict such uses. That which follows shows some of the typical areas for which documentation of business systems has been assembled and used.

DOCUMENTATION IN THE LIFE CYCLE
OF A MANAGEMENT INFORMATION SYSTEM

This discussion of documentation follows the life cycle of a systems development shown in Chapter 3. As shown in Figure 6–1, the amount of documentation expands as a study progresses through the phases of the cycle. Documentation can be useful, in varying degrees, in each phase of the life cycle. The very describing of what decisions are to be made in each phase is helpful, in itself, in getting better decisions

FIGURE 6–1

DOCUMENTATION EXPANSION THROUGHOUT LIFE CYCLE OF A
MANAGEMENT INFORMATION SYSTEM

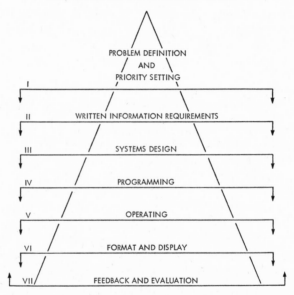

during the phase. In this sense, documentation is a tool of analysis. It provides the basic description of the situations with which the analyst is working and it acts as a point of departure for the improvements he seeks to accomplish.

In addition to its use in a phase, documentation also transmits description between phases. This is particularly helpful when different people become involved as the phases change. In this sense, documentation facilitates passing the work along with minimum need to redo previous work. If, however, a need arises to check a previous decision, the evidence is available and can be reviewed. Thus, the same set of evidence can be many different things to different people.

Documentation of a system or parts of a system can be done in a careless or in a careful manner. In some cases, scratch pads and all other working papers are simply thrown in a file drawer (or perhaps a wastepaper basket). At the other extreme, every detailed decision made is carefully reviewed, indexed, written up in some standardized manner, and filed for easy retrieval. Both extremes are rare; actual practice is usually somewhere in between.

The degree of care in documentation should be determined in each organization and often should vary from system to system. This is simply a recognition that documentation can be very expensive and should not be carried beyond a point of diminishing returns. The guide for selecting the form and amount of documentation is similar to the basic question for any information design problem: What will be the need to know, and in what degree of breadth and depth?

Documentation, as a term, is usually reserved for the phases associated with systems design and computer programming. Here, however, we will follow the generation of evidence down through the entire life cycle of a system's design.

PHASE I: IDENTIFY PRIORITY PROBLEM FOR SELECTED ATTENTION

Chapter 4 included rather simplified examples of the need to select priority areas for systems study and design. Many and various choices are normally available for selections, and for the assignments of personnel.

This phase is the most difficult, from a documentation point of view, primarily because opportunities for systems studies come to us in hints and possibilities and not in well worked out and clear detail. In the examples used in Chapter 4, the Executive Committee performed the filtering action. Presumably, they had the best perspective of the organization and were able to sense where there were opportunities for making improvements. They formalized their best judgments into recommendations for study by the systems department. These recommendations became more firm as the systems department made decisions to assign budgeted dollars to specific projects. Further concreteness became possible as study-generated reports gave better guidance for decisions.

At each level of the spelling out of the decisions, some form of documentation could and should take place. When a "peer group," such as the Executive Committee, records its recommendations, these selections should represent the prime guidance for organization improvements. In the traditional sense, this is policy guidance for the best interests of the organization. Understandably, such guidance in the early phases of a project is quite general and is usually written in simple

English sentences. This is in sharp contrast to the detailed logic diagrams and machine codes referred to below in the description of documentation in phases III and IV.

PHASE II: WRITE INFORMATION REQUIREMENTS

Once a priority area has been chosen for formal systems study, a need appears for gradually determining the particular types of information that should be produced by the system when it is put into operation. The documentation of these information requirements is an important phase in assuring a successful system's design. Only as these requirements are carefully chosen and documented is it possible to formfit the design of the system to individual manager's needs to know.

Typically, information requirements will be expressed in the vocabulary of the manager's field of specialization. The development and the relations of a management vocabulary to systems design documentation are presented in Chapter 8.

PHASE III: DEVELOP SYSTEMS DESIGN

We have now shown that systems design is not the first, but rather the third, step in the development of a management system. We hope we have also demonstrated that, unless phases I and II are carefully prepared, phase III of systems design has no clear-cut objectives. Without at least a reasonable problem definition, and some expression of the information requirements, this phase of systems design can be a waste of effort. In fact what often happens is that the systems designer, by himself, creates his problem definition and his view of the information requirements. As noted earlier, the difficulty here is that he may not know the "local" languages and may have only a superficial knowledge of the practical problems. There is no substitute for experience in conducting phases I and II. A professional systems designer will do his best to bring all available experience into the documentation on which he will base his design of a system. He recognizes that his efforts anticipate the day when he must go back to the managers and ask: "Does this fit your needs?"

PHASE IV: WRITE PROGRAMMING SPECIFICATIONS FOR MACHINE PROCESSING

Computer programming serves two major purposes. The logic of the systems design is converted into a format that recognizes the logic of the way the computer works. Quite often it is appropriate for the computer programmer to go back to the systems designer and discuss possible changes in order to take full advantage of the machine characteristics. The second purpose is the translation of the logic into *ma-*

chine language, the coded instructions that the machine requires to perform the right actions in appropriate sequences.

By the time a systems development enters the programming phase, there is usually a great quantity of detail which must be controlled. Special types of documentation are available to serve this purpose. Examples are shown in Chapter 10 (Programming Design Background) as part of the coverage of programming design.

PHASE V: DEVELOP PROCEDURES FOR OPERATING THE SYSTEM THROUGH A COMPUTER FACILITY

As with all expensive operations, a computer facility justifies careful attention to administrative procedures. These procedures should cover methods for scheduling, maintenance, inventory of in-stock programs, and inventories of data in processable form. Because each procedure ties directly into the classifications and codes used in systems design and programming, it is worthwhile to align the documentation of these procedures with the documentation provided by the designers and programmers.

Mistakes in program or data identification can result in lost time, as well as in the (perhaps more costly) incorrect production of output. Documentation in operations is important to both the quantity and quality of work accomplished in a computer facility.

PHASE VI: DESIGN OUTPUT FORMAT AND DISPLAY CHARACTERISTICS

The end results of a data processing system, to a large degree, are represented by what comes off the computer in hard copy or in visual display form. Documentation of the specifications for such output represents a logical follow-through on the documentation provided in the preceding phases of a system's development.

The work done in documenting the information requirements in phase II can be put to good use again in this phase of output analysis. These requirements provide at least general specifications that should be met by the system's output.

There are many formats in which information output can be presented. The sequence, as well as the content of presentation, is subject to study and decision. Much creative work is being done in this phase of systems development.

PHASE VII: PREPARE FEEDBACK ANALYSIS AND OVERALL EVALUATION OF SYSTEM

For certain relatively simple projects, this phase can almost be ignored. The outputs in such cases are obviously in line with what was required, and no further analysis is needed. In many instances, especially in the initial use of new systems, adjustments and revisions are to be expected. This feedback for the user's evaluation of the output of a system can lead to a recognition that he is not getting what he asked for, or a recognition that he needs what he had not previously asked for. This, of course, means adjustments of the documentation all through the cycle of the system's development. It often happens that documentation in the first cycle of a development is quite thorough. Later changes, however, are ignored, and the documentation therefore does not give an up-to-date picture of the existing system.

A sufficient and consistent attention to documentation throughout a system's development provides the best possible basis for the overall evaluation that should take place after the system is installed. The rhyme and the reason for each step that has been taken can be available in the documentation. Areas for improvement can be pinpointed and specific changes can be made.

THE CONTRIBUTION OF DOCUMENTATION TO THE INFORMATION PRODUCTION PROCESS

In Chapter 3 an analogy was made between the production of physical and information products. It was pointed out that production of physical products depends on the availability of standard nomenclature, uniformity in dimensions, and quality specifications. These needs are now becoming apparent in the production of information for business uses.

Just as we have needed good documentation to be able to produce physical commodities, we now see the merit in providing the same sort of guidance for decisions on data processing. In this sense, documentation for management systems development is a special kind of data, those data which are uniquely collected for the sole purpose of effective processing of all other kinds of data. Though this may sound strange at first, it is no different from physical production, where all types of data are created for the purpose of specifying product characteristics.

Progress has been made in manufacturing, and not only because of new machine methods. Careful attention to the documentation of answers to the questions of what should be produced, how it should be produced, when it should be produced, and where it should be produced has had much to do with the effectiveness of modern manufacturing methods. Documentation of answers to these same questions for modern data processing can produce similar results.

OTHER APPLICATIONS FOR DOCUMENTATION

The preceding sections introduced the idea of documentation as it applies in and between the phases of a system's development. These are not the only system uses for the evidence of which decisions to make and how they should be made.

The function of business auditing also has great interest in such evidence. This includes both internal auditing and auditing by external parties. Accurate and sufficient documentation facilitates such audits. The ability to trace through systems, especially now that they are intertwined with machine processing, is aided by appropriate documentation. At a minimum, documentation provides the key points of entrance into a system for such tracing.

The ability to trace through a variety of systems has another major use in systems designers' search for interrelationships among systems. The approach of this book emphasizes the design of a single system, but systems designers are making major efforts to see how various systems relate and interact. This type of compound analysis is in large measure dependent on the availability of good documentation techniques.

Another important use of documentation is in selecting computer hardware and related communications equipment. Such selections are based upon analyses called feasibility or augmentation studies. Computers, obviously, come in a variety of shapes and sizes. They, like shop equipment, should be matched with the requirements of the work to be done. Good documentation of the data processing work to be done should be an integral part of any feasibility study. Such evidence should include processing steps, volumes, and time-schedule requirements in sufficient detail to indicate what size machine should be obtained and which processing characteristics it should have. In feasibility studies it is, of course, necessary to estimate future systems work loads. To the degree possible, such projections should also be expressed in the standard documentation format.

DEVELOPING A PROGRAM FOR DOCUMENTATION

One significant service that a systems department can provide is guidance and monitorship in the organization's program of documentation. In effect, the systems department has a "license to meddle" in all areas of a business. Because of this exposure, such a department can do much to influence the quantity and quality of documentation. It should also play an active part in decisions regarding arrangements for retention, dissemination, and disposal of documentation files.

All too often, duplication of work takes place because previous studies have not been well documented or—even if they were well documented—the documentation has been mislaid. A program of documentation should be designed to minimize these difficulties. This is one place where the idea of standardization can make important contributions to management planning and control. Careful attention to how the written evidence of the business is selected and recorded will influence planning and control at the level of specifics. Such efforts build a degree of consistency and confidence into studies of any part of the business.

A formal program of documentation should include a Documentation Manual for distribution to all concerned. Let us take such an assignment as an example of a project that the Management Systems Department might initiate on its own, that is, without formal direction from the Executive Committee. No code number is assigned and work is done as time allows. Periodic reviews, however, include this project. After some period of time, the following report might be made at a Department Review Meeting.

Report on Documentation Project:

Ten man-days were spent on this project in the last three months (that is, only 10 man-days of this project were charged as "fill-in" work). We are finding that more and more time is being spent on documentation problems within all our other assignments. At a minimum, this project has provided some bench marks for coordination. We have as a result received many worthwhile suggestions over and above those developed in the ten man-days of effort on the project.

It appears that we could prepare a Documentation Manual at this time that would at least be a start in the right direction. With this in mind, we propose that the manual include the following sections:

SMART Corporation

Documentation Manual

(*Proposed Outline of Content*)

1. Importance of Documentation

This introduction would describe the benefits of documentation and its relationships to key management planning and control activities. Included would be statistics demonstrating the volume of present documentation and an estimate of what such work now costs the Company.

2. Scope of Manual Coverage and How to Use It

This section would delimit the areas for which guidance is to be provided in the manual. Inasmuch as documentation (written evidence) can include every piece of paper received by or produced in the Company, the manual would have to be encyclopedic to cover them all. If the manual is well done, it should serve several purposes. We propose that it not be limited to documentation for systems design and programming of management information systems. This section would explain why certain documentation areas are selected, and how these areas will be gradually refined and extended in later versions of the manual.

3. Documentation at the Level of Searching for and Selecting Key Objectives

We emphasize this area, for it is here that the initial guidance for monitoring the company's success is organized. Formal documentation at this level can, however, be considered only as an aid to managers when they grapple with large and complex situations. This type of documentation depends to a large degree upon the way in which the top management structure is arranged, and upon the manner in which this group stresses formal or informal methods at its level of planning and control.

4. Documentation at the Level of Selecting a Methodology for Making a Study

The selection of a management methodology determines to a large degree the type of documentation that can be used for a particular study. Here management specialties come into play as specific techniques are matched to particular types of problems. Stressing documentation at this level serves to emphasize the need for careful selection of study techniques. It also provides opportunity to refer back to the written record of how and why particular techniques were selected. The array of possible techniques for applications to management studies is rapidly increasing. It is becoming more and more important that the reasons for choice of a particular technique be identified and documented. We propose that a simple form be designed which would include a checklist of certain standard techniques and a space in which to identify other selections. Examples of standard techniques would include such approaches as:

Forecasting	Flow Charting
Marketing Services	Activity Analysis
Economy Study	Work Measurement
PERT Charting	Simulation
Linear Programming	Waiting Line Analysis
Plant Layout	Product Mix
Questionnaire Development	Work Sampling
Cost Estimating	Job Evaluation

The first purpose of such a checklist is to have the responsible party take time to ask himself: What technique should I use? The list obviously is not meant to be all-inclusive. It does demonstrate, however, that there are many choices, and that the results of a study can be limited by the choice of techniques. The existence of a document that records such choices will facilitate the further processing of any study. Thus, the second purpose is to provide guidance to all who work on the particular project.

5. Documentation Used when a Study Requires the Development of a Management Information System

After an initial problem definition has been written and preliminary information requirements have been stated, certain projects will be processed using the techniques related to designing a management information system. For such developments, a somewhat standardized approach to documentation is gradually evolving. These methods will be described in this section, and, wherever possible, details will be handled by references to documentation standards such as those developed by the American Standards Association. Copies of these standards will be available from the Management Systems Department.

The Management Systems Department has a particular interest in this section of the manual because dissemination of such standards outside of the Department can be a means of acquainting all personnel with the approaches to management information systems. This is, of course, most necessary, especially in the phases of problem definition and information requirements.

The above outline has been written in the form of an information requirement for company documentation. It is, admittedly, a preliminary statement, and we request your comments and suggestions.

A documentation program in a company serves as a rallying point for gradually improving the effectiveness of management information systems. Documentation touches every level and every specialty in an organization. The variety of languages with which the business is operated can cause confusion and consequent inefficiencies in operations. Documentation, at a minimum, highlights these problems. It gets them out in the open where something can be done about them.

As noted earlier, documentation is a special kind of data. It consists of those data which are uniquely collected for the sole purpose of effectively processing all other kinds of data. The development of an organization documentation manual provides a firm foundation for all types of management studies. This is especially true when the study concerns the design of a management information system.

The remaining chapters of this book look at each phase of a management information system's development in greater depth. The chapter headings, therefore, follow the levels shown in Figure 6–1. In each chapter examples are given of the types of documentation that are being used in business today. Because documentation is so important, constant efforts are being made to improve related concepts and techniques. New approaches to documenting are receiving much attention at the research and application levels. That which follows in these chapters seeks to provide certain fundamentals. The study of these fundamentals should be viewed as preparation for understanding the new approaches to documentation as they are developed. And of course, the reader may wish to do some of this development himself.

Chapter 7

SETTING SYSTEMS PRIORITIES:
INITIAL PROBLEM
DEFINITIONS

Chapters 7 to 14 seek to present the primary ingredients of each phase in the systems development cycle: from Problem Definition to Evaluation. This means, of course, that this coverage represents great breadth and depth in systems development. The following materials, however, should be considered as introductory; they were selected to provide a useful framework in which to treat systems development. They obviously do not include all the specifics, which must be learned from experience on the job. These comments are particularly appropriate to the first phase, in which the initial problem definition is made and initial priorities are assigned. The two questions, "What is it?" and "How important is it?" are very important throughout all phases of a system's development, but they are particularly critical in the first phase.

What is a management priority? The word "priority" means a preferential rating assigning rights to scarce management resources. It implies that some order has been established in which jobs will be done. In the case of management problems, a priority refers to the relative amount of resources—men, machines, materials and money that are to be used on a specific project. The typical business situation always provides more possible things to do than can be supported by the resources available. There is also the profit motive which necessitates doing only those things which promise returns above the costs of the work.

SITUATION ANALYSIS

For any situation of significance a management can ask, "What is it?" and "What do we do about it?" At any point in time and experience, a first glimmer of a situation may appear. We can say that a situation is a relative combination of circumstances. This means that certain factors are significant and that these factors have interrelationships. A difficulty, of course, is that *the situation is rarely clear*. In many business situations we are not sure of the factors, their significance, or their interrelationships. It is in the context of such vague situations that management problems are first identified and stated. This is the threshold level where the preliminary question is asked and the problem is stated for the first time. As with succeeding statements of the problem, the initial statement should represent the best possible effort at that time.

Note that we are suggesting that it is useful to think of situations as the *unstated existence* of matters of concern to a management. We further suggest that the formalization of a situation into written questions represents the *stated existence* of a management problem. A problem, of course, can exist in unstated form, but good systems development practice requires that problems be put down in writing as soon, and as carefully, as possible.

This chapter provides some thoughts which may help a manager or analyst in this difficult phase from which are developed all the tasks and assignments which can be given to organization personnel. That this is a most difficult part of management work is apparent from the very lack of explicit techniques for sensing situations and writing down problems.

Let us consider what is involved in sensing situations in a typical organization. We can identify two levels of situations: (1) those in our environment over which we have no control, and (2) those which we can do something about. Figure 7–1 makes one further separation of situations; it shows external and internal situations. External refers to circumstances such as those involved in the marketplace, with government regulations, and with suppliers of goods and services. Changes in buyers' preference, changes in government regulations, and changes in the prices we pay to our suppliers are examples of external circumstances which can be significant to a management.

Internal situations refer to difficulties involved in identifying and using the particular set of resources available to operate the firm. At a moment in time, certain quantities and qualities of men, machines, and materials are available. A management, however, does not automatically know the characteristics of these available resources. People quit, machines break down, and materials disappear. Today's situations are not necessarily the same as those of yesterday. Constant surveillance is a necessity if a management is to know (with any degree of confidence) its resource capacities.

We are suggesting that the term "situation," as applied to both the external and internal areas, be used as the general label for circumstances which exist but which have not been formally identified. Such reasoning provides a bench mark, or a point at which formal identification starts to take place. Figure 7–2, where the two triangles come

FIGURE 7–1

MOVING FROM THE UNSTATED TO THE STATED

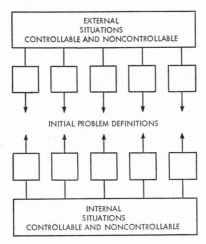

together, represents this point. The upper triangle symbolizes all the circumstances that may influence the business. The tapering of this triangle results from the fact that any organization has only so much environmental surveillance going on. This limits, at a moment in time, the possibilities for identifying critical problems. The lower triangle and its expansion is taken directly from Figure 6–1, which shows the phases in the life cycle of a system's development.

This symbolizing of situations provides, at a minimum, recognition of certain basic difficulties that must be handled in the development of management information systems. In the final analysis, no system can be evaluated except as it serves some purpose. The purpose can be spelled out only as we are able to provide effective surveillance of situations and an arrangement for formally initiating problem definitions.

THE IMPORTANCE OF SURVEILLANCE IN PRIORITY SETTING

Surveillance refers to all those activities by which a better perspective of an organization and its environment is obtained. It includes coverage of both external and internal situations. It includes immediate and longer-range circumstances. In effect, it can cover every aspect of an organization, but practically, an organized surveillance effort seeks to be selective. Experience and intuition are used by management as a guide in selecting the more critical areas of their environment for concentrated attention. Experience tells them where things have gone wrong in the past and where opportunities are likely to appear; intuition provides a sensing of where new factors or combinations will have an impact.

FIGURE 7–2

RELATING SITUATIONS TO SYSTEMS DEVELOPMENT

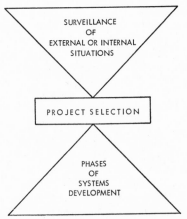

Problem definition for systems development does not have to take place in a vacuum. An effective arrangement for environment surveillance is the best insurance that the most important problems will be selected and that they will receive meaningful definitions. This is, therefore, the starting place for setting management priorities and for allocating resources. Recognition of both strengths and weaknesses of environment surveillance is extremely important in the first phase of systems development.

EXAMPLES OF PRIORITY SETTING IN THE ENVIRONMENT OF THE SMART CORPORATION

In Chapter 4 the SMART Corporation was described as a medium size firm producing electronic instruments and automatic control systems. The environment of this company is a most interesting one, for many developments have been taking place that have a direct impact upon this industry. Technological advances in industrial automation have increased both the quantitative and the qualitative requirements for the output of automatic controls and instruments. More, and larger, firms are entering the industry, and competition is increasing in all forms. Meanwhile, costs have increased in every class on the chart of accounts. As we saw earlier, SMART sales were up but profits were down. What priorities should this company's management set?

It appears that from one level of surveillance (i.e., the Executive Committee), it was decided that much more formal methods of priority setting should be developed. As a result, the Management Systems Department was activated. Arrangements were then made to pass selected and formal assignments to this department. In Chapter 4 we saw ten examples of these assignments:

1. Product Line Analysis
2. Shipping and Receiving
3. Purchasing Department Study
4. Inventory Control Problems
5. Typing Pool Study
6. Policy Formulation and Compliance
7. Automatic Factory Study
8. Executive Information Display Center
9. Clerical Work Measurement
10. Self-service Stockroom Study

Note that these assignments were not made to the heads of the functional departments. The priorities for these projects were high enough to provide a special department to work on assignments. Note also that this new department provides an additional dimension of surveillance as a basis for improved problem definitions. Thus, at least three separate groups are somehow involved in setting priorities among these assignments. These are the top management, represented by the Executive Committee, the people in the functional divisions, and the systems development group in the Systems Department. Priority setting obviously is not a one-man job nor a one-shot proposition. The initial problem definition, and related priority, must be developed in a blending of viewpoints and evaluations.

In practice, this takes place through a rather informal process of meetings and conversations. "Yes, but . . ." is a familiar part of such conversations. Factors are added and deleted; viewpoints regarding the significance of factors are blended and reblended. At some point, someone sits down and produces a written statement that is, in effect, the first real problem definition. Progress has been made, but immediately a reaction sets in and a game called "Murder Board" is played. In this game, everybody finds fault with the first statement of the problem. New participants enter the game, bringing new rules with them. Gradually, through a process of elimination, the time arrives for a revised problem definition to be written, but there may be several "semi-finals" before an acceptable initial problem definition is written.

We might assume that a similar process was used in arriving at the SMART Executive Committee assignments to the Systems Department. In each organization there is something comparable to this point where an authoritative group "signs off" on a document and a project is activated.

Now let us look at the ten assignments from a relative point of view: How are relative weights of importance developed for each project? All we knew initially was that the Executive Committee felt these particular assignments had some importance. For demonstration purposes, make the oversimplifying assumption that these ten assignments cover all of the areas that will be worked on for some period of time. Though simplified, this is still a scope of major proportions. For perspective at this point, we suggest that you re-read the short descriptions of these assignments, starting on page 47.

If you went through the exercise of assigning priorities in Chapter 4, you have the benefit of hindsight. You know, within the limits of the case, which projects are the "best," that is, have the highest returns for money spent to make studies. Typically, you still have some doubts as to how good the estimates of savings and costs were. This is understandable, for it would be unrealistic to expect that such estimates could be made with a high degree of accuracy in every study area. We do not want to understate the difficulty of this analysis because, in practice, the problem of making such estimates demands careful attention; and even then the results may be only approximations.

Priority setting requires that each assignment be evaluated, and that these evaluations be brought together so that each assignment receives a relative position in the priority scale. Figure 7–3 shows these assignments ranked in order of the actual savings that were achieved *after* complete studies had been made. Also shown are the first estimates of potential savings as they were anticipated in the early phases of each project. Note that estimated and actual savings were quite close in some cases and far apart in others. In the Policy Project, savings were much better than originally anticipated; the reverse was true for the Executive Information Display study. Hindsight, of course, is not available at the beginning of a study. The only alternative is to try to estimate what will actually result by extrapolating presently available knowledge and making estimate adjustments as the studies progress.

The last two columns in Figure 7–3 show some initial judgments which could have been made in the Systems Department. The depart-

FIGURE 7-3

SCALING OF ASSIGNMENTS

Final Ranking Order	Project Number	Project Title	Initial Estimate of Savings	Final Actual Savings (Scale Values)	Skill Level Required	Type of Analysis Required
1	1	Product Line..........	$900,000	$848,000	Leader	Simplification Diversification
2	7	Automatic Factory...	750,000	842,000	Leader	State of the Arts Prototype Evaluation
3	6	Policy..........	450,000(?)	747,000	Senior	Classification Analysis
4	4	Inventory..........	180,000	350,000	Senior	Flow Charting
5	2	Shipping, Receiving....	240,000	276,000	Senior	Flow Charting
6	10	Stockroom..........	220,000	268,000	Junior	Economy Study
7	5	Typing Pool..........	300,000	141,000	Junior	Work Distribution Time Study
8	9	Clerical Measurement....	300,000	107,000	Junior	Standard Time Data
9	3	Purchasing..........	200,000	106,000	Senior	Flow Charting
10	8	Information Display....	500,000(?)	51,000	Senior	Classification Analysis Flow Charting

ment manager had to decide what types of skills he would use and what management technique would be applied. Possible results of these decisions are shown in the last two columns. There is a close relationship between priorities and the package of talents and techniques that fit each project. The language in which the criteria of success for a project are expressed is very close to the vocabulary involved in describing talents and techniques used on the project. Priorities should, where feasible, be backed up by statements spelling out the criteria for a successful project. In the Manpower Planning and Control Project (No. 11–0), for example, the initial problem definition (shown on page 69) could be rewritten as a criteria statement:

Criteria Statement, Code 11–0, Phase I: Manpower Planning and Control
Wages and salaries in this company approximate $15,000,000 per year. This is $.40 per sales dollar shipped. According to our best intelligence, our competitors average $.32 per sales dollar shipped. Some part of this difference is due to our inability to get higher utilization of our personnel. These two figures, our ratio and that of competitors, should be considered as broad criteria for this study. It is recognized that many other factors influence this ratio. This measure, therefore, should be used with due regard for these other factors.

A more specific criterion for this study area is one representing the quality of data kept in the Employee Records File. Samples of these records indicate that at least one mistake exists in one out of every five employee records. This figure can be a bench mark criterion for checking improvement in quality of data.

A sample has also been taken to find out how many man-hours are involved in processing the data for a typical transfer of an employee. The sample shows that over five hours are required. This figure can be used as a basis for comparison when the new system is installed.

The foregoing criteria have stressed the cost and the efficiency with which employee records are maintained. Criteria are also needed to measure the effectiveness of such records as they are put to use. Who uses them? How are they used? How important are these uses? What difference would it make if these records were not available? Obviously, no one word as a criterion will suffice here. What we need are a few concise paragraphs in which are described the basic uses for Employee Records, the detriments of a bad system, and the benefits of a good system. The following three paragraphs are but a first effort for such a statement. As the study progresses, this statement should be refined, and, where appropriate, expanded.
1. *Uses:* The basic uses for employee records are to serve legal requirements, manpower planning, and employee benefits. Legal requirements are set by local, state, and federal regulations. Manpower planning includes the setting of job requirements and the matching of these requirements with personnel skills. Employee benefits include working conditions, services, and various forms of compensation.

2. *Detriments:* With poor records, the following negative things can happen. Legal requirements may not be met and cash and other penalties may result. Job skill needs may not be anticipated and therefore may not be available to meet schedules. Poor quality of work may arise from the use of inadequate skills. Business may be lost. A higher grade of skill may be placed on a job than is needed, with resultant higher costs. Mistakes in employee benefits can also lead to high costs or, if they impact unfairly on the employee, to undesired quits and additional training costs.

3. *Benefits:* With good employee records, the following positive things can happen. A fundamental benefit—but difficult to evaluate—is that good records give the users a confidence factor in support of their decisions. Accuracy and precision in records minimizes the need and costs of double checking and making corrections. More importantly, employee records put a "backbone" in manpower planning and control. Facts can replace guesses and offset bias in job placement and promotion. Hiring and training can be done with much more specific goals. Flexibility to meet shifts in job requirements can provide management with important assets in servicing customers.

Criteria statements are logical extensions of initial problem definitions. Note how the above criteria statement on the manpower study has identified certain additional problem elements. At the same time, it has provided at least preliminary bench marks for testing the success of the project. Criteria are those English words with which we express the bases upon which we make choices. Any system that purports to aid decision making should be designed with conscious attention to criteria. Criteria become more meaningful when we are able to attach weights to the English words, and thereby make relative comparisons. This type of thinking is important in designing a system. It is especially important in attempting to set priorities among systems. Criteria statements can be quite useful when a management is attempting to compare and contrast projects and to set meaningful priorities. We will return to the study of criteria in Chapter 14, as we complete the cycle of systems development in the phase of feedback and evaluation.

USING A MASTER CLASSIFICATION SYSTEM AS A GUIDE IN SETTING PRIORITIES FOR MANAGEMENT STUDIES

The development of assignments in the SMART case appears as a rather random process. Projects are sent to the Systems Department one at a time, whenever the Executive Committee decides to do so. Now let us assume that someone recognizes that this is too informal a way to run a business, and he proposes that better methods be developed. More specifically, he has raised the following questions at a meeting of the Committee:

Executive Committee Memo:

For some time this Committee has been making recommendations for management studies. In reviewing these assignments, it appears to me that there is duplication and overlap between some of these assignments. Further, I see no overall framework in which to compare and contrast all possible projects. Sure, we can compare the present projects among themselves, but is this enough? We should have available at least some broad set of classifications of possible management problems that could provide a context in which to consider each specific project. Do we have anything of this nature?

As you have probably guessed, this became assignment 12–0 and was sent to the Systems Department for study. In due time the following report was received:

Preliminary Report on Project 12–0:

Attached is a general classification system, proposed as a grid or map upon which to consider the placing and interrelations of individual projects. In making these selections we have attempted to apply the "See-Saw Rule" for classification refinements. We have sought to limit the number of classes and subclasses to give an optimum balance between too many classes and too few. With too many classes, projects would have to be at a very detailed level before they could be placed in the classification system. In initial study phases, this is obviously impossible. With too few classifications we would be in trouble because we could not match even a few subclasses in a possible project. The attached classification can be expanded, or made smaller, if experience in use makes such a change desirable.

This classification system separates external surveillance problems from internal operational problems. The classifications for management studies are placed between the external and internal classifications. The management studies classifications are labeled under the Search and Select Objectives heading. This, of course, is where the Executive Committee and the Systems Department have their primary focus. This overall classification system, for example, is a tool for use in this area of search and selection. The subclasses under Search and Select were chosen to identify five significant places where management measurements can be applied. These subclasses, we believe, can be cross-referenced to many, if not all, of the other classes and subclasses.

The numbers in parentheses placed on the classification profile [Figure 7–4] are the numbers of the ten projects received to date. A quick look at the location of these numbers shows where we are allocating study resources, and where we *are not* allocating resources. A given number for a project placed in more than one classification indicates the compound nature of the project. It appears that we have a bias (right or wrong) toward material problems, and a concentration on problems of productivity.

We also have available the classification developed for the project on

Policy Formulation and Compliance, Code 6 [see Appendix, 267]. At this writing, we are analyzing the policy classification system to see if it can be merged or cross-referenced to the master classification presented here. At a later date we hope to do a similar analysis considering our chart of accounts [p. 60].

The above report can represent the start of a program in which management can search and select its projects with more careful atten-

FIGURE 7–4

SMART CORPORATION'S MASTER CLASSIFICATION FOR MANAGEMENT STUDIES

EXTERNAL ENVIRONMENT				
Government	Organized Labor	Marketing	Community	Suppliers

(6) (8) SEARCH AND SELECT OBJECTIVES				
Forecasts	Market Share	Product Line (1)	Productivity (5) (7) (9)	Profits

INTERNAL ENVIRONMENT		
Organization Specialization Functionalization Authority Structure Coordination	*Finance and Accounting* Profit Planning Budgeting Financial Statements General Accounting Cost Accounting	*Physical Facilities* Land Buildings (7) Shop Equipment Office Equipment Utilities
Personnel Manpower Planning Wage and Salary Labor Relations Employee Services Personnel Records	*Production Planning and Control* Authorization Scheduling Routing Dispatching Follow-Up	*Material* (3) Purchases (4) Inventory Control (2) Traffic (10) Receiving and Warehousing Quality Control

tion to interrelationships and overall relative priorities. This master classification can be useful as a "map" of areas wherein arrangements for surveillance can be analyzed. What individuals or groups are responsible for intelligence in each of these classes? Where are we weak in coverage? These questions can be better phrased and answered if a master classification framework is available. The classification also provides a vivid demonstration of the need for the combined organization/information structure discussed in Chapter 2.

At a given moment in time, a company has only so many types and quantities of resources. It also has what amounts to fixed commitments through management studies. Whatever this represents in budgeted dollars, it should be given the attention that is appropriate for any management investment.

The existence of a management systems department is, in itself, symbolic of priority setting. Top management has, in effect, said there are certain problems that require, and will receive, special attention over and above that which could be given in any one functional department of our business. This does not mean that the functional divisions will not make studies. It *does* mean that functional department studies will be made only after they have been checked out for consistency with the studies being made by the organization systems department. Further, it is expected the functional department managers will lend support (make their personnel available) to studies monitored by management systems department. Such policies, when backed up by the top management, provide the first level of structure in setting priorities for management studies. The effect is that more specific attention must be given to organization assignments and to the possible rates of return on these assignments.

The Management Systems Department in the SMART Corporation is not limited to assignments that involve computer-based data processing. In recent years too many companies have set up departments with this limitation. The difficulty, of course, is that this isolates such groups from the main stream of broader studies and from the related priority setting process. As noted earlier, this can mean the data processing effort is working in a vacuum. The benefits of an arrangement for setting priorities can apply to data processing projects only if such projects can be compared and contrasted with other types of management studies.

Of the ten projects (see Figure 7–3) half of them appear to be candidates for computer-based data processing. These are noted in the last column of Figure 7–3 by reference to a flow-chart type of analysis. These projects are probably the only ones that could be carried down through all the phases of the life cycle of systems development:

I Problem Definition and Priority Setting

II Written Information Requirements

III Systems Design

IV Programming

V Operating

VI Format and Display

VII Feedback and Evaluation

This does not mean that the computer could not be used at all on the other projects; it means that techniques other than data flow must be used in these projects.

In the next chapter we will analyze the types of information that can be required for a variety of management situations. This chapter has suggested that we think of situations as "circumstances waiting to be described." When selected circumstances are described for the first time, we should think of this as the initial problem definition. As we will see, a good initial problem definition is a prerequisite for the analysis of information requirements.

Chapter 8

INFORMATION

REQUIREMENTS

DESIGN

The fundamental question, What information does a manager need to do his job? is *so* fundamental it is almost meaningless! There are so many managers, in such a wide variety of situations, that the best we can do is carefully select the more critical situations and then work on these.

Remember that we are working through a special set of circumstances. The approach developed here is designed to collect and direct *certain* management problems into a *somewhat standardized* sequence of analytical steps. The point is that many management problems will not enter through this gateway to formal exposition and detailed analysis. This is as it should be. We should not use a formal approach if the state of management arts does not provide at least a minimum guarantee that analysis will give better payoffs than experienced intuition. Simply, we are saying that rigorous analysis for the sake of rigor may be an interesting exercise, but it is not necessarily good management.

Information requirements should be stated as clearly and as concretely as possible. "Nice to know" and "rare occasion" information should not be included in the framework we are designing. If we could afford such information in our systems, there would be fewer objections. We are, however, seeking efficient systems within the normal limits associated with shortages of men, material, machines, and money.

96

INFORMATION RESULTS FROM SELECTED REQUIREMENTS

Information, we have noted, informs only when there is a recognized need to know. A recognized need to know requires a stable basis, or at least a context in which we can separate the interesting from the truly useful information. This idea that information requires an identifiable setting is extremely important. It means that we should spend at least some of our resources to provide meaningful descriptions of such settings. Only as this is done can we have any degree of confidence that we have been selective. Selection is a refining process. A professional in any field should be able, after he has made a selection, to identify what he has *eliminated* as well as what he has *retained*. Otherwise, how does he know he has made a selection?

Typically there are great pressures that work against a conscious retention of what has been eliminated during any study. We tend to concentrate on what is retained as a result of the selection process. This may absorb our whole span of attention and leave little or no capacity for reflecting on that which was eliminated.

If this emphasis seems strange, remember that the only way we can determine the importance of any information is by putting it in a setting. This is where our purposes are spelled out and our guides for priorities are developed. Navigation has made full use of such bench marks as the stars and the horizon. The plotting of a course for selected management information systems requires similar points of reference. These points can be available only as we build them through the surveillance activity described in the preceding chapter. Without pretending that a "total system" will ever be achieved, a framework *representing* the total universe of possible situations can be extremely useful. The Master Classification for Management Studies (shown in Figure 7–4) is an example of a gross context for surveillance, initial problem definition, and information requirements. As noted in the preceding chapter, this form of organization-wide classification can be useful as a device for locating and identifying the scope and relationships involved in particular management projects. Certain information requirements can, in the same way, be tied to these various classes. We are going to suggest, however, that the Master Classification for Management Studies be thought of as most useful during the first phase of setting systems priorities and initial problem definition.

That which follows is a classification that would be useful when managers ask "What information is available from our systems today?" Note that the Management Studies Classification aids in constructing better information systems. The classification discussed here, however, is designed to get the most out of systems that are already in existence.

With two such classification systems available, it is possible to identify a basic conflict that must be treated when designing management information requirements. The dichotomy develops as one set of forces leads to changing management systems, and another set of forces provides a need for stability. In effect, if an organization is constantly changing its information systems, it is much more difficult to know what information is available in those systems. With a stable set of systems, people can learn the classifications and logic. This familiarity facilitates getting into and out of the system whatever information is available.

Because a systems designer has to work with what is already available, and at the same time consider how the existing systems can be replaced or changed, we suggest that he will be aided by having the two classifications: one to initiate change and the other to identify the content that exists in present systems. We show an application of this latter classification in Chapter 13 on Output Format and Display. But for now let us discuss the content classes and the reasoning behind them.

KEY INFORMATION CONTENT CLASSIFICATIONS

Dollars	Facilities	People
Items	Locations	Programs

These six terms represent a set of key areas which, individually or in combination, can encompass a large number of management need-to-know situations. We are going to use this set of areas as a framework in which to consider the assembly of information for management report purposes. This is admittedly an arbitrary selection of areas; many other selections are possible. As you read the following, however, we suggest that you test this classification and decide for yourself how useful it is. We are saying that this set of six terms can at least represent a firm's "hard core" of its critical need-to-know situations.

Even starting with this six-class breakdown, it is still an enormous framework of analysis. This size results from the large number of possible subclasses, plus the increasing number of combinations that are possible as subclasses are added. For our demonstration purposes it is not necessary to handle large numbers of subclasses; in practice, however, the system may have to include a large number of them.

Each manager, at any level, has a certain set of questions that he can ask. The classification described here is made up of key words that expand into many of the most significant areas in which managers, at all levels, plan and control. Definitions for these classes follow.

1. *Dollars:* the monetary units by which measures of certain management situations are expressed.

2. *Items:* covers the catalog of materials from raw stock to finished goods. Can be individual items or commodity groupings. Can be names of services provided by nonmanufacturing organizations.

3. *Facilities:* includes all physical properties; land, buildings, and equipment (see *Items* for materials).

4. *Locations:* identification of geographical locations, from the largest to the smallest. A location can be a marketing territory or a shelf in a warehouse at a depot.

5. *People:* this is the "who?" question; it includes names and title of individuals and names of organization components at all levels. There will be overlaps with the location questions ("where?") in those cases where organization components are named by geographical area.

6. *Programs:* this is a general class that includes any formal assembly of goals to be accomplished. It covers names for budgets, projects, studies, program packages, contracts; any grouping of work efforts that can be formally identified and assigned.

Figure 8–1 shows the six key classes. It symbolizes the breadth dimension by combinations of these classes, and depth by addition of subclasses.

FIGURE 8–1

BREADTH AND DEPTH OF INFORMATION REQUIREMENTS: KEY CONTENT

CLASSES

		SUBCLASSES					
		Dollars	Items	Facilities	Location	People	Programs
SUBCLASSES	Dollars	X					
	Items		X				
	Facilities			X			
	Location				X		
	People					X	
	Programs						X

CONTROLLING THE EXPANSION OF INFORMATION REQUIREMENTS DETAIL

Figure 8–2 represents the hierarchy as subclasses lead out of the six key classes shown in Figure 8–1. Figure 8–2 demonstrates how subclasses can build up exponentially as succeeding levels are added. Each

FIGURE 8–2

EXPANSION IN LEVELS OF SUBCLASSES

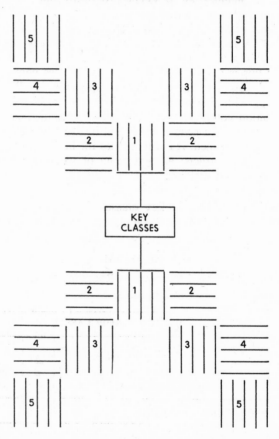

organization has such a structure, which can be identified as expanding out of the key classes of dollars, items, facilities, locations, people, and programs. The identification of this structure is a major step in any attempt to write explicit statements of an organization's information requirements. A written inventory of these main classifications provides (at least) the existing and relatively static structure from which changes (seeking improvements) can be considered. More importantly, each element class is a basic building block on which other characteristics can be assembled to design a particular piece of information.

The six key classes in combination give 63 (2^N-1) possible interrelationships about which a manager could inquire. When we consider how many subclasses can be placed under each major class, the size of the problem of selected information requirements becomes apparent. It is because of this magnitude that efforts should be made to provide an overall framework in which both managers and systems designers can find common reference points. We repeat; a framework *representing* the total universe of possible situations can be extremely useful. To narrow to selected information requirements, it is necessary that at least a representation of the whole be available. Such a representation can be as informal as the mental images of scope held by a variety of managers with differing experiences, or it can be a formal, documented classification. Arguments for building and using such a classification are many. The gist of these arguments is that it is nice to have a map of an area before choosing a route through that area. Think of this classification in this sense, and not as a device for building the so-called total system. Our goal is to build selective systems and to produce selected information.

THE ELEMENTS AND STRUCTURE OF A PIECE OF INFORMATION

Figure 8–1 can be such a framework for selection. In effect we are, in this classification, predicting a variety of questions that managers will ask. With this prediction available, we can then proceed to select those particular questions for which we will design systems and provide answers.

Figure 8–3 shows certain other factors that must enter into information requirements. A question and its counterpart answer need more than the identification of the selected classes of information shown in Figures 8–1 and 8–2. Decisions must be made as to the elements and structure of the particular pieces of information required. The following example demonstrates these requirements:

QUESTION: How many Heat Recorders, Type A, does the Chicago Warehouse have in stock today as contrasted with the number in stock one year ago?

ANSWER: The Chicago Warehouse has 250 dozen Heat Recorders, Type A, in stock as of this date, June 1st, as contrasted with 200 dozen Heat Recorders, Type A, one year ago. Inventory thus is up by 25 percent.

To ask and answer this relatively simple question, certain identifiers had to be used. We have classified them as follows:

Name of the Class. These are derived from the Key Content

Classification. In the above example the class is *Items;* the first subclass is *Heat Recorders,* and the second subclass is *Type A.*

Units of Measure.   These are all the terms in which measures can be expressed. Each management action area has its specific units of measure: tons of material, man-hours, pieces per machine per minute, etc. The unit of measure in the example is *dozens* of recorders.

Forms of Information Presentation.   Form refers to the shape in which the answer is presented. Note that, in the example, the answer could be shown by two separate simple counts: numbers last year and this year. An alternative form could be to put these two numbers in a

FIGURE 8–3

ELEMENTS OF A PIECE OF INFORMATION

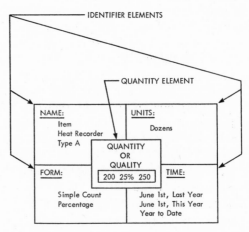

ratio and express this as a percentage. This was done when the answer stated that inventory had increased by 25 percent.

Thus, form depends to a large degree on the methodology that is used to assemble the information. The wide variety of statistical measures are good examples of the forms in which information can be presented. Form provides the tie between information requirements and management techniques. Another way to say this is that a given management technique will produce a particular form of information.

Time Dimension.   Information usually needs a time context. The primary "when" considerations are a *date* and/or a *period* at which, or during which, events are planned, happen, or do not happen. Time dimensions are particularly important for scheduling and controlling. Time is also important for determining the relative currency of events and situations wherein deterioration or obsolescence could occur.

Three time dimensions are used in the example: today, one year ago, and a comparison of these two points in time.

Quantifiers Related to Identifier Elements. These four classes—name, units, form, and time—give the basic identification to many types of management information. Note that these are all factors which are prerequisites to writing down a piece of information. The actual quantity or quality that gives weight to these factors is a separate consideration, as shown in the center box in Figure 8–3. Picture the overall figure as a file card on which (in this case) inventory information is kept up-to-date. All identification information could be pre-printed on this card. The box in the center, however, would be used to write in the actual counts of inventory. As inventory changed, the count shown in the box would change. This demonstrates the difference between the identifying classes and the data which is processed through these classes.

SEQUENCING IN INFORMATION SYSTEMS

At the practical level, the work in the identification of information requirements amounts to a refining of a systems priority and the problem definition. This refining is not a one-time effort; it continues throughout any study. Anything that provides a degree of stability in this process of change is a great aid to the systems designer. The above classifications give such a basis for reference. They also keep the designer humble by reminding him how the detail in his project can quickly multiply if he is not careful.

In this phase of information requirements it is important that we keep in mind both the overall management framework and the framework in which a specific piece of information can be retrieved once it is in a system. By viewing both ends of the process, we can then seek to design a system that is based upon information requirements that recognize important needs *and* which are feasible of accomplishment.

We suggest that information requirements are facilitated when the class name is viewed as the carrier to which are attached the other elements of units, form, and time. The next step is to view the process of the assembly of a particular piece of information as a sequence of changes in name, units, form, and time. This is shown in Figure 8–4. In blocks 1 to 6, the quantity of data is recorded for the first time with appropriate names, units, form, and time characteristics. Blocks 7 and 8, as examples, show the simple processing steps of adding and subtracting. In each case, all the information elements except quantity, must be exactly the same or the action of add and/or subtract cannot occur. This, of course, is the old story of not adding apples and oranges; there must be dimensional stability for a meaningful result to occur.

In blocks 9 and 10, however, the elements do not have to be the same in order to get meaningful results. It is quite possible (and usual) for changes in the information elements to take place in the processes of multiplication and division. A truck that goes 50 miles, carrying a ten-ton load, has accomplished 500 ton-miles of work. Note how the *units* have been joined in this step. A similar (but reversed) process

FIGURE 8–4

Sequence in a Management Information System

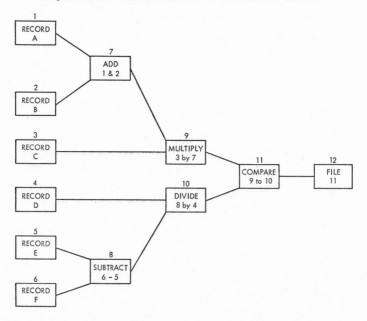

takes place in a division action. The truck carrying the materials 50 miles in two hours has traveled at a rate of 25 miles/hour. The result is that the units show the same action (division) as that which was performed on the quantities.

In blocks 11 and 12, again we see situations where common units of measure must exist for the actions (comparison and filing) to take place. In this case the identifier elements would be identical, and the comparisons or filing would take place on the quantity element in each piece of information.

In summary, we can say that the state of a piece of information at a point in time is a function of its place in the processing sequence, and this, in turn, is determined by changes in: (*a*) names of classes, (*b*) units of measure, (*c*) forms resulting from actions taken, and (*d*) time identifiers.

The quantity (or quality) a piece of information carries is determined initially by the weights at all entry points, and thereafter by the actions called for in the form desired at each step in the sequence of processing. This description of a piece of information is appropriate to all quantitative information used in business and to much of the qualitative information. By looking at a piece of information at the elements level we are able to analyze information requirements in quite specific terms. We at least know what to look for as we gradually assemble information requirements.

EXAMPLE OF A SET OF INFORMATION REQUIREMENTS

Let us use the SMART assignment, code 11–0, to demonstrate the analysis involved in writing a set of information requirements:

Development of Data Bank for Manpower Planning and Control, Code 11–0:

Please investigate the possibilities for improvements in the Employee Records Division of our Personnel Department. We are spending over $80,000 a year on salaries alone in this Division. What are we getting for our money? What services does this Division perform? Is it feasible to develop a computer program that can improve these services?

This initial problem definition was used for demonstration purposes in the chapter on Classification and Coding Approaches. A preliminary study report was presented, starting on page 69. In essence, this report found that there was much duplication in the system and that the classifications and codes used were in need of a thorough reevaluation.

On page 90, the initial problem definition was rewritten as a criteria statement. This statement includes uses, detriments, and benefits associated with an Employee Records system. Now let us take a specific situation in the context of manpower planning and see what can be done to provide an information requirement statement.

Assume that the following letter to the Personnel Department from the Manager of Marketing was given to analysts in their preliminary study of employee records. It was given to analysts as an example of the requests received and to point up the difficulty of satisfying such requests by the Employee Records Division.

To: Division Manager, Employee Records, Personnel Department
FROM: Manager of Marketing

The approved budget of the Marketing Department for next year includes funds ($10,000) to hire a Sales Convention Arrangements Manager. Job Specification No. 103764 has been designed to identify the characteristics desired in candidates for this position. Will you please provide me with a list of our employees who qualify under this specification?

This letter pinpoints the specific information need of a manager in a particular situation. The "need to know" is to be satisfied by the capacity of the Employee Records Division to select only qualified individuals, who will then be given personal interviews by the Marketing Department (see Figure 8–5). The universe from which selections

FIGURE 8–5

SMART CORPORATION: JOB SPECIFICATION No. 103764

Title: Sales Convention Arrangements Manager
1. Age: 30+
2. Sex: Male
3. Education: Bachelor's degree (any field)
4. Experience:
   3 years' sales related to our product line
   2 years' knowledge of our factory operations
   1 year of our accounting (general or cost)
5. Temperament:
   Personable, good conversationalist
   Energetic
6. Physical Characteristics:
   Makes good appearance
7. Miscellaneous:
   Willing to travel
   Citizen
   Military service completed
   Character references approved

---

can be made is represented by the term "our employees." The information required must be provided through a process that identifies those who do not qualify, and also those who qualify but who for some reason would not be available for the job. The latter could include those who are at a level of pay above the $10,000 budgeted for salary, or those who are being developed for other jobs of equal or better pay. These are some of the ingredients, or open questions, that a formal information system must encompass to effectively process the request of the marketing manager.

In the next chapter we will follow this example through the phase of systems design; that is, the start of answering the question: How do we satisfy the information requirement? The remainder of this chapter will concentrate on getting this information requirement spelled out in appropriate detail. Again, let us view this through the eyes of systems analysts who have been given an assignment. In this assignment they have reached the phase where they are to prepare written information requirements for a system that can meet requests of the nature described in the marketing manager's letter.

Report on Project 11–0, Phase II
Information Requirement Specifications:

The Company has a job analysis program including job evaluation, the requisite job descriptions (what is done on the job), and job specifications (characteristics a candidate should have). In the present job specification, seven general classes of characteristics are identified. Thus, managers have been provided a set of classes in which they can express their job specifications. In effect, the acceptance and use of these classifications standardizes the language in which managers can express their job position needs and, in this case, their information needs regarding available candidates.

Six primary classes are included: age, sex, education, experience, temperament, and physical characteristics. The seventh class is a catch-all for miscellaneous characteristics. These classes, and the form used, have been checked and approved by legal counsel. We see no need for changing these classes as long as the managers are allowed to use the miscellaneous class for citing other characteristics desired.

We have studied the variety of questions that managers may submit regarding the Company's personnel inventory. The following list of questions was developed after interviews with Employee Records personnel, managers, and the head of a local employment agency.

Information Requirement Situations:

1. Straight matching of job specifications against records in employee files.
2. Checking specific records to verify other sources.
3. If there are no complete matches, are there some employees who almost qualify: who have two years and eleven months of experience instead of three years?
4. Can the process be reversed? The manager has a man with a particular set of characteristics. He wants to know if there are other openings in the Company for this man.
5. The manager has been told that no employee meets his specifications. He asks how he can go about outside-the-Company recruiting.
6. The manager is trying to make equitable recommendations for salary adjustments. He asks for the job specifications and salaries in the Company that are comparable to those of a particular job in his department.
7. The manager is asked to provide an evaluation of a former employee's abilities and personal traits. He wants to review the man's record.
8. Outside organizations request data on past and present employees. This includes private and public agencies.
9. An employee asks to see his record, and, on occasion, will even ask to be given data about other employees.
10. The union representatives request access to employee records.

We have deliberately resisted the temptation to answer any of these questions, even in the interviews. We understand that our job in this phase is to express requirements and not to evaluate how these requirements might be satisfied. The answers to some of the above questions may be obvious. If so, this will be verified in the next phase of this study.

The above questions go beyond those asked by a manager. The original assignment stresses the development of a data bank. We have therefore included other potential customers who might be serviced from these records.

Even though we have recommended that the present classes continue to be used, we took the time to ask the managers what they did with the data in each class. Some interesting answers were received. These ranged from a blunt "It's none of your business!" to "We could use your help in applying these data." We cite this situation to demonstrate that the way in which the manager uses the output of a system can be just as important as the way we get the output to him. In this case we noted a wide range of interest and competence in putting employee record data to use.

We append a short statement regarding applications under each of the seven classes:

1. *Age.* The age of an employee is considered mainly from two points of view. Age is generally correlated with maturity and experience. This reflects the past, and what the employee has accomplished so far. The second view looks to the future and considers how an employee of a certain age can be further developed in his capacity for more responsible positions. A consciousness of an age scale, spanning the period from hiring to retirement, provides an overall context for analysis. Age distribution by job positions aids in the planning of training programs and replacement schedules. A manager would want to know the age of a candidate in order to see the effect on his desired pattern of age distribution.

   More specific requirements are determined by legal, insurance, and medical restrictions. A manager must know these restrictions, or a control must be exercised by the Personnel Department to assure compliance.

2. *Sex.* Tradition is probably the most significant factor here. Managers are influenced by the precedents of whether certain jobs have been handled by men or women. There are some jobs that, legally, women cannot do. There are also restraints on hours of work and on working conditions that preclude women. The more significant factor is that a woman may decide to operate her own business (a household) and depart the company. Despite much lip-service to equal job rights, managers rarely break with tradition on assignments to men or women.

3. *Education.* Successfully completed years of education are considered as a testimonial to residual abilities in an individual. If one was not able to obtain a certain amount of education, one cannot be sure he

has the capacity to handle the job. However, if the record shows that, in fact, the individual has passed the educational test, the confidence level is increased.

4. *Experience.* A manager seeks help in a literal sense. He wants people who can produce effectively with a minimum of supervision. Inexperienced help means too much instruction and too little confidence in results. Experience is an important factor in any job of significance. One observed difficulty is that of spelling out just what kind of experience is pertinent to particular job positions.

5. *Temperament.* The attitudes and personality of employees cannot substitute for talent, but they can surely make talent ineffective. This is particularly true when the job requires much interpersonal contact and many acts of persuasion.

6. *Physical Characteristics.* These requirements refer primarily to the shop environment jobs, those that depend upon muscles or dexterity. Mechanization, especially in materials handling, has done much to reduce the extremes of physical requirements in today's extractive, fabrication, and assembly operations.

Physical characteristics can also refer to appearance. Again, this is considered particularly important in situations where persuasion is important. Often, however, this really means that the individual should not have a negative appearance; it rarely means that the candidate must be a fashion plate, or can qualify for a beauty contest.

A man's present state of health and his record of past medical experience can be of significance in any job demanding high-effort levels.

7. *Miscellaneous.* This, of course, encompasses a wide variety of possible characteristics. Among the more representative are those related to character and community standing. Family responsibilities, military service status, and even hobbies and avocations can be desirable information for a prospective employer. One manager stated that he wanted a picture of the "whole" person he was considering for placement. The miscellaneous class gives opportunity to formally note any important characteristics not taken care of in the other classes.

These statements regarding the use of employee record data for employee selection and placement demonstrate that many variables are involved in a manager's decision to hire a given individual. In each instance the manager must choose what he considers to be the significant characteristics, and he must also choose relative weights of importance for these characteristics. Any system designed to provide him with information must start with a rather full recognition of his situation. Further, it must complement (or substitute for) his abilities to choose among available candidates.

We propose that a fairly narrow study be made concentrating on the logic involved in designing a system for matching job descriptions to employee record files. We suggest this with full recognition of the many other uses for employee records. Our reasoning is that even the limited study will require five man-months of senior analyst effort. As this study proceeds, certain opportunities for enlarging its scope may appear, which can be evaluated at that time. Our cautious attitude results from what we have seen so far. This can be a bottomless pit, with no end to the types and combinations of data that might be processed. Under our present suggestion, any additional coverage must stand careful scrutiny before resources are committed.

At this point we are not at all sure that this is an area where the computer can be applied. Until at least a preliminary systems design is available, it will be impossible to estimate a price for either the manual or the machine processing of such requests. We have been told that there were about 10,000 requests last year for employee data from the employee records files. This is less than 40 per day, or 8 per hour. Obviously, we should not jump to the conclusion that this is a machinable job. The systems designer should consider whether manual or machine methods should be used *after* he has developed the specific scope and logic for the system.

The above information requirement specifications represent a narrowed-problem definition, which should now go to the Systems Design Division of the Management Systems Department.

This report identifies information requirements which are primarily associated with the name of the class of information content. It leaves open many questions associated with units, form, time, and quantities. This is typical in the information requirements phase of systems development. Only as we move through the succeeding phases will we see that the identification and analysis of the specific identifier elements are expansions and adjustments of the initial statement of information requirements. In the next chapter, this expansion takes place under the heading of Systems Design. Here we see the assembly of more specific names, units, and forms. These elements are gradually selected and built into the sequences which give the logical structure of a representative systems design.

Information requirements have to be stated before they have any meaning to anyone. To be able to phrase an information requirement, a perspective of how information is collected and processed is required. We will return to this point in Chapter 13 when we discuss the formating and display of information.

It is obvious that a manager can ask an infinite variety of questions. The approach used in developing management information systems must include this recognition. It should also recognize that no set of systems can ever anticipate and have ready all the answers for all the possible requirements that all managers can state. There is, however, certain work that a systems designer can do prior to the actual writing of information requirements. He can, for example:

1. Identify the formal and informal statements of a given manager's missions, his responsibilities, and those of his subordinates. To the degree that these statements have been well thought out, they provide guidance for developing information requirements.
2. Determine the needs of the manager with regard to the breadth and depth of his information requirements. Can he work with summarized data and exception reporting, or does he feel he has to get down to the "nuts and bolts" level of analysis?
3. Determine if the manager wants to receive his information packaged to include conclusions and recommendations for actions.

The documentation of answers to these questions, in combination with explicit information requirements for specific projects, provides a firm foundation for all that must follow in a system's development. In the next chapter we see how information requirements are used in the phase of systems design.

Chapter 9

SYSTEMS DESIGN: EXTENDED
PROBLEM DEFINITION

In the next few chapters we face the problem of specifics, i.e., the responsibility of a management to know that it is in control of the appropriate level of details in its business. A reading of these chapters will give a grasp of why it is necessary to be specific in computer-based management information systems. Any manager, even though he is not directly involved in systems design or computer programming, should have an understanding of this problem of specifics and its impact on the development of the management systems he would like to have.

It should be apparent by now that the development of a management information system does not have the nice, neat, compartmentalized phases that we have been using. These phases, as in all classification systems, contain grey areas where one phase overlaps another. If this worries you, treat this overlapping as a recognition of the need for coordination between phases of the study. The important use of these phases is that they provide at least a general set of activities and events in which to organize a systems study.

The activities and events in the systems design phase are related to those in choosing and describing the method by which information requirements can be satisfied. The phases of problem definition (with priority setting) and information requirements design are both for purposes of establishing clear, initial statements of need. The last two chapters gave examples of the level of documentation used to prepare for the systems design phase. In the case study on manpower planning, we have seen how the analysts gradually develop the initial problem definition and the criteria statement, and (in the last chapter) the information requirements for a systems design. They suggested a study restricted to the matching of job specifications to employee record files.

Before going into how the systems phase for candidate matching can be organized, consider how the study has already proceeded. The action started with the Executive Committee. The Systems Department provided manpower to do the initial, exploratory study. In the first two phases the analysts had to work very closely with a wide variety of functional managers and certain staff divisions. The point to be observed here is that these analysts were *not* telling anybody how to do a better job; rather, they were acting as official documenters. People were telling *them* what was involved as background for the writing of a problem definition and for the derived information requirements. In the first two phases especially, the analysts should consider themselves as dependent upon functional and other personnel. They are dependent in the sense that good definitions and requirements can be obtained only if the experience and insight of the responsible managers is made available. This attitude is very important.

Too often the systems design personnel take the posture that, because they were given a particular assignment, this means they have "ownership" of the functional area. This presumption is psychologically immature and politically dangerous. Look at the facts. To some degree, someone is already responsible for the area covered by the assignment. The systems effort cannot help being, to some extent, a conflict of interests, and a good analyst does not compound this situation by exaggerating his importance. This is not necessary where his project is truly supported and appropriately publicized by top management. With such support, the analyst can make most efficient progress by "doing his homework" in the study area and demonstrating his appreciation of the manager's problems.

This "maturity" is critical to a successful systems development. It applies in every phase. In this systems design phase we will see that the analyst cannot go off in a corner and do "his" design work. Only as he stays in touch with the managers on the "firing line" does he build into a study the appropriate refinements and restraints. In effect, the analyst doing systems design should be pictured as returning repeatedly to phases I and II to double-check his study direction.

THE APPROACH OF THE SYSTEMS DESIGNER

Now let us look at the systems design phase more specifically. A systems designer has a kit of tools that he applies to the existing problem definitions and information requirements. In this book we are concentrating on those tools that are applied to processing a flow of data. As we have noted, this involves a special set of circumstances, and there are many management problems for which this approach provides little, if any, help.

A generalized picture of a data flow situation is shown in Figure 9–1. It is in this framework that data of any kind are processed. The systems designer's job in a particular study, is to know (or to learn) the content necessary in each box on the diagram, and, especially, to describe what should happen in the lines connecting each box to other boxes.

Obviously it is impossible to do this job in one all-inclusive effort. Rather, the designer learns to move through successive stages, gradually refining and relating additional details. He "block diagrams." He traces what he considers to be the primary patterns of data flow in his

FIGURE 9–1

Elements of a Data Flow Situation

(A Simplified View of Figure 3–1)

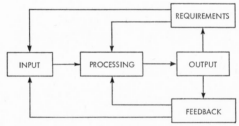

problem area. He concentrates on one part of the problem for awhile, moves to another part, and then considers both parts for relationships. Because of the increasing amount of detail that enters his analysis, he uses certain documentation techniques to record his findings and to communicate and test these findings with other interested parties. He is, typically, a very busy man. The techniques do not do his job for him, but they help him compare, contrast, and remember. In the vocabulary of psychology, the techniques reinforce his span of attention.

DEVELOPING THE LOGIC DIAGRAM

In the information requirement specification for this project (page 109) the systems designer has been told to limit his study to the design of a system for matching job descriptions to employee record files. *Job descriptions* are those statements that list the characteristics of *work* to be performed in particular job positions. *Employee record files* contain the detailed data describing the characteristics of *individual employees*. The designer's basic task, therefore, is to:

1. Identify the array of content in the company's job descriptions;
2. Identify the content of the employee record files;
3. Provide a system which will allow particular job descriptions to be matched against the record files to see if there are employees who can qualify for the job openings.

The designer immediately faces a problem. Job descriptions, as noted, are written to describe the job and not the man. Employee records are the reverse; they give the "man characteristics." The designer must somehow translate job characteristics into man characteristics, or vice versa. Fortunately, a procedure exists which can help here. Typically, in personnel work, another document is usually pre-

FIGURE 9–2

JOB DESCRIPTION EXAMPLE

SMART CORPORATION JOB DESCRIPTION No. 103764

Title: Sales Convention Arrangement Manager

Plans convention programs one year ahead. Prepares budget and is responsible for program accounting.

Meets with convention bureau executives and negotiates for space rental. Must be able to recognize prime display space and to negotiate on variety of "special charges" typical to convention operations.

Prepares exhibits and plans demonstrations showing the unique qualities of our product line.

Reports to management on impressions of market situations as part of Company's surveillance program.

---

pared that is called a *job specification*. This is derived by asking what sort of man is needed to do the work called for in the job description. The job specification therefore is (or can be) written in the same language as that which is used in the employee record files.

Let us demonstrate the functions of job descriptions and job specifications by use of the example shown earlier on page 105. This refers to the request by the marketing manager for help in finding out whether or not a present employee can qualify for the position of Sales Convention Arrangement Manager. Figure 9–2 shows this position written in the form of a job description. Note how it emphasizes the type of work and responsibility. It does not say what kind of background and other factors a man should have to be able to do this job. (This, of course, is just why the job specification is written.) Figure 9–3 shows both the job description and the job specification. In this figure a translation has taken place, as the requirements on the right now describe the desired man characteristics. The systems designer therefore includes this step of providing the job specifications in his development of the logic for the system.

Figure 9–4 shows the overall, generalized logic which the systems designer has chosen to encompass in the project. As noted above, at this level he is attempting to represent the major events and activities in the problem area, and is not trying to include very much detail. Each box represents what he considers to be a major reference point in the

FIGURE 9–3

EXAMPLES OF MATCHING DESCRIPTIONS AND SPECIFICATIONS

Job Description *Requirements*	Job Specification *Requirements*
Plans convention program one year ahead. Prepares budget and is responsible for program accounting.	Education: Bachelor's degree Experience: 1 year of our accounting (general or cost)
Meets with Convention Bureau executives and negotiates for space rental.	Age: 30+ Sex: Male Physical: Makes good appearance Miscellaneous: Willing to travel
Prepares exhibits and plans demonstrations showing the unique qualities of our product line.	Experience: 3 years our sales 2 years our factory
Reports to management on impressions of market as part of company surveillance.	Temperament: Personable, good conversationalist Experience: 3 years in our sales

problem area. Let us assume that he has checked this diagram with all interested parties and has received general approval. He has tried to draw his chart so that it is self-explanatory. Let us, however, look at his chart and inspect his choices.

He has identified (block 1) the initiation of a request for personnel to do a particular job. This request normally comes from a department head somewhere in the organization. This request can be quite formal or quite informal. When it is to be processed through a system, there is no choice: the request must be made in a specified manner. This is recognized in block 2, when a formal job description is written. As mentioned above, the next step is to convert this description of work into a specification for a person to do the work. Block 3 shows this as the written job specification. (We return to this block later to show how the analysis must proceed into more specific aspects before the system can be made operational.) Blocks 1, 2, and 3 provide one leg, or input sequence, for the system which is being designed.

FIGURE 9–4

GENERALIZED DIAGRAM OF CANDIDATE MATCHING

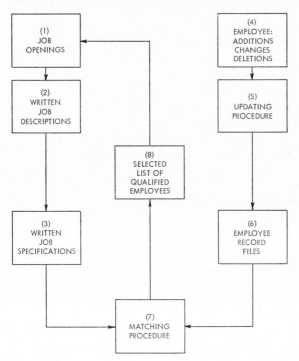

Blocks 4, 5, and 6 provide the other input sequence. Block 4 cites the significant problem of how to record all the changes, that is, the original entry of change data into the system. Block 5 recognizes that, once the changes are noted, they must somehow be processed so that block 6, the employee record file, is up-to-date when it is interrogated.

Block 7 shows the comparison of a job specification (block 3) to the employee record file (through a matching procedure). In effect, the system will identify the specific characteristics on the job specifications and will ask the employee record file for names of those who have these specific characteristics. The result is the selected list (block 8), which is then sent back to the department head for his final screening and candidate selection.

PROBLEMS OF CLASSIFICATION

Obviously, these blocks give a greatly skeletonized view of the problems involved in this process of candidate selection. Let us demonstrate this by returning to block 3 to see what is required. To write job specifications that can be processed through a system, it is appropriate to remember what was said earlier about classifications and codes. In Chapter 5 we said ". . . the fundamental idea is that classifications are built to facilitate decisions. Decisions involve both the making of comparisons for similarities, and of contrasts for differences. A good classification system has already built in certain significant comparisons and contrasts."

If the matching of characteristics in this systems design is to be logical, there must be careful attention to the classifications that will be used for this matching. On page 106 we showed the example of the job specification for the Sales Convention Arrangements Manager; and this same information was shown on the right side of Figure 9–3 in this chapter. Note that seven major classifications of employee characteristics were shown. Again, this is a simplification, for, as we will demonstrate, there will typically be a much larger number of classifications that must be included. For our present purposes, let us look only at these seven classes and question the logic involved. The reader should also review the information requirements specifications which were written for this project, starting on page 107. These specifications stress the use of the output of the system being designed, and they act as a reminder that the inputs we are now considering must ultimately satisfy these uses.

1. Age.   The company does not hire anyone under 18, and, with few exceptions, employees are retired at 65. The systems designer therefore must provide an arrangement for classifying and coding that covers this range. He could set up this scale as going from 18 to 66, with 66 representing any exception over 65 years of age. Assume also that he decides there is no need to work with time units less than a whole year. He thus has 48 discrete time points at which he can identify employee age.

2. Sex.   Here the designer has to provide the two classifications. Data recording and retrieval are thus matters of either–or.

3. Education.   The problem now becomes quite a bit more complicated. Details under this heading must cover both the type of education and the time span of such education. Decisions must be made as to which types of education will be identified and classified. An appropriate number of years must also be chosen to show the time dimension. Figure 9–5 gives one possible set of these classifications. Note that times are not necessary for grammar school, because the company does not employ anyone with less than grammar school education. Times are necessary for the other levels, however, because the job specifications are written identifying the years of education at these levels. A third dimension is that which recognizes the type of specialty. We have symbolized these specialties by simply noting that lists A through D have been established and are available to the system's designer.

FIGURE 9–5

EXAMPLES OF CLASSIFICATIONS

FOR EMPLOYEE CHARACTERISTICS

(1) Age_____   (2) Sex_____

(3) Education Classes

Level	Time	Specialty
Grammar		
Vocational School	1, 2, 3, 4	List A_1, A_2, A_3
High School	1, 2, 3, 4	List B_1, B_2, B_3
Associate Degree	1, 2	List C_1, C_2, C_3
Bachelor's Degree	1, 2, 3, 4	List C_1, C_2, C_3
Master's Degree	1, 2, 3	List C_1, C_2, C_3
Doctor's Degree	1, 2, 3	List C_1, C_2, C_3
(Other?)	1, 2, 3, 4	List D_1, D_2, D_3

(4) Experience Classes

Specialty	Level	Time
Budgeting	1 to 7	1 to 25
Clerical Supervision	"	"
Cost Accounting	"	"
Factory Supervision	"	"
General Accounting	"	"
Industrial Engineering	"	"
Industrial Sales	"	"
Marketing Research	"	"
Production Planning	"	"

FIGURE 9–5 (Continued)

(5) Temperament Classes

Trait	Gradations
Ambition	1 to 4
Courage	"
Decisiveness	"
Initiative	"
Forcefulness	"
Leadership	"
Personable	"
Perseverance	"
Persuasiveness	"
Responsibility Attitude	"

(6) Physical Characteristics Classes

Characteristics	Gradations
Appearance	1 to 4
Dexterity	"
Drive	"
Energy	"
Health	"
Strength	"

(7) Miscellaneous Classes

Class	Gradations
Citizen	Yes or No
Community Activities	1 to 4
Military Service Completed	Yes or No
Oral Presentation	1 to 4
References	1 to 4
Willing to Travel	Yes or No
Written Presentation	1 to 4

(Later in this chapter we will return to this classification for further analysis, and in Chapter 11 we will use this classification to demonstrate the computer programming design steps necessary to operate this system. Note that we are gradually narrowing down the scope of what we are presenting in these chapters as the amount of detail increases.)

4. Experience. A similar situation exists in the classification of experience. Therefore, the same three headings are used: Specialty, Level, Time. In this case we have shown specialty first, followed by level and time. This reflects a judgment that we normally check experience qualifications in this order: What specialty, what level, and for how long?

5. Temperament. This can be a particularly complex major class for it requires the identification of pertinent personal traits and an associated set of scale values for these traits. "Personable" is a trait, but how do you describe *how personable* an individual is? The normal procedure is to set up a somewhat arbitrary set of boxes with names that give gradations to the trait: *very personable, personable, withdrawn,* and *negative personality.* For our purposes here, let us take the traits shown in Figure 9–5 and assume the numbers of trait gradations as shown in the right column.

6. Physical Characteristics. Physical requirements are rather standardized. A representative selection of classes is shown in Figure 9–5.

7. Miscellaneous. This classification, as noted earlier, is the "catch-all" class. Over a period of time a set of these miscellaneous classes will gradually evolve for a particular company. Figure 9–5, again, shows such a set.

The detail in the above seven classes has been deliberately kept to a minimum. In practice, it can be expected that a greater number of classes must be incorporated in the typical systems design. For our purposes the present choices are sufficient to show the problems of establishing a system's logic.

Assume that for our simplified case this set of classifications has been reviewed and accepted as the total number of classes that will be handled, at least initially, in this system. This means that arrangements must be made to see that these classes are used in the writing of job specifications, and they must also be included in the classifications used in the employee record file.

Let us take one more step in the phase of systems design. Consider the classification of Education. We chose three subclasses under this heading: level, number of years, and specialty. Figure 9–6 shows the structuring of the classes and codes that must be put in the format no matter what the medium of processing is going to be. This is the problem of establishing the positional relationships needed to represent all types of data. We have added "name of school" to demonstrate how code numbers can increase quickly as an increased variety of classifications is included in the systems design. Note that the length of the code word which is needed to describe just these four classifications requires a ten-position code.

At some point the addition of a new class will involve more processing costs than are justified in light of the use to which the additional data can be put. The identification of such a point of diminishing returns in systems design is very important, and the point can be established only through close and cooperative analysis by both the managers and systems designers.

The phase of systems design is used to try to anticipate as many specific problems as possible, considering the logic of what is desired and what is feasible. These are extensions of the factors developed in the phases of problem definition and information requirements, but

FIGURE 9–6

EXAMPLE OF BUILD-UP OF CODE POSITIONS IN A RECORD

	Education Level	Field of Study	Number of Years	School
Number of Positions	1	3	4	2
Entries	0–9	100–999	0001–9999	01–99

now carried into further refinements. The logic of what is desirable in the design of a system should be developed initially, ignoring *how* the data will be processed. Note that there was no reference here to whether manual, punch card, or computer methods would be used. Only after the logic is established is it appropriate to see what adjustments may have to be made in consideration of the possible processing methods available.

Because we are emphasizing computer-based information systems, we will carry this example through the phase of the design of computer programs. (We will return to this example in Chapter 11.) Before going to the problem of programming design application, we will review what the computer is and what it takes to make it operate. The next chapter provides this review.

FLOW CHARTING SYMBOL STANDARDS

In the next few chapters we will make use of more specific flow charts. For this reason we have added to this chapter a brief section on the types of flow chart symbols that are used in systems design and in computer programming.

ABSTRACT OF
AMERICAN STANDARDS ASSOCIATION'S
PROPOSED AMERICAN STANDARD*
MARCH 26, 1963

FLOWCHART SYMBOLS FOR INFORMATION PROCESSING

1. *PURPOSE AND SCOPE*

1.1. *PURPOSE*

This standard establishes symbols for use in the preparation of flow-charts for information processing systems, including automatic data processing systems.

1.2. *SCOPE*

This standard prescribes and defines symbols used on flowcharts to represent both the sequence of operations and the flow of data and paperwork of information processing systems.
This standard does not cover:

    a. identifying, descriptive or explanatory information written inside or adjacent to a symbol;
    b. pictorial type flowcharts that utilize pictures or drawings to depict a system.

2. *FLOWCHART SYMBOLS*

2.1. *SYMBOLS REPRESENT FUNCTIONS*

Symbols are used on a flowchart to represent the functions of an information processing system. These functions are: input/output, processing, flow direction, and annotation.
A basic symbol is established for each function and can always be used to represent that function. Specialized symbols are established which may be used in place of a basic symbol to give additional information. The size of each symbol may vary but the dimensional ratio of each symbol shall be maintained.

---

* From Radio Corporation of America *Manual on Flowcharting Standards for Information Procession.*

2.2 *BASIC SYMBOLS*

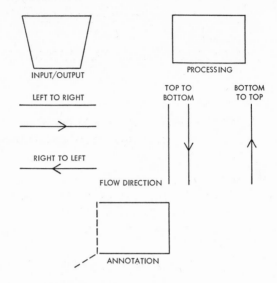

2.3. *SPECIALIZED SYMBOLS*

2.3.1. *Specialized Input/Output Symbols*

Specialized I/O symbols may represent the I/O function and, in addition, denote the medium on which the information is recorded or the manner of handling the information or both. If no specialized symbol exists, the basic I/O symbol is used.

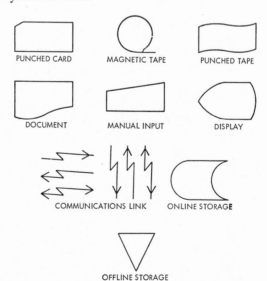

2.3.2. *Specialized Processing Symbols*

Specialized processing symbols may represent the processing function and, in addition, identify the specific type of operation to be performed on the information. If no specialized symbol exists, the basic processing symbol is used.

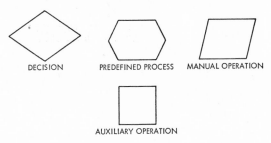

DECISION   PREDEFINED PROCESS   MANUAL OPERATION

AUXILIARY OPERATION

2.4 *ADDITIONAL SYMBOLS*

CONNECTOR   TERMINAL

Chapter 10

PROGRAMMING DESIGN
BACKGROUND

What does the executive-manager need to know about the computer and the languages used to make it work? It may not hurt the manager to know a lot about the computer, its internal circuitry, and the variety of ways the computer can be programmed. It is, however, more and more necessary that executive managers know at least the fundamentals of how these machines operate. Without this knowledge they are at a loss to understand modern management systems. This chapter, then, is specially written to provide such a statement of fundamentals.

INFORMATION PROCESSING BY MAN AND MACHINE

It appears that much of the thinking and deciding that a human being does is accomplished by his abilities to reshape the information stored in his brain. The information is reshaped by moving the data about in his mind while undertaking two types of mental actions. One group of actions, in effect, involves the mathematical procedures of addition, subtraction, multiplication, and division.

His images of anything become larger as he adds or multiplies. These images get smaller as he subtracts or divides. Through combinations of these four forms of mental actions he proceeds through his thought processes, changing the information held in his mind until he reaches a shape and content of information that is much more useful to him.

The second class of actions is the making of logical decisions based on some property of the information. If the information is numerical, the decisions are based on the numerical values. Some areas of human

126

thought do not lend themselves to numerical evaluation; therefore, some qualitative measure is applied. The like or dislike of music is an example of a qualitative decision.

A computer operates much the same as the human brain, with the exception that it is a much simpler device. Electronic computers are machines with a very limited repertoire of actions. A computer can add, subtract, multiply, and divide; make two simple, logical comparisons; put data into the machine, move it about, and send it out. Moreover, the storage capacity of the computer memory is very limited in comparison with the human brain. This is true regardless of the cost and size of the machine. The question, therefore, arises, How can a computer do so much?

The power of a computer comes primarily from two aspects of its design. One is the speed in which computer operations can be performed. Computers now in everyday use can perform arithmetic operations in two microseconds, that is, two-millionths of a second. This means 500,000 operations can be done in one second. Computers which are forecast for the near future will operate in the nanosecond range, that is, in billionths of a second. Thus, even though many simple operations are required to perform a function, the speed in which the work is done overcomes the limitations imposed by the machine's simplicity.

The second characteristic which gives a computer its great power is its ability to follow long programs of instructions. These instructions are stored internally in the computer and can be easily changed. This ability to store and change instructions enables a computer to perform processing tasks which involve a large number of steps. Since the time required for each step is extremely short, complicated tasks can be performed efficiently and rapidly.

FLOW OF OPERATIONS THROUGH THE COMPUTER

Computers are made up of five structural sections.[1] They are the input, memory or storage, control, arithmetic/logical units, and the output. The normal flow of operations is as follows:

1. By an operator's command, a program of instructions is fed into the computer's memory. These instructions tell the machine what is to be done.
2. Once the instructions are stored, the operator tells the machine to perform the first instruction.
3. Generally, the first series of instructions read the first batch of data to be entered into the computer's memory.

---

[1] In some instances the input and output are considered together since they may be physically the same piece of equipment.

4. Where the instructions call for arithmetic or logical operations, the data to be manipulated is brought to the arithmetic/logical unit. All of the numerical and logical operations are done in this unit.
5. When these operations are completed, the data are returned to the memory area, though not necessarily to the same place in memory.
6. In like fashion, many series of operations can be performed until the last desired processing has been completed and the resulting data are passed to the output unit. Other batches of data can then be read into the machine and the cycle retraced until all the data has been processed.
7. Throughout this operating cycle, the control unit performs the switching necessary to make the computer follow the actions dictated by the program.

FIGURE 10–1A

COMPUTER CONFIGURATION

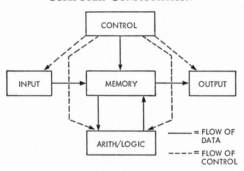

Figure 10–1A is a graphic representation of the five computer sections. Figure 10–1B depicts the flow of data through a computer. Of particular note is the fact that no processing is performed in the

FIGURE 10–1B

COMPUTER DATA FLOW

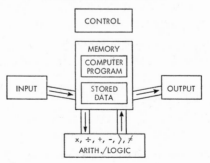

memory area. All operations are carried out in the arithmetic/logical unit. With this brief introduction to computer hardware, let us consider what has to be done to harness a computer for management purposes.

TREATING COMPUTERS AS A PROBLEM IN LANGUAGES

In order to take advantage of the benefits of electronic computing equipment, someone must be able to communicate instructions to the computing equipment. To do this at present, he must be able to "speak" the language of the machine. Moreover, to efficiently use the equipment he must understand another language, the language which the computer "speaks" to itself. This language is responsible for both the strengths and limitations of the equipment. Learning to use a computer, therefore, is closely parallel to learning a foreign language.

Two steps are involved in the process of mastering any language. One is to learn the words of the language, the other is to understand the grammar of their usage. The same is true with respect to computers. This is not to say that the ability to use any language relies only on the rote ability to memorize vocabulary and grammar. There are many degrees of ability to express oneself in a language. However, basic to this ability is an understanding of the fundamentals of the language.

For example, in order to understand and use a balance sheet, a manager must be familiar with the vocabulary of accounting—debits, credits, etc.—and with the basic rules to be followed in developing accounting reports. This does not mean every manager must be an accountant, that is, a person who is fluent in using the accounting language. Nevertheless, a manager who has no knowledge of accounting is surely severely limited in understanding the operations of a company.

The same is true with respect to computers. While a manager does not have to be fluent in computer languages, he cannot expect to flourish in a business environment in which computers are a vital link unless he is familiar with the basic language and grammar. Only then can he understand computer operations as they apply to his problems and information needs. With this fact in mind, the remainder of this chapter will be devoted to presenting the basic language and grammar of a computer.

BINARY NUMBERS: THE LANGUAGE SPOKEN IN THE DIGITAL COMPUTER

Numbers to the Base 2. All computer languages are based on some form of the binary numbering system. Binary numbers are numbers whose base is 2. To understand this, consider the number

673: a decimal number, a number to the base 10. Mathematically speaking, 673 can be written:

$$3 \times 10^0 = 3$$
$$7 \times 10^1 = 70$$
$$6 \times 10^2 = 600$$
$$\overline{673}$$

or as:

10^2	10^1	10^0
6	7	3

Each digit of the number is equal to that number times a power of ten. In the rightmost column, ten is taken to the zero power. Any number to the zero power is equal to 1. Therefore, 3 times 10^0 is equal to 3×1, or 3. In the next column, 10 is taken to the first power. A number to the power 1 is equal to itself, or in this case 10. Thus, 7 times 10^1 is equal to 7×10, or 70. In the leftmost column, 10 is taken to the second power, which is equal to 10×10, or 100. Hence, 6 times 10^2 is equal to 600. Adding 3, 70, and 600 together yields the decimal number 673.

In each column, from zero to nine units may be expressed. That is, in the 10^0 or unit column, for example, we may have either:

$$0 \times 10^0 = 0 \qquad 5 \times 10^0 = 5$$
$$1 \times 10^0 = 1 \qquad 6 \times 10^0 = 6$$
$$2 \times 10^0 = 2 \qquad 7 \times 10^0 = 7$$
$$3 \times 10^0 = 3 \qquad 8 \times 10^0 = 8$$
$$4 \times 10^0 = 4 \qquad 9 \times 10^0 = 9$$

The same is true for all other columns of the number. In each column, one of ten numbers, 0 through 9, may be used.

The same logic is followed in the binary number system, except that the base is 2 and not 10. The rightmost digit column in binary numbers is 2^0. Moving to the left, the next digit column is 2^1, the following 2^2, and so forth: $2^4 / 2^3 / 2^2 / 2^1 / 2^0$.

In each column, however, only two choices are available. They are 0 and 1. To write a number in the binary system, either a 1 or a zero is written in each column. To write the number 5, a 1 is placed in the 2^2 position, which yields 4. This is the highest power of two which is less than 5. Moving to the right, a zero,

2^2	2^1	2^0
1		

$(1 \times 2^2 = 4)$,

must be placed in the 2^1 column. If a one was placed there, our number would be:

$$1 \times 2^2 = 4$$
$$1 \times 2^1 = \underline{2},$$
$$6$$

which is greater than 5. In the 2^0 column,

$$\frac{2^2 / 2^1 / 2^0}{1 / 0 /},$$

a one must be recorded:

$$\frac{2^2 / 2^1 / 2^0}{1 / 0 / 1}.$$

Our number now reads:

$$1 \times 2^2 = 4$$
$$0 \times 2^1 = 0$$
$$1 \times 2^0 = \underline{1}$$
$$5$$

The reason electronic computers use the binary system and not the conventional decimal system can now be put forth. Computers are fundamentally built from a series of switches. The switches are either on or off. They either conduct, or do not conduct, electricity. How does this relate to binary numbers? In computers, when a switch is not conducting, it is equivalent to a zero; when it is conducting it is equivalent to a 1. Thus binary numbers can be represented with a simple set of on–off switches. If another number system, such as the decimal system, was used, the switches would have to show some qualitative aspect. In the decimal system they would have to represent values from 0 to 9. In the binary system they only need represent 0 or 1. Thus no qualitative measure is required; the switch is either on or off.

The Quantitative Processes.   Using the binary language, a computer can accomplish the *four* basic mathematical operations of adding $(+)$, subtracting $(-)$, multiplying $(\times)$, and dividing $(\div)$. To illustrate this, consider the problem of adding 5 and 6. In binary:

$$101 \quad (5)$$
$$110 \quad (6).$$

To accomplish the addition, the computer need only be built to follow three simple rules:

1. If current is added to no current, the result is current. That is, $1 + 0 = 1$.

2. If current is added to current, the result is no current, with current being shifted to the left: $1 + 1 = 10$.
3. Adding no current does not change the form of the switch.

Applying these rules to the addition problem:

$$\begin{array}{r} 101 \\ 110 \\ \hline \end{array}$$

(adding 5 to 6) gives:

Current to no current equals current:

$$\begin{array}{ccc} 1 & 0 & 1 \\ & & \downarrow \\ 1 & 1 & 0 \\ \hline & & \downarrow \\ & & 1. \end{array}$$

No current to current yields current:

$$\begin{array}{ccc} 1 & 0 & 1 \\ & \downarrow & \\ 1 & 1 & 0 \\ \hline & \downarrow & \\ & 1 & 1. \end{array}$$

Current to current yields no current and shifts current to the left:

$$\begin{array}{cccc} & 1 & 0 & 1 \\ & & \downarrow & \\ 1 \leftarrow 1 & 1 & 0 \\ \hline & 0 \downarrow 1 & 1. \end{array}$$

No current to current yields current:

$$\begin{array}{cccc} 0 & 1 & 0 & 1 \\ & \downarrow & & \\ 1 & 1 & 1 & 0 \\ \hline \downarrow & & & \\ 1 & 0 & 1 & 1. \end{array}$$

Looking at the resultant we see:

$$\frac{2^3 / 2^2 / 2^1 / 2^0}{1\ /0\ /1\ /1}$$

$$\begin{array}{rcl} 1 \times 2^0 &=& 1 \\ 1 \times 2^1 &=& 2 \\ 0 \times 2^2 &=& 0 \\ 1 \times 2^3 &=& 8 \\ \hline & & 11. \end{array}$$

The reverse procedure is followed for subtraction. Subtracting 5 from 6:

$$\frac{110}{101}$$

Current from no current yields current, and current is borrowed from the next column[2]:

$$
\begin{array}{rrr}
1 & 1 & 0 \\
-1 & 0 & 1 \\
\hline
& & 1.
\end{array}
$$

No current from no current gives no current:

$$
\begin{array}{rrr}
1 & 0 & 0 \\
-1 & 0 & 1 \\
\hline
& 0 & 1.
\end{array}
$$

Current from current equals no current:

$$
\begin{array}{rrr}
1 & 0 & 0 \\
-1 & 0 & 1 \\
\hline
0 & 0 & 1
\end{array}
$$

Multiplication can be done in a similar fashion. To multiply, the rules are:

1. Current times current yields current.
2. Current times no current yields no current.
3. No current times anything yields no current.

These are simple rules. The only multiplication table needed is the one table. One times one is one. Following the same multiplication rules as learned in grade school, 6 times 5 in binary is:

$$
\begin{array}{l}
101 \ (5) \\
110 \ (6) \\
\hline
000 \\
101 \\
101 \\
\hline
11110,
\end{array}
$$

$$
\begin{array}{ccccc}
2^4 & 2^3 & 2^2 & 2^1 & 2^0 \\
1 & 1 & 1 & 1 & 0 ,
\end{array}
$$

---

[2] This is the same in the decimal system as subtracting 9 from 10:

$$
\begin{array}{r}
10 \\
-9 \\
\hline
1.
\end{array}
$$

$$0 \times 2^0 = 0$$
$$1 \times 2^1 = 2$$
$$1 \times 2^2 = 4$$
$$1 \times 2^3 = 8$$
$$1 \times 2^4 = \underline{16}$$
$$30.$$

In a like fashion, the rules for binary division could be presented. However, the purpose here is not to teach binary arithmetic but to show that a computer, using a series of switches representing zeros and ones, can do addition, subtraction, multiplication, and division.

The Comparison or Choice Processes.   If a computer could only accomplish arithmetic operations, it would not differ significantly from a desk calculator, despite its other virtues. Obviously, therefore, a computer can do more. It can perform two types of logical comparisons. The two comparisons which can be made are the equalities comparison:

$$A = B \text{ or } A \neq B$$
(A is equal to B or A is not equal to B),

and the inequality comparison:

$$A > B \text{ or } A \leq B$$
(A is greater than B or A is less than or equal to B).

An indication of how this is done follows. Reconsider the two binary numbers for 5 and 6.

$$110$$
$$101$$

If a computer were programmed to see if the numbers were equal, one number would be subtracted from the other:

$$110$$
$$\underline{101}$$
$$001.$$

The machine then looks to see if any current is in the remainder; that is, is any switch set to the one position? If none is, the values are equal, while if any switches are set to one, they are unequal.

Rather than consider how a computer determines if one value is greater than another, let us consider the nature of the decision:

$$A > B \text{ or } A \leq B.$$

Notice that three alternatives are possible. A can be greater than, less than, or equal to B. However, in a computer, only yes or no type decisions can be made. Either all switches are set to zero and no current is flowing, or one or more switches are set to one and current is flowing. No measure is made of how much current (how many switches are set to one) is flowing; it is a yes or no situation. Therefore, the inequalities decision, like all other computer decisions, must have only two paths, either:

$$A > B \text{ or } A \leq B.$$
$$\text{or}$$
$$A \geq B \text{ or } A < B.$$

It cannot be $A > B$ or $A < B$ or $A = B$. The equality case must be part of either $A \geqq B$ or $A \leqq B$. The form that is used varies according to computers, and is not of prime importance. What is important is that a systems designer must be able to state all logical operations to be done in a computer in a yes or no fashion. This point will be developed to a greater extent later in the chapter.

The Processing of Alphabetics. Early computers used pure binary numbering systems for all operations. This seriously limited their application; since they could not handle alphabetics, they were not much use for data processing. Further, the necessity of the user to use binary numbers limited his desire to use the computer. To expand the area in which computers could operate, and to satisfy the user, decimal and alphabetic forms of binary numbers were developed. Of the various forms used for data processing the most common is the binary-decimal system.[3] First, let us see how this system handles decimals, and then how it treats alphabetics.

In this language, binary numbers are used to represent decimals. Four binary positions, or switches, are used for each decimal digit. The number 973 is represented as:

9	7	3	
1	0	0	2^3 position (8)
0	1	0	2^2 " (4)
0	1	1	2^1 " (2)
1	1	1	2^0 " (1)

Any decimal number can be written in this form. In practice, computer "words" of five decimal positions, or multiples of five positions are used most often.

---

[3] This system is also often called the binary coded decimal system.

To do arithmetic, the binary equivalents of the decimals are employed. For a simple illustration consider adding:

6	7	2		3	5
0	0	0		0	0
1	1	0	and	0	1
1	1	1		1	0
0	1	0		1	1.

To accomplish this, the rightmost digits are added first:

2	5	7
0	0	0
$0+1$	$=$	1
1	0	1
0	1	1

Then the next set of digits is added, and so forth. If a number greater than 9 (1001) occurs, one is carried to the next left position and (1010) is subtracted from the number greater than 9:

6	7	2		3	5		7		0	7
0	0	0		0	0		0		0	0
1	1	0	+	0	1	=	1		0	1
1	1	1		1	0		1		0	1
0	1	0		1	1		1	←	0	1.

In order to perform the comparison operations in binary coded decimal, the individual binary equivalents of the decimal numbers are compared. For example, to determine if 672 is equal or not equal to 35, the binary equivalent of 2 is subtracted from 5 and the remainder checked for switches set to one. This is the same procedure as was followed for a pure binary number, except that only one column is done at a time.

To express *letters* in the binary-decimal system, two more binary positions are needed. These positions are called zone positions. If the zone positions are both zero, the binary number represents a decimal. If either, or both, zone positions is a one, it represents an alphabetical symbol.

P	A	1	
1	0	0	Zone 1
0	1	0	Zone 2
0	0	0	(2^3)
0	0	0	(2^2)
0	0	0	(2^1)
1	1	1	(2^0)

To the computer, A is the binary value 010001. When A is typed in, it is recorded as 010001. When 010001 comes to the output, it again becomes A.

Notice that the addition of the zone positions has not changed the way arithmetic is done. The binary number for 1 is 000001. Since zeros are added to the left, the numerical value is not changed. Any numerical operation can still be performed. However, before allowing an instruction to perform some arithmetic operation, the zone codes are checked. If either or both have ones, no arithmetic can be done, since alphabetics cannot be added. Adding an A to a B is meaningless.

However, since letters have a binary numeric value, alphabetics can be logically compared. In data processing applications this allows checking names and alphanumeric codes for matches.

EXAMPLES OF BINARY REASONING

This completes the discussion of the internal computer language. The following aspects bear repeating for emphasis. First, only the basic arithmetic operations of $+$, $-$, $\times$, $\div$ can be performed. All compli-

FIGURE 10–2

COMPUTER LOGIC FOR A THREE-VALUE COMPARISON

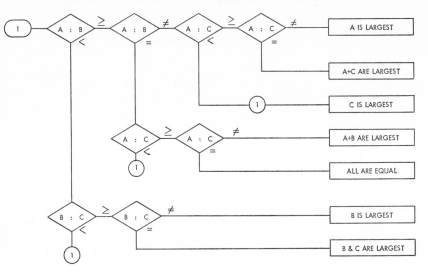

LEGEND:
$\geq$ IS GREATER THAN OR EQUAL TO
$=$ IS EQUAL TO
$\neq$ IS NOT EQUAL TO
$<$ IS LESS THAN

cated numerical procedures, such as square roots, must be done with these operations. Second, only two yes or no type comparisons can be made. Anything that a user desires a computer to do must be done within these limits.

Using a computer therefore forces the programmer to think in binary terms, that is, in the language of the computer. A simple illustration will show the mechanics of this type of logic.

In order to determine which of three numbers, *A, B,* and *C* is greatest (using computer logic), eight decisions must be made. Figure 10–2 is a graphic presentation of the logic. To see the logic of the chart, read across the top line. In the first decision *A* was greater than or equal to *B.* Therefore, another decision was required to determine if they were equal, a valid condition. The necessity for this decision derives from the inability to make more than a yes or no decision at one time. The first decision established that *A* was > or = to *B.* The second that it was not equal to *B,* therefore it must be greater than *B.* In like fashion, across the top line *A* was compared to *C* and found to be greater.

This, however, is the logic path followed only when *A* is greatest. Paths must be provided for all alternatives. The alternatives are:

> *A* is greatest
> *B* "   "
> *C* "   "
> *A* and *B* are greatest
> *A* " *C* "   "
> *B* " *C* "   "
> *A, B* " *C* "   " .

If one of the alternatives is omitted, an incorrect answer would be obtained at some point. This illustrates why many computer programs operate correctly for a period, then suddenly furnish an incorrect answer. The set of instructions was not complete. One or more possible alternatives was not included, or was included incorrectly. Where that path was used, the error occurred.

Let us complicate the problem somewhat. Suppose a computer were to play a simplified poker game in which only one pair, two pairs, three of a kind, and four of a kind were valid hands. How could the computer determine the value of a hand? Stated in another form, what logic is involved in determining the value of a hand? To attempt this problem in the manner of the previous example would be folly since so many possibilities exist. Therefore, a more efficient approach must be found.

One possible approach is to combine the mathematical and logical aspects of a computer, and one feasible solution is illustrated in Figure

10–3. The logic is to compare the first card to the second, third, fourth, and fifth, and—if they are the same—to add 1 to M. M is initially equal to zero. After the first card is compared to the others, the second card is compared to the third, fourth, and fifth cards. In like fashion, the other cards are compared.

Figure 10–3 represents this comparison process. After the ten comparisons are made, the value of M is checked. If it is 1, one pair exists;

FIGURE 10–3

LOGIC TO DETERMINE NUMBER OF PAIRS IN A POKER HAND

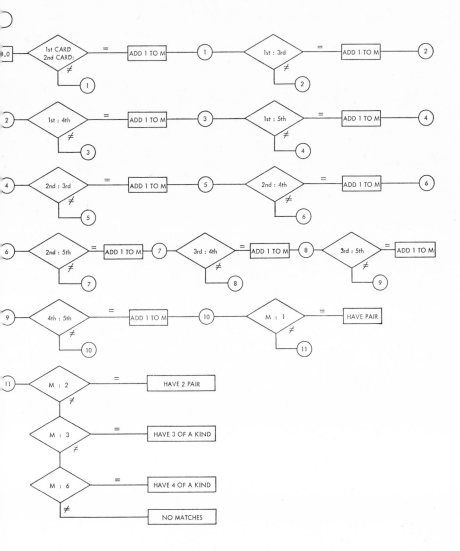

if it is 2, two pairs exist, and so on. This example is included to show that the ability to innovate with the simple computer language is great. In fact, careful study of most problems will reveal an efficient approach.

THE SIGNIFICANCE OF COMPUTER CHARACTERISTICS TO MANAGEMENT PRACTICE

At this point our discussion of computers ends. What does it all mean to a manager? First, any classification of characteristics must lend itself to precise definition. Second, the classification structures and the aims of the system must fit into a logical machine approach.

This means that the logic must be minutely detailed, but not that the manager himself must develop the detail. It does mean that his approach must be capable of logical development. Virtually any decision process can be broken down into yes or no steps. To do so, however, requires a clear understanding and a good statement of the problem. This means that management must be able to state its desires or thoughts lucidly. It cannot fall back on half-definitions.

If half-definitions are given, the programmer must come back to the manager for more specific statements, or the programmer must make the detailed decisions himself. These, of course, will be only as good as the programmer's knowledge of the problem area.

As was noted in the previous chapter, the programmer and the systems designer must work very closely together. Both, in turn, must work closely with the functional manager, checking, refining, extending, or narrowing the scope of the content of the system. Only through such an interplay of talents is it possible to obtain computer-based systems that meet manager's needs-to-know and that operate at relatively low costs.

The manager provides the knowledge of which factors are important and how they relate to other factors. He identifies the information requirements and refines these requirements, seeking to be as specific as is possible in given circumstances. The systems designer provides the ability to convert the manager's requirements into block diagrams, and more specific flow charts, so that a picture of the logic of the system's design can be provided. Gradually, through approximation and careful trial and error, a logic is developed that can be discussed and agreed upon by all concerned. The programmer contributes his knowledge of equipment and of the languages necessary to communicate the systems requirements to, through, and out of the computer.

We have treated programming here as a separate position having particular skills. There are many situations, however, in which the systems designer—and to a lesser degree, the functional manager—

may do at least preliminary programming. Whether or not these people do actual programming, it is important that they appreciate the computer's capacities and limitations. This chapter has been presented to give a background of what we consider to be the minimum that managers and systems designers must know about the computer. In the next chapter we move to an example of applying this background in a further refinement of the candidate screening system.

Chapter 11

PROGRAMMING DESIGN
APPLICATION

This chapter will merge the candidate matching system design as discussed in Chapter 9 with the requirements of the computer as discussed in Chapter 10. The systems design provides the general outline of the overall system. The peculiarities of the computer require that this general outline now be expressed in the specific language that the computer understands.

THE COMPUTER FLOW CHART

The first step in computer programming design is to lay out the major aspects of the system design at the more detailed level of the computer. In the candidate matching project there are two major areas to be considered. These are the retrieval and file maintenance problems. A general systems flow chart including these functions is presented in Figure 11–1.

As shown in the diagram, the retrieval area is concerned with matching requests for personnel with the information in the firm's personnel file. For a new job, a rough job specification is written by management and sent to the Personnel Department. This department evaluates the request and, together with management, draws up the final job specification. In turn, this specification is coded, punched, and run on the computer. The computer run checks the personnel records of the firm's employees. When an employee's record matches the request, his personnel record is printed. This list of matches is edited and furnished to the manager to aid him in selecting a person for the new job.

Of particular note at this point is the fact that the computer pro-

FIGURE 11–1

GENERAL SYSTEMS FLOW CHART FOR CANDIDATE MATCHING

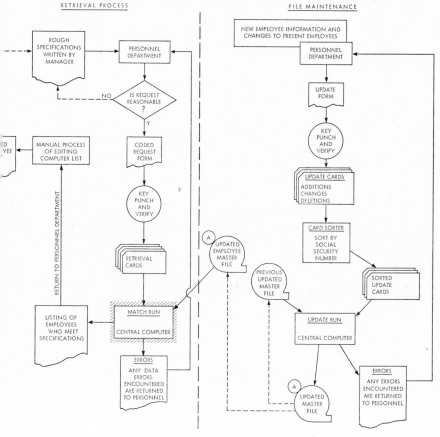

grams are only part of the system. Many other types of operations are involved, both before and after the computer operations. The problems, which are part of the input tasks, will be discussed in the following chapter, while those relating to output will be presented in Chapter 13.

The file maintenance portion of the system covers the assimilation and updating of the personnel records. Data relating to new employees and to changes in old employee data are funneled through the Personnel Department. This department classifies and codes the data according to the procedures discussed in Chapter 9. The coded data is then punched, verified, and run through the computer. The result is an updated master file with the latest personnel data for every employee.

Once the general systems flow chart is designed, the next step in the process is to detail the operations within each step of the plan. This is a narrowing process, a movement from generalities to detail. It is analogous to the movement from broad information classes to specific information classes, illustrated in Chapter 9.

As an example, let us look at one block of Figure 11–1, the Match Run block in the retrieval system. The purpose of this computer run is to search the master file for individuals who meet a particular set of job specifications. Very quickly a question arises, "How do you define *meets?*" If, for instance, 20 characteristics are desired and an individual only meets 19, should we select him? Certainly that depends on what the one characteristic is. As an alternative, we could decide to print this individual's record out and let management decide if it matches their desires. This evades the issue, however. If management is supplied with records for individuals who match 19 out of 20 of the desired characteristics, should they get records which meet 18, or 17, or 16 characteristics? Some decision must be made as to what constitutes a match. The programmers cannot decide this, as it is a managerial function. It therefore is management's task to make this decision. Systems analysts must gain from management a further definition of the problem. This illustrates the fact that, in designing a programming package, management will often be called upon to clarify specific issues. The more incomplete the original systems design, the more often this will occur.

Notice that in this discussion we are approaching the limitations of computers presented in the previous chapter. For the computer to operate, the decisions must be based on a series of simple yes or no answers. The matching problem, however, is not simple. Perhaps through a long series of yes or no decisions the questions can be resolved to yes or no answers. The cost of obtaining a flow which will cover all of the cases may be more costly in systems time, programming time, computer time, and, above all, in management time, than it is worth. As a result, systems analysts must obtain a feel of what level of depth the system should treat and what should be an exception. Generally, systems will not cover 100 percent of the cases. Ninety-five percent may be all that can be systematized. Since this is so, some way must be found to treat the cases which the programming system will not handle. In Figure 11–1, and in the following charts, exception printouts from the computer are programmed for this purpose.

The exceptions are of two types. The first group consists of those cases containing a mistake. It may result from a bad code, a programming mistake, or from one of many other sources. This type of exception is printed out so that it may be corrected. The second type of exception represents a true exception. It can be broken down into two classes. One, it can be a condition which was foreseen in the original programming but was easier to treat as an exception with special handling. Two, it may be the result of unforeseen conditions which are not a mistake but represent a condition not covered by the program.

SPELLING OUT THE COMPUTER LOGIC

The gist of this discussion is that many complex decisions must be made to redesign the system into the logical pattern required by the computer. In our example we will present the simple case where a match must be 20 out of 20 items. Figure 11–2 presents, in computer logic, the processing steps involved in the match program. It uses the same type of logic that is illustrated in the simple logic diagrams in Chapter 10. For example, the first line of the chart is devoted to reading into the computer the specifics of a job for which management desires to find qualified personnel. A card is read into the computer and checked to see if it is the sentinel card placed at the end of the input to tell the computer it has completed the processing. If it is, the computer tapes are rewound and the machine stopped. If the card is not a sentinel, processing begins. The area on the card which carries the codes for previous experience is checked. If the field is blank, signifying "no experience is needed for the new job," the program will move to 3 where the educational requirements of the job are checked. If some experience is required, the nature of the experience will be determined through a series of yes or no questions. The nature of the experience needed determines the sequence of the subsequent steps in the processing.

CARD AND TAPE LAYOUT

To support the logic of the computer, the design of the input cards which hold the description of the new job, and the computer tapes which carry employee data must be determined. A programmer can only tell a machine what to do if the precise form of the data is known. In the description of the match program a sentinel card was used to tell the computer when to stop processing. To check for the sentinel, the exact location on the card, and the specific type of symbol which will be used must be known. In this example a 1 in the 80th column of the input card signifies the end of the input. To continue the example, blanks (spaces) in the first experience field of the input card signify that "no experience is required." If experience is needed, the code describing the experience must range between 0 and 999. In like fashion, the location and specifics of the information on the master

FIGURE 11–2

Candidate Matching Logical Flow Chart

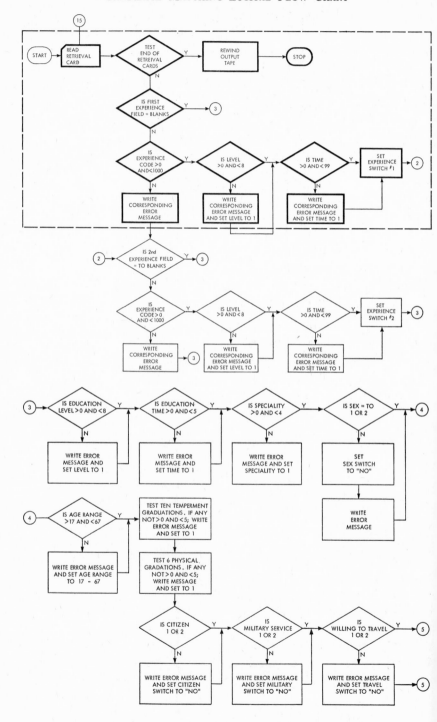

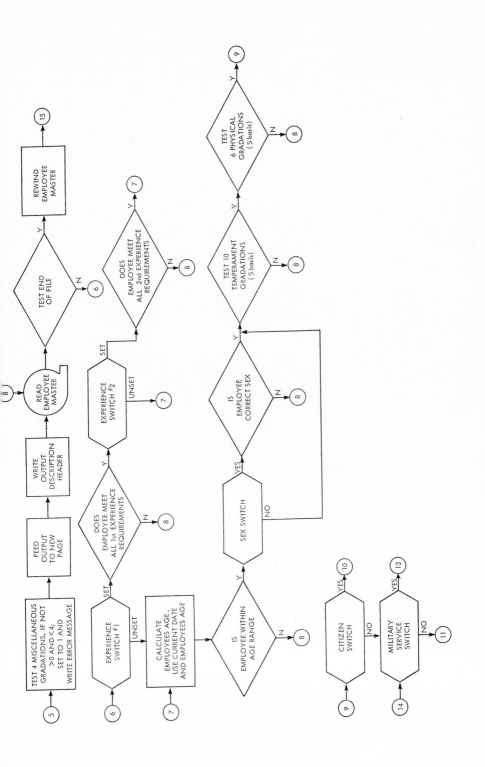

FIGURE 11-2 (cont.)

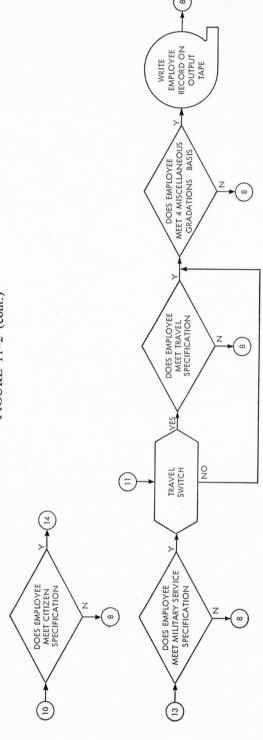

personnel tape must be specified. Figure 11–3 presents the format and the layout of the master file computer tapes. In the record the first nine positions will contain the employee's social security number; positions 10 through 25 the employee's last name, and so forth. Every position of every record must be specified.

CODING THE COMPUTER INSTRUCTIONS

The final step in the design of the matching system is to code a logic sequence for the computer to follow which will accomplish the operations required. In the preceding chapter we presented the internal language of a computer. This is the language in which the computer speaks to itself. The language that enters the picture now is the language with which the programmer speaks to the computer.

For every computer there is a set of codes which tell the computer what operations to follow. A sample list of such a language, for the Honeywell 200 computer,[1] is shown in Figure 11–4. The instructions are broken into three groups: arithmetic, logical, and movement. Movement may be further subdivided into control (movement of data inside the machine) and input-output (movement of data in and out of the machine). The three primary classes of instruction were covered in the previous chapter; that is, a computer can do arithmetic, some limited logic, and move data about.

To illustrate the use of the language, consider a few of the steps from the Match program. They are represented on Figure 11–2 by blocks which have a heavy outline. The command language coding for these steps is shown in Figure 11–5. Each individual computer operation must be specified. The first instruction reads the card into the computer. The next step is to check to determine if the 80th column (sentinel) is a one. If it is not a one, the program moves to test the experience fields. If it is a one, the tapes are rewound and the machine stops.

Each instruction required to accomplish the bold type area of Figure 11–2 is presented in Figure 11–5. An explanation of what is done is shown for each instruction. To accomplish these simple tasks requires 21 instructions. Each has three parts: Location, Operations Code, and Operand. A mistake in any instruction will invalidate the entire program. The amount of work and the detail necessary to do machine level coding means that the task is cumbersome, lengthy, costly, and difficult. In order to correct this condition other levels of

---

[1] The command languages for other computers are similar. The same is true for the use of the language.

language have been developed. These languages are composed of some form of short English statements (called psuedo-English). These statements are then fed into the machine and the machine translates them into its internal command language.

To illustrate this, consider a computer that only understood German. If someone who only spoke English wished to communicate with

FIGURE 11–3

EMPLOYEE MASTER FILE

TAPE FORMAT

Digits		Information
1–9		Social Security number
10–25		Last name
26–38		First name (Initial, if used)
39–59		Address
60–79		City and State
80–90		Telephone number
91		*Sex:* 1 = male, 2 = female
92–97		*Birth Date:* MMDDYY
		MM = month, DD = day, YY = year
98		*Education Level* (1 to 7)
99		Time for above (1 to 4)
100		Specialty for above (1 to 3)
101–103		*Experience Specialty* (001 to 999)
104	1st	Level for above (1 to 7)
105–106		Time for above (01 to 99 years)
107–112	2nd	Experience specialty, etc.
113–119	3rd	Experience specialty, etc.
120–125	4th	Experience specialty, etc.
126–131	5th	Experience specialty, etc.
132–137	6th	Experience specialty, etc.
138–147		Ten *Temperament* gradations in sequence (1 to 4)
148–153		Six *Physical* gradations in sequence (1 to 4)
154		Citizen: 1 = yes, 2 = no
155		Military Service completed: 1 = yes, 2 = no
156		Willing to travel: 1 = yes, 2 = no
157		Community Activity gradation (1 to 4)
158		Oral presentation gradation (1 to 4)
159		Written presentation gradation (1 to 4)
160		References gradation (1 to 4)
161–180		Blank (possible future use)
		(Each employee will have one record on tape with the preceding information.)

FIGURE 11–3 (cont.)

RETRIEVAL CARD FORMAT

Columns	Information
1–6	1st *Experience requirement:* CCCLTT
	CCC = code (001 to 999)
	L = level (1 to 7)
	TT = time (01 to 99)
7–12	2nd *Experience requirement* (same as above)
13–15	*Education:* LTS
	L = level (1 to 7)
	T = time (1 to 4)
	S = specialty (1 to 3)
16	*Sex:* 1 = male, 2 = female
17–20	*Age Range*
21–30	*Ten temperament gradations*
31–36	*Six physical gradations*
37	*Citizen:* 1 = yes, 2 = no
38	*Military Service:* 1 = yes, 2 = no
39	Willing to travel: 1 = yes, 2 = no
40–43	*4 Miscellaneous gradations* (1 to 4)
	1. Community
	2. Oral presentation
	3. Written presentation
	4. References
44–49	Current date (MM DD YY)
50–80	Output description

the machine and tell it what to do some translation would have to be done. The English would have to be translated into German. This could be done outside the machine with a dictionary. However, if the machine had a translator program it could translate the English into German itself. The German instructions could then be followed and the processing completed. This is precisely the path followed with the higher order computer languages commonly termed compiler languages. The English is translated by a program written in the computer command code into its own command code. Then this program can be run. Figure 11–6 illustrates the process. At the bottom of the figure, commands written in a special form of English are fed into the machine along with a program which translates the English into machine language. When the translation is completed the commands in computer language and the data to be processed are fed into the computer. The output is the processed data.

FIGURE 11–4

COMPUTER INSTRUCTIONS

(Example: Honeywell 200 Computer)

Mnemonic	*Function*
	ARITHMETIC INSTRUCTIONS
BA	Binary Add
BS	Binary Subtract
A	Decimal Add
S	Decimal Subtract
ZA	Zero and Add
ZS	Zero and Subtract
	LOGIC INSTRUCTIONS
EXT	Extract (Logical Product)
HA	Half Add (Exclusive Or)
C	Compare
SST	Substitute
BCE	Branch if Character Equal
B	Branch
BCT	Branch on Condition Test
BCC	Branch on Character Condition
	CONTROL INSTRUCTIONS
SW	Set Word Marks
SI	Set Item Mark
CW	Clear Word Mark
CI	Clear Item Mark
H	Halt
NOP	No Operation
CSM	Change Sequencing Mode
CAM	Change Addressing Mode
RNM	Resume Normal Mode
MCW	Move Character to Word Mark
EXM	Extended Move
MAT	Move and Translate
LCA	Load Characters to A-Field Word Mark
SCR	Store Control Registers
LCR	Load Control Registers
MCE	Move Characters and Edit
POT	Peripheral Data Transfer
PCB	Peripheral Control and Branch

FIGURE 11–5

MACHINE CODING*

Location	Operations Code	Operand	Explanation
Start	POT	Match, 12, 41	Read Input card to memory area. Match using the 2nd Read-Write Channel with card reader control assigned to memory location 41.
	BCC	Rewind, End, 02	Test the Character on the card called End. If it is equal to 1 go to Rewind. If not continue in sequence.
	B	Experience	Go to Experience for next instruction.
Rewind	PCB	Stop, 00, 23, 40	Rewind tape 3. If tape in use go to Stop. After rewind release tape.
Stop	H	Rewind	Stop machine. If run button pressed go to rewind.
Experience	C	Experience Field, Blanks	Compare the 1st experience field by blanks. If it is equal go to three.
	BCT	Three, 45	If not continue in sequence.
	C	Experience Code, Con 1	Compare Experience Code to Con 1 (1000). If Excode is greater than 1000 go to
	BCT	Error, 41	Error. If not stay in sequence.
	C	Excode, Con $\emptyset$	Compare Experience Code to Con $\emptyset$ (0). If Excode is less than 0 go to
	BCT	Error, 44	Error. If not stay in sequence.
	C	Level, Con $\emptyset$	Compare Level to Con $\emptyset$. If Level is less than 0 go to Updat, if not stay
	BCT	Updat, 44	in sequence.
	C	Level, Con 8	Compare Level with Con 8 (8). If Level is greater than 8 go to Updat,
	BCT	Updat, 41	if not stay in sequence.
Time in	C	Time, Con $\emptyset$	Compare Time with Con $\emptyset$. If Time is less than 0, go to Updat 1. If not
	BCT	Updat 1, 44	stay in sequence.
	C	Time, Con 9	Compare Time with Con 9 (99). If Time is greater than 99 go to Updat
	BCT	Updat 1, 41	1. If not stay in sequence.
	A	Con 1, Switch 1	Add 1 to Switch 1, setting it to 1.
	B	Two	

* This is done in assembly language so mnemonics can be used instead of numbers, to facilitate the reader's understanding.

There is one other significant advantage to these higher order languages. Compiler languages are much simpler to write and understand than machine language programs. Figure 11–7 shows the COBOL (Common Business Oriented Language) commands for the same section of the match program as was written in machine language. The difference between the two languages is immediately obvious. The COBOL program is far less complicated, and is easier to understand and write. For example, to read the input cards, check the sentinel, and

FIGURE 11–6

TRANSLATION PROCESS FOR
HIGHER ORDER COMPUTER LANGUAGES

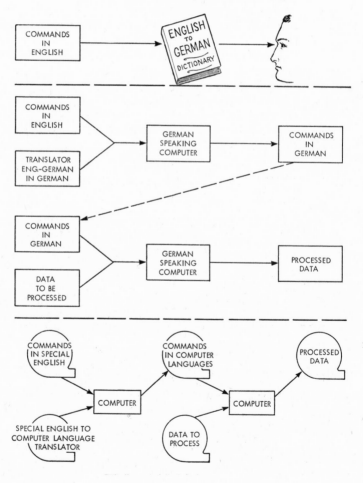

proceed to take action, we simply write: *Read Retrieve Record; at End Go to Rewind Routine.* Removing the need to learn the meaning of specific symbols and returning to a form of English makes a great difference to the programmer. If the pseudo-English language is precisely defined, translator programs for various computers can be writ-

FIGURE 11–7

COBOL OPERATING STATEMENTS*

Statement Identification	Operation	Program Name
00 60 10	Open Retrieve	Match
00 60 20	Read Retrieve Record; At End go to Rewind Routine	Match
00 60 30	If First-Experience-Field is Equal to Blanks go to three	Match
00 60 40	If Experience-Code is not less than 1000 and not greater than 0 go to Error Routine	Match
00 60 50	If Level is not less than 8 and not greater than 0 go to Corresponding-Error Routine	Match
00 60 60	If Time is not less than 99 and not greater than 0 go to Error-Write Routine	Match
00 60 70	Set Switch to 1	Match

* Only the procedure section for these operations is shown.

ten. Thus, the same pseudo-English program can be used for various computers. This is a distinct saving over command languages, since each computer has its own command language, and to use a program written in command language for one computer on another requires rewriting. Properly written, COBOL programs may be translated and run on a variety of computers.

To recapitulate the material in this chapter:

1. The general systems design was extended to consider the requirements of the computer.
2. The detailed programming system was developed.
3. A part of the program was coded.

At this point the match program must be tested and corrected until it is in operating order. The same steps followed for the match program must be followed for all other stages of the program package. The development of the computer program is, however, not the end of developing the personnel system. The system must be put into operation. This involves the development of operating procedures. In the following chapter the operating procedures are detailed and the responsibilities for developing the procedures of various groups, such as systems design, programming, and management, will be discussed.

Chapter 12

SYSTEMS OPERATIONS:
DAY-TO-DAY PRODUCTION

Operating a management information system on a daily basis requires careful planning and control. No matter how well the systems requirements are determined or the design and programming done, there is always a need for clear directions to keep the system operating smoothly. These operating instructions must cover every aspect of the process, from the origination of the data to the processing and distribution of information.

At this point in the text the reader might conclude that all of the facets of the candidate matching system have been designed. This conclusion, however, would not be correct. What has been designed is the machine portion of the system. In Chapter 2 a set of relationships between organization and systems was stated. The basic point was that systems are combinations of man and machine activities. To this point only the machine activities within the system have been developed. The manual tasks have not been considered.

THE MANUAL OPERATIONS

What are these tasks? A look to Figure 11–1 from the previous chapter should clarify this. The figure is divided into two major areas. One is the maintenance of the employee record file. The other is the matching of specifications for new jobs to the inventory of skills represented in the file. If the matching activity is to be valid, the employee record file must be as complete as possible. This updating function cannot be left to chance. If it were, some records would be up-to-date and others would not. Some records would be coded incorrectly, and some records would be missing in their entirety. Therefore, some systematic means of assuring that the employee record will be up-to-date must be included in the system.

A similar condition exists with respect to the matching activity. It is not enough that the data being fed into the system must be up-to-date. The program package which manipulates the data must reflect the *latest* management requirements. Management's problems do not remain the same over time. This means that the computer programs which furnish information for the decision process must lend themselves to updating. It is not uncommon for up to one-third of a company's computer programmers to be involved in changing and updating programs. As with the updating of the employee record file, this cannot be a chance activity. Therefore a systematic way to make the changes and to place the responsibility for the changes must be incorporated into the overall system.

Since the two updating activities (employee record file and program design) involve different problems, let us consider them in turn. First we will treat the maintenance of the employee record file, and then we will cover the matching operation.

MAINTAINING THE RECORD FILES

The major problems involved in updating the employee record file are:

1. To ascertain that all changes in status of employees are entered, and
2. To be sure that the information is in the precise form required for the computer operations.

The first requirement is obvious and needs no development at this time. The same is not true for the latter area, and therefore, a brief discussion is in order.

All of the data in the employee record file are kept on a coded basis. A sample of these codes was presented in Chapter 9 where a portion of the codes for educational background was detailed. The educational codes, however, only cover one area of an individual's personnel record. A complete record must cover many other aspects. To give the reader some idea of the volume of data which is needed to describe an employee, Figure 12–1 is included. Thirteen 80-column punched cards are needed to capture all of the data on the form.

The data on these cards must be exact and it must be in the specified position on the card, or the computer output will be incorrect. A simple recording error could change the entire meaning of the information in an employee's record. For example, consider Figure 12–2 where a set of codes for fields of educational study is shown. A transposition in code numbers from 213 to 312 would change the record of an

Example of Detailed Personnel Record

PERSONNEL RECORD

EMPLOYEE NAME

ADDRESS — NUMBER AND STREET | CITY | STATE OR PROVINCE | SEX — M F | MARITAL STATUS — MARRIED / SINGLE / WIDOWED / DIVORCED / SEPARATED | DATE OF BIRTH — MO. DAY YR.

IS EMPLOYEE — FULL TIME / PART TIME

CD | EMPLOYEE | IDENT. NO. 1

CITIZENSHIP — NATIVE BORN U.S. / NATUR. ALIZED U.S. / NATIVE BORN CANADIAN / NATUR. ALIZED CANADIAN / OTHER

AGES OF DEPENDENT CHILDREN (OLDEST FIRST - MAXIMUM OF 10 AGES — USE LAST 2 DIGITS OF YEAR OF BIRTH)

NUMBER OF DEPENDENTS OTHER THAN CHILDREN

DOES EMPLOYEE — OWN HOME / RENT

IS EMPLOYEE EXEMPT — EXEMPT / NON EXEMPT

IF EXEMPT, IS EMPLOYEE — EXEC. / ADMIN. / PROF. / OUTSIDE SALES

PRESENT RANK

NO. OF CITATIONS

CD | EMPLOYEE | IDENT. NO. 2

MILITARY SERVICE HISTORY AND PRESENT STATUS

BRANCH — ARMY / NAVY / AIR FORCE / MARINE CORPS / COAST GUARD / MER. MARINE / OTHER

NUMBER MONTHS SERVICE

RANK AT DISCHARGE

TYPE OF DISCHARGE

ENTRY DATE — MO. YR.

RESERVE STATUS CODE

DRAFT STATUS

TYPE OF DISCHARGE

RANK AT DISCHARGE

ENTRY DATE — MO. YR.

MONTHS SERVICE

CD | EMPLOYEE | IDENT. NO. 2

SERVICE AWARD — DATE OF LATEST — MO. YR.

CONTINUOUS SERVICE DATE — MO. DAY YR.

ANY BREAKS IN CONTINUOUS SERVICE? — YES / NO

DATE FIRST EMPLOYED — MO. DAY YR.

EMPLOYEE PHYSICAL — DATE OF LAST COMPANY EXAM — MO. YR. — WAS IT ANNUAL? YES / NO

IS EMPLOYEE COVERED BY MANAGEMENT DEVELOPMENT PROGRAM — YES / NO

MAJOR PHYSICAL DEFECTS — NAME — CODE

CD | EMPLOYEE | IDENT. NO. 3

FOREIGN LANGUAGES

LANG. — R E A D / W R I T E / S P E A K

SPECIAL SKILLS — NAME — CODE

OFFICE MACHINES OPERATED — NAME — CODE

CD | EMPLOYEE | IDENT. NO. 3

EDUCATION (LIST COLLEGES IN CHRONOLOGICAL ORDER)

HIGHEST LEVEL OF EDUCATION ACHIEVED

COLLEGE (USE MAXIMUM OF 15 CHARACTERS) — CODE

YEAR GRADUATED

HONORS

MAJOR FIELD CODE

MAJOR FIELD (USE MAXIMUM OF 10 CHARACTERS)

DEGREE

RANK IN CLASS — QUARTER 1 2 3 4

% EXPENSE EARNED

CD | EMPLOYEE | IDENT. NO. 4

DATE THIS EMPLOYEE PERSONNEL RECORD ISSUED — MO. YR.

CD | EMPLOYEE | IDENT. NO. 5

FIGURE 12-1 (cont.)

EMPLOYEE BENEFIT STATISTICS

	HOSPITALIZATION		MAJOR MEDICAL		IN-HOSPITAL MEDICAL			SURGICAL		LIFE INSURANCE FREE			DISABILITY OR EARNINGS /WKS		
	TYPE COVERAGE	COVERAGE			TYPE COVERAGE			TYPE COVERAGE		$ SCH. A.	SCH. B.		$ /WKS TABLE		
CD. EMPLOYEE	CONTRI-BUTORY	NON-CONT.-RIBUTORY	CONTRI-BUTORY	NON-CONT.-RIBUTORY	CONTRI-BUTORY	NON-CONT.-RIBUTORY		CONTRI-BUTORY	NON-CONT.-RIBUTORY				CONTRI-BUTORY	NON-CONT.-RIBUTORY	
NO. IDENT. 6		2		2		2			2		1	2		2	

PENSION INFORMATION

		TYPE OF PENSION	AMOUNT OF PENSION	BASED ON AVERAGE EARNINGS OF	AGE AT RETIRE-MENT	AGE OF SPOUSE	LENGTH OF SERVICE	NATURE OF RETIRE-MENT	AMOUNT OF LIFE INSURANCE CARRIED OVER
			$ PER MONTH	$ PER MONTH	YRS. MOS. TRS. MOS.		YRS. MOS		

TERMINATION

DATE	REASON
MO. / YR.	

CD. EMPLOYEE	COMPANY (USE MAXIMUM OF 15 CHARACTERS)		DATE STARTED MO. / YR.	NUMBER YEARS SERVICE	COMPANY (USE MAXIMUM OF 15 CHARACTERS)	NUMBER YEARS SERVICE	PRESENT SALARY GRADE	PRESENT SALARY $
NO. IDENT. 7				2		2		

CD. EMPLOYEE	TYPE OF WORK (USE MAXIMUM OF 15 CHARACTERS)		TYPE OF WORK CODE	TYPE OF WORK (USE MAXIMUM OF 15 CHARACTERS)	TYPE OF WORK CODE	AMOUNT OF LAST INCREASE $ PER MONTH	DATE OF LAST INCREASE MO. / YR.
NO. IDENT. 8							

PRESENT JOB INFORMATION

CD. EMPLOYEE	JOB TITLE (USE MAXIMUM OF 20 CHARACTERS)	JOB CODE	TYPE OF WORK (USE MAXIMUM OF 15 CHARACTERS)	TYPE OF WORK CODE	DIVISION	DIVISION CODE	LOCATION	LOCATION CODE
NO. IDENT. 9								

EMPLOYMENT HISTORY (LIST LAST 3 POSITIONS IN CHRONOLOGICAL ORDER - OMIT PRESENT POSITION)

CD. EMPLOYEE	JOB TITLE (USE MAXIMUM OF 24 CHARACTERS)	JOB CODE	TYPE OF WORK (USE MAXIMUM OF 15 CHARACTERS)	TYPE OF WORK CODE	JOB LOCATION CODE	DATE STARTED MO. / YR.	DIVISION	DIVISION CODE	DATE STARTED MO. / YR.	LOCATION	LOCATION CODE
NO. IDENT. 10											

CD. EMPLOYEE	JOB TITLE (USE MAXIMUM OF 24 CHARACTERS)	JOB CODE	TYPE OF WORK (USE MAXIMUM OF 15 CHARACTERS)		DATE STARTED MO. / YR.	DIVISION		LOCATION	
NO. IDENT. 11									

CD. EMPLOYEE	JOB TITLE (USE MAXIMUM OF 24 CHARACTERS)	JOB CODE	TYPE OF WORK (USE MAXIMUM OF 15 CHARACTERS)		DATE STARTED MO. / YR.	DIVISION		LOCATION	
NO. IDENT. 12									

PROFESSIONAL SOCIETY AND TRADE ASSOCIATION MEMBERSHIP

CD. EMPLOYEE	ORGANIZATION	CORP. OR INDIVIDUAL MEMBER	MAJOR OFFICES HELD	ORGANIZATION	CORP. OR INDIVIDUAL MEMBER	MAJOR OFFICES HELD	ORGANIZATION	CORP. OR INDIVIDUAL MEMBER	MAJOR OFFICES HELD
NO. IDENT.									

FOREIGN COUNTRY EMPLOYMENT

COUNTRY	NO. YEARS	WITH Gov't YES NO	COUNTRY CODE	COUNTRY	NO. YEARS	WITH Gov't YES NO	COUNTRY CODE	COUNTRY	NO. YEARS	WITH Gov't YES NO	COUNTRY CODE

employee's educational history from management to pharmacology. Computer programs generally have no way of knowing when codes are in error as long as the codes represent possible combinations. The programs merely match one set of numbers' against another and, based on the outcome of the match, take an action. This places a great burden of accuracy on those who prepare the input information. The lack of good procedural instructions to facilitate the accurate preparation of good input can spoil an otherwise effective system.

Returning to the central discussion, some means for correctly and uniformly updating the employee record file must be established. Phrased another way, a standard operating procedure for updating the file must be designed. The procedure must state when the file will be updated and precisely how this will be done. Figure 12–3 contains a standard operating procedure designed to accomplish these aims for the candidate matching system.

The standard operating procedure lays out the ground rules for the entire system. By scanning it, the reader will see that eight different input reports (*A* to *H*) are employed in the system. This means that the eight different forms must be designed and precise instructions for completing these forms must be developed. If this is not done, the varieties of interpretations of how to fill out the forms will destroy the computer system. To illustrate the degree of detail required, consider the instructions which outline steps for the completion of the Employee Personnel Record, Figure 12–1. An excerpt of the instructions is presented in Figure 12–4. The instructions pinpoint the number of characters allowed to describe an employee record and the precise form of the input data. To obtain consistency every detail must be specified. This is programming a human operator, and is in fact very similar to programming a computer.

Even the information in Figure 12–4 is not the end of the detail since, in order to follow the instructions, a code manual must be consulted. This manual contains all of the coding classifications used to complete the personnel forms. Samples of these codes were already presented in Chapter 9.

In total, the standard operating procedure for the candidate selection system would include five sections:

1. General Systems Procedures
2. Instructions for Completing Forms
3. Classification and Codes
4. Sample Forms
5. Glossary of Significant Terms

FIGURE 12–2

CODES FOR EDUCATIONAL STUDY AREAS

Major Fields of Study Codes

Code	Major Field	Code	Major Field
	CHEMISTRY 100		ALLIED SCIENCES 300
101	General Chemistry	301	Agronomy (soil management)
102	Analytical		
103	Bio	302	Bacteriology
104	Inorganic	303	Biology
105	Organic	304	Botany
106	Radio	305	Entomology
107	Physical	306	Forestry
108	Agricultural	307	Geology
109	Pulp and Paper	308	Medicine
110	Rubber	309	Metallurgy
111	Textile	310	Mycology (fungal life)
112	Industrial/Chemical Technology	311	Nursing (RN and BAO)
		312	Pharmacology
113	Polymer	313	Physics
114	Thermochemistry	314	Veterinary Medicine
115	Pharmocological Chemistry	315	Zoology
		316	Pomology (fruit growing)
116	Physical-Organic		
199	Miscellaneous Chemistry	317	Mechanics
	ENGINEERING 200	318	Ceramics
		319	Mineralogy
201	Aeronautical	320	Industrial Hygiene
202	Architectural	321	Physiology
203	Basic/General	322	Geophysics
204	Chemical	323	Pharmacy
205	Civil	324	Plant Physiology and Pathology
206	Electrical		
207	Industrial	325	Limnology (study of fresh waters)
208	Mechanical		
209	Mining	326	Food Technology
210	Petroleum	327	Agriculture
211	Metallurgical	328	Physical Education
212	Corrosion	329	Silicate Technology
213	Management	330	Architecture
214	Refrigeration	331	Nuclear Physics
215	Sanitation	332	General Science
216	Textile	399	Miscellaneous allied sciences
217	Agricultural		
218	Systems		
219	Electronics		
299	Miscellaneous Engineering		

FIGURE 12–3

STANDARD OPERATING PROCEDURE
FOR PERSONNEL SELECTION

1 Personnel Department will complete Employee Personnel Record (Form A) on all employees.

2 Division, Subsidiary, and Laboratory Personnel Departments will arrange for completion of the Employee Personnel Record (Form A) on all employees in their respective jurisdictions who are covered by the system.

3 Computer Operations will arrange for entry of the personnel data obtained on Form A Employee Personnel Record into the computer system.

4 To maintain the personnel salary information, Payroll Change Authorization (Form B) will be used as the source information on changes in job title and status, present salary, date and amount of last salary increase, pension information and termination information.

5 To maintain the Management Development information, Development Review (Form C) will be used as the source information. Development Review Transmittal (Form D) will be used to transmit this information to computer operations.

6 As salaried employees retire, the Personnel Department will furnish pension information, in addition to that obtained on Form B and Pension Data Transmittal (Form E).

7 Once each year the Personnel Department and the Operating Department will arrange for updating of items of information in existing personnel records not updated as provided in paragraphs 4 through 6 by completing the Annual Employee Personnel Supplement (Form F) for employees in their respective organizations.

8 This information will be put into the system as per paragraph 3.

9 An Employee Personnel Record (Form G) will be printed for each employee and distributed as follows:
    a) 2 copies: Personnel Department
    b) 1 copy: Appropriate Operating Department

10 Personnel information will be retained in the system for an indefinite period on all pensioned and terminated salaried employees.

11 All requests for periodic or special reports will be forwarded on Personnel Report Request (Form H) to the Personnel Department for clearance.

12 Systems and Procedures and Computer Operations will arrange for completion of reports provided for under paragraph 11.

For a system such as the one presented, the material would take 70 to 80 pages. The number of pages in itself means nothing. It does, however, serve to indicate the amount of work that is required to systematize the task. As stated in Chapter 2, management can delegate operations to its organization or to a system. To do the latter requires

FIGURE 12–4

INSTRUCTIONS FOR FILLING OUT THE EMPLOYEE RECORD FORM

Instructions for Completion of Employee Personnel Record

The following instructions are to be used as a guide in order to complete the Employee Personnel Record.

Strict adherence to the instructions noted is urgently requested since IBM cards will be punched directly from the Employee Personnel Record. Accuracy and legibility of the information to be recorded are of paramount importance.

The items explained below are presented in the order in which they appear on the Employee Personnel Record.

PLEASE PRINT ALL INFORMATION

Line 1	
Item	Instructions
0. Employee Identification	List will be provided with the Employee Identification and the Employee Name. Insert this 5-digit number on any line on which data on the employee appear.
1. Employee Name	Use maximum of 18 characters for the last name. Space is also provided for up to 3 initials.
2. Address	*a*) Number and Street: Use maximum of 20 characters, including spaces, hyphens, etc. *b*) City: Use maximum of 15 characters. Readable abbreviations permitted. *c*) State or Province: Use abbreviation found in Manual page 8.
3. Sex	Circle appropriate digit (1 or 2)
4. Marital Status	Circle appropriate digit (1 through 5)
5. Date of Birth	Month-day-year. Use preceding zeros, e.g. (06/09/25).

complete spelling out of all aspects of the system. As much of the operation must be made routine as possible; that is, as much of the judgment factor as possible should be included in the system.

MAINTAINING THE COMPUTER PROGRAMS

At this point, let us shift from the generation of input data for the maintenance of the personnel file to the problem of maintaining the computer programs for the system. The discussion of the computer programs involved in this system should be considered as indicative of the problems which arise with all computer programming packages. If the nature of the problems management faced in the selection of individuals for jobs remained fixed, the discussion of this system would be at an end. The whole tenor of this book, however, points to the fact that systems normally do not remain fixed. Since the data coming from the system can only become information if it relates to management's problems, a means of changing the output data to conform to management's problems must be built into the system. In practice, this means that the system must be sufficiently documented to enable a programmer or systems designer to make the changes.

Why is the documentation necessary? Let us start by showing what will happen without the proper documentation. Without documentation a programmer has two sources of information relating to the computer operation. They are (1) the actual computer program, and (2) his, or other programmers' knowledge about the program. The actual computer programs themselves will not serve as a basis for making changes. The complexity, length, and individual programmer touches involved in a computer program make it virtually useless as a referral document. After a few months, programmers may not even be able to follow their own programs without considerable effort. It may take several weeks to re-enlighten themselves. For another programmer to understand the operations may take several months. In some cases it is easier for a new programmer to start over and write a new program rather than try to understand and change the old one.

In the same fashion, the knowledge which a programmer has about the program will not do. Even if he could quickly re-educate himself, the problem of his not being available to do the work arises. He may have left the company, been transferred to another activity, or simply be on vacation when the need for the change arises. Therefore, an auxiliary means of documentation must be available. What form this documentation should take is arguable. In most cases logical flow charts are maintained.[1] These charts are annotated and supplemented

---

[1] Examples of these charts and the annotating are presented as Figure 11-2 and Figure 11-3 in Chapter 11.

with written information so that as complete a description of the programming activity as possible can be maintained. Armed with this information a programmer can make changes swiftly and economically.

While the answer to this problem seems simple, in practice, it is not. Most programmers are motivated by the challenge of getting their programs operating. The task of drawing and annotating flow charts is repugnant. Therefore, without close supervision the documentation often is not completed. Even worse, it may not be done at all. To assure that it is available, and accurate, the documentation should be done as the program evolves. If it is not, the program will be in use while no documentation exists. A case in point from a large computer center should illustrate this. After over one man-year of programming an inventory and standard cost program was put into operation. No documentation existed. When management realized this, the programmers were directed to document their work. Unfortunately, changes had to be made to the programs before the documentation was completed. The changes that were made affected other parts of the program and, instead of getting an up-to-date program, two months were spent clearing up the problems created by the changes. This is not an isolated, or bizarre, example. Without good documentation, dynamic systems are impossible. It is plain foolishness not to pay for reasonable documentation.

To this point in the chapter the tremendous amount of detail that is involved in systematizing an area has been emphasized. This was not done to frighten or confuse, but rather to give an accurate picture of what is involved. With this background it should be clear why systems to develop operating information are more susceptible to systems design than those which aim at the development of management information. Operating information systems cover relatively routine activities which are stable relative to management's information needs. Moreover, these involve areas where much of the work to systematize the activity is already known. Consequently, the cost of building an operating system and the time involved is smaller than for the more ill-defined management reporting area. Another important aspect is involved. The cost of building a complicated operating information system must be compared to the savings resulting from the system. Processing costs can be measured. Using a computer to accomplish what is being done in another fashion can be measured costwise. It is the same as evaluating a new lathe to replace an old one. With respect to management information systems, this is not so.

DAY-TO-DAY SCHEDULING AND CONTROL

Up to now our discussion of the day-to-day aspects of systems operations has dealt with the problems involved with input preparation and systems changes. This leads us to the point where we can consider the processing activities themselves. When the candidate matching system program is put into production it will join a long list of other operating systems which must be processed through the computing equipment. Since the individual systems have varying priorities, operating times, and schedule requirements, some control must be placed over the operation of the computing facilities.

The operation of a computer center is analogous to the operation of a manufacturing facility. All of the elements present in the production control activity play a role. Manufacturing production control is traditionally divided into five segments. They are: authorization, scheduling, routing, dispatching, and follow-up. The same elements are present in the operation of a computer facility. Let us consider them in sequence.

Before a system can be put on a production basis, some form of authorization must be presented to the computer operations group. This authorization is the signal for computer operations to process the data. The authorization is divided into several sections. One, the programming activity must release the computer programs. This implies that the programs are ready to be operated without the aid of the programmer. To do this, all of the instructions necessary to run the program must be furnished to the operating group. This includes a specification of the equipment to be used, the machine settings required, the length of time the input and output data is to be kept, the type of forms to be used, the frequency the program will be run, when and in what form the input will be available, and, if applicable, the day of the month the program will be run.

With the information in hand, the computer operations group can proceed to design processing schedules. These schedules are usually developed first on a monthly basis, then on a weekly basis, and, finally, down to a daily basis. Some items are even scheduled on an hourly basis.

To build a production schedule, the sequence or routing for a job through the various types of equipment must be known. In most instances there is only one path the job can take. This routing is specified by programming when the task is turned over to production. In developing a schedule, production must determine the processing load for each type of processing equipment on a daily basis. To do this the estimates of required machine time for the individual jobs are accumulated and compared with machine hours available. Because of the nature of data processing, schedule peaks are common. Month's end, and year end accounting needs may cause severe time pressures. It is not unusual for the processing load to exceed the capacity. If this happens, processing priorities must be established. A first-in-first-out priority system, or some other simple procedure will not do. Payroll applications cannot be held up by processing some trivial tasks which were ready for processing at an earlier time. The determination of processing priorities is not a production function. Processing priorities should be established by management in the same fashion as the setting of priorities for new systems projects.

Since the production schedule is generally broken down to a daily basis, the task of prescribing when during the day each phase of the job should be done arises. This is the task of dispatching. Someone must continually audit the status of the jobs and keep the equipment occupied. This is not a simple task. To state when the input for a job should be ready does not mean it will be ready. Therefore, operations must be flexible. The essence of dispatching is to put pieces of jobs on the equipment in such a fashion that the day's production is completed.

If all of the variables in the process were under the control of the operating group the task would be simple. However, many aspects are not under this direct control. The input data, for example, may be bad. Everything may be set up and ready for processing and the processing begun. Suddenly, machine activities may stop and an error printout stating that the input is bad may come from the computer. Another job must be ready to be run while the corrections to the input are made. Without these jobs on standby, idle machine time will result.

The final step in the production control is the follow-up activity. This involves the generation of information for the management of the operating facilities so that they can detect and correct inefficiencies. In effect, we are back at the beginning of the book, asking how can we design an information system for computer operations.

Oddly, or perhaps not so oddly, many data processing managers who are ready to show how systems activities can help the overall organization, believe that it cannot be applied to their area. Being close to the complexities of their job, they believe data processing too complicated for good scheduling. In fact, scheduling a data processing activity is generally much less complex than scheduling a large production facility.

To begin with, rough measures of the efficiency of the processing operations are readily available. The most important measure is the relation of functional time, the time the equipment is actually operating, to the chronological time which has elapsed for the job. If operations are inefficient, the chronological times will be much greater than the functional time. The difference is the time spent in getting the input ready, setting up the machine, or in detecting equipment malfunctions. Let us illustrate how this occurs by viewing the input area a bit closer, since this is the most common area of lost time.

To minimize lost machine time, all of the inputs required for a job must be where they are needed at the proper time. If this is so, the old program tapes can be quickly taken off the machine and the new tapes mounted. In some instances, the tapes for the new job can even be mounted while the old job is being run. If the tapes are not available, the operator must leave the machine area and search the files for them. This is costly and results in poor machine efficiency. Moreover, laxness in this activity is generally indicative of a similar state in other operating areas.

In a well-run operation the tapes needed for the daily schedule are taken from the files and placed in the order of their priority at the computer. A storage area for the processed data is also nearby. The operator takes the jobs in order. If something occurs which prevents the processing of a job, the next job can be put on the machine while the trouble is remedied.

The aim in discussing a planning and control system for production processing is not to outline what is good and what is bad. The goal is to reiterate the fact that data processing is a production activity and can and should be treated as such. Once the decision of how or when to process the data is made the production aspect is the same as the fabrication of a physical product in a manufacturing plant. In fact, banks, insurance companies, and stock brokerage firms can be likened to paper work factories. What they process is data. On the scale in which they operate, efficiencies in processing are as important as efficiencies in mass production.

This concludes the discussion of the day by day operating considerations of management systems. From this chapter it should be apparent that a tremendous amount of detail work is involved in operating a system. Errors or inefficiencies in this level of specifics can only lead to chaos. Well-conceived and well-designed systems sometimes fail miserably because of ineffective operations.

SUMMARY OF MANPOWER PLANNING:
CANDIDATE MATCHING PROJECT

To demonstrate the type of analysis appropriate to each phase of the cycle of systems development, we have used as a case study the project for Manpower Planning and Control. This project was gradually narrowed in scope to candidate matching as we moved through the phases described in each chapter.

The following is a detailed index of the materials presented on this case study in the various chapters. This index provides a summary view of a systems development:

This index highlights the major considerations that are typical to the development of a computer-based information system. To some readers this index will appear to have a surprising amount of detail. Other readers will recognize that we have shown but a skeleton of the specifics that must be encompassed for a thorough job of systems development.

Although we have summarized the case example here, there remain two more phases of systems development that require attention. In the next chapter we analyze the problems of Output Format and Display. We then complete the coverage of the phases of systems development in Chapter 14, with an analysis of Feedback and Evaluation of System's Effectiveness.

Chapter 13

OUTPUT FORMAT
AND DISPLAY

With the present ability of organizations to produce all sorts of documents in high quantities, there is great need for attention to the design of format of such output. The first question, of course, is: What do we need to know? The next question is: What form of this needed information would be most advantageous? To answer the second question we need to know at least what format design alternatives can be available.

FORMAT DESIGN IS AN ART

Format design is still an art. It is appropriate that we consider who is practicing this art today. Interestingly enough, it appears that it is the advertising copy writers who have been giving the most specific attention to this problem. They concentrate on catching the eye of the potential customer and then present a carefully formated message. Unless you have gone through the experience, it is hard to realize how much time and concentration goes into even minute advertising questions concerning message content and format layout. Packing a message into a medium is understood by the advertising business.

The art of journalism and the other lively arts all stress interpretation and presentation. Simple, complex, concrete, and abstract messages are given form for the observer. These fields have developed principles and styles for presentation. This has taken a long time and we can expect that the art of information presentation for management will be slow in evolving.

As demonstrated in the SMART assignment, code 8–0, Executive Information Display System, the primary problem is to be able to identify what managers need to know to do their jobs. This is what we have described as the message content problem. The earlier chapters covering priorities, information requirements, and systems design focused on this problem. Here we are considering, once message content is describable in general terms, how to present the information to the eye or ear of the manager.

THE MAN-MACHINE-DISPLAY SYSTEM

Figure 13–1 shows the manager on the job seeking to recognize his problems and searching for additional information with which to improve his decisions and actions. We will consider the less glamorous work involved in preparing and using plain paper reports later, but for now, let us look at the possibilities for using visual displays monitored by large capacity computers. In the figure, a display console is

FIGURE 13–1

MAN-MACHINE-DISPLAY SYSTEM

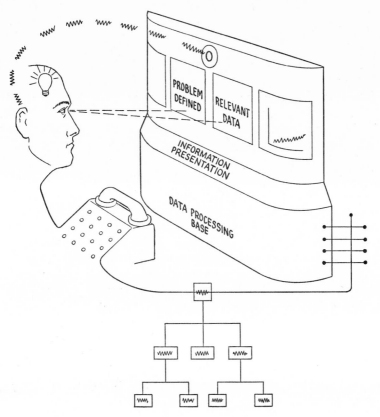

mounted on a computer. The computer, in turn, is tied to the event generating environment through a switching station and a communications network. This environment is symbolized by the organization chart shown on the diagram. The pushbuttons on the telephone represent the manager's ability to communicate with people or with the data stored in the system. For the moment, assume that there are no state of the arts limitations to this setup and concentrate on what should be shown on the display. Note that the display screen has been split into two parts—one reserved for describing a situation (problem definition) to the manager, and the other side for aiding the manager as he asks, "What can be done about this situation?"

DEFINING WHAT IS IMPORTANT

We must also assume that, typically, there is already in the manager's mind some image of a situation and some relevant data. Efficient display should correct any wrong impressions the manager has and add any available new information. The results are produced when he says, "I did not know that, and it is important!" It may be that someone else thinks a certain situation is critical but the manager does not. The burden then is for that someone to convince the manager by putting impressive value dimensions into the situation portrayed on the screen. This tells us that we have to format both the situation characteristics and their relative significance.

Situation characteristics, as noted earlier, come from the surveillance activity of a company and then are converted into problem definitions as formal (and, if possible, written) statements are prepared. Many situations can exist for which it is not yet possible to be explicit regarding either situation characteristics or their relative significance. A well-organized systems development effort will, however, keep the pressure on for describing the particular classes of problem elements and their relative weights wherever possible. The borderline between nonexplicit management problems and explicit management problems is a critical one. This line represents the boundary which must be moved if a management is to claim that it is making progress.

Progress can be measured only if there is available good evidence of where we are and good statements of where we want to go. An organization that seeks to improve its overall situation will classify its problems by degrees of difficulty, from simple and concrete to complex and abstract. A general consciousness of these differences among situations facing a management is a prerequisite to making decisions regarding the importance and the practicality of attacking particular problems. It is only when the classification of degrees of difficulty can be related to the information identifier classification that managers can get a full picture of a situation.

In Chapter 8, on Information Requirements Design, a classification was presented with six key information content classes. These classes referred to the context in which managers can ask for information. Let us use this classification here to represent the information content which might be stored in an organization system at a point in time and from which selected information can be formated and presented to a manager. Chapter 8 also showed a set of the elements that give structure to a particular piece of information. These were broken into identifier elements covering names of classes, units of measure, time dimensions, and the information forms resulting from processing. The element representing the quantity or quality of a piece of information was described as that part of a piece of information which is attached to give weights to the rest of the assembly of elements.

It was proposed that this skeletonized view of the assembly of information through a management information system was useful in both the design of a system and, once a system was in operation, when a manager was seeking to retrieve information from the system.

In Chapter 8 we emphasized that realism demanded that we consider both the *importance* of various kinds of management information and the *practicality* of having such information available through our systems. We now know that this availability is affected by many different factors, including:

1. Our ability to recognize important events in our environment;
2. Our ability to record these selected events with best choices of names of classes, units of measure, time dimensions, and form;
3. Our ability to design a sequence of processing that assembles the raw data initially recorded into new classes, units, and forms which are more meaningful for managers' purposes.

ELEMENTS OF AN INFORMATION DISPLAY SYSTEM

Figure 13–2 represents the screen on our information display console. The words shown surrounding the screen are reminders to the manager of the elements which must be identified in the information processing procedure. He knows that it is from these elements that he must phrase his questions, and it is from these same elements that answers can be provided to him.

The Manager's Information Menu.   Because these words around the screen are but the generalized reminder of information systems content, it is necessary that the specifics of such content be made available to both the askers and the answerers of questions. The book shown in front of the screen on Figure 13–2 contains a selection of descriptions of the organization classification systems and an appropriate level of documentation of information classes, units, and forms available in certain information systems. This book is labeled the Manager's Information Menu. The "menu" concept is appropriate for it is a reminder that we must be selective within the range of what is available. The variety of our choices is limited by what we are able to prepare with the ingredients available. "Special orders" will take longer and be more expensive. With the information menu on hand, both the asker and the answerer have a positive basis for making choices. The information menu operating in combination with the information dis-

FIGURE 13–2

MOCK-UP FOR

INFORMATION DISPLAY ANALYSIS

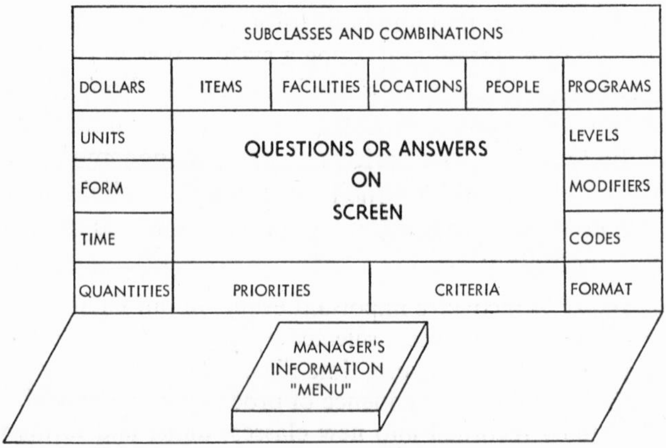

SUBCLASSES AND COMBINATIONS					
DOLLARS	ITEMS	FACILITIES	LOCATIONS	PEOPLE	PROGRAMS
UNITS	QUESTIONS OR ANSWERS ON SCREEN				LEVELS
FORM					MODIFIERS
TIME					CODES
QUANTITIES	PRIORITIES		CRITERIA		FORMAT

MANAGER'S
INFORMATION
"MENU"

play can also provide a means for identifying what is not available in our systems. It, therefore, can give guidance as to where additional management studies might be made.

Priority and Criteria Reminders. The words Priorities and Criteria, shown under the screen, remind us of the need to keep a consciousness of the relative importance of our problems and to seek clear criteria for spelling out the measures upon which we can make our decisions. The place of priorities was analyzed earlier. In the following chapter we review the priority problem and give an analysis of the manner in which criteria relate to organization structure and information structure. Here let us note only that a view of priorities and criteria is necessary in order to decide which questions should be asked at the console and to decide how far into detail it is worthwhile to go.

The words at the top and left of the screen were defined in Chapter 8. Now let us look at the four words at the right of the screen. These four words, Levels, Modifiers, Codes, and Formats, provide for many of the subtleties and complications that must be handled in assembling information.

Levels. This term refers to the degree of grossness or detail at which information must be assembled. This is always a difficult problem for managers and systems designers. Whenever possible managers would like to be able to make good decisions without having to go into a large amount of detail. If this is to be possible, it is only because systems have been designed which handle the detail and in which managers can have confidence. Levels, in particular, consider the detail in the key classes of dollars, items, facilities, locations, people, and programs. By knowing what levels of detail are available, the manager can "find his place" relative to his responsibility at a given organization level. He can then decide on whether he can work with summarized data or must get into the details. In a situation where an information display console is available, the manager can work with gross information but call for lower and more detailed information, on occasion, to double-check his reasoning.

Modifiers. Any element in a piece of information provides some degree of modification. This classification refers, then, to modifications which are not taken into account under the other classes. There is a wide array of such modifiers. Examples of such terms are:

Estimated	Deferred	Total	Confirmed
Actual	Discounted	Unit	Average

These terms give more specific dimensions to information requirements and information provisions. A separate and selective list of these modifiers can be made and included in the documentation provided in the information menu arrangement.

Codes. This term was discussed in Chapter 5. There it was pointed out that codes are shorthand expressions for classes. They therefore reduce the burden of detail which can exist in a system. The price paid for this advantage is that code conversions must be available and understood by systems users and systems designers. Separate arrangements must be provided to make relatively easy any conversions from classes to codes or codes to classes.

Format. This term will be covered in more detail later in this chapter. For now, let us note only that format refers to the effectiveness of information display, that is, for a given message, what can be done to facilitate transfer of this message to those who have a "need to know"?

These four words to the right of the screen remind the manager to consider additional refinements in his requests for information. Thus, these terms can guide the manager's inquiries out to the limits of his ability to conceive questions. This, in turn, means that, at some point, the limits of answers available in the system will be identified and decisions can be made by managers and systems designers as to whether or not it pays to go looking for additional information. The use of an information display facility, such as portrayed here, can gradually bring out refinements in the array of questions that are important to managers. In this sense, the setup can be used as a "test bed" for the further design and test of information systems proposals. In other words, when the display is not being used for presentations to managers it can be used for experimental purposes. A systems development department, for example, can use a mock-up of such a display facility long before it is ready to recommend installation of a full computer-based video or chart-generating display facility. This mock-up has a back-projected screen and can be used with standard slide-making processes to test the variety of content and format appropriate to selected management information systems. The results would gradually be refined and documented in the information menu book and its subreferences. This "bread-boarding" of systems content can be extremely useful, whether or not an automatic display is ultimately justified. Even without the automatic display, all of the above elements must be built into the system.

HARD COPY DISPLAY

Although the ideas of display of information on a screen are receiving much attention, there still remains the competitive advantage of low-cost display held by a plain piece of paper. This will be true even when the state of the arts of assembling console operated displays is perfected. Even with such displays it would be important to have a button to push that would cause a hard copy to be made of what is being displayed on the screen. This statement is made here to suggest that the development of any display of information on a screen or on paper goes back to the same basic elements with which we have been working.

The above-described computer-based information display supported by high-speed communications can be, of course, an expensive proposition. It was used here to pinpoint the critical factors involved in the formating and display of information. The reasoning should hold even when less sophisticated means are used to display information. Displays on plain paper are no different in the sense of their preparation and their ultimate usefulness. A sheet of paper has the same rectangular surface as a fancy display screen. On this surface must be shown the information that aids managers as they bring problems into focus and as they evaluate data that may support their reasoning in solving such problems.

The reasoning that we are using here applies to any form of information display. Most display of information today is provided by paper medium. The cost of preparation of paper copy in the aggregate is estimated at $150 billion dollars per year. This figure, however, does not include the cost of having to read this output. Here we are concentrating on how effective this paper production is when we consider that somebody has to put it to use.

THE HUMAN AS A RECEIVER OF INFORMATION

Let us take a little time and consider just how the human being is equipped to receive information. We can then go back and discuss the best means for presenting such information. The human has five ways in which to receive information. These are the five basic senses: sight, hearing, touch, taste, and smell.

Unless we are willing to consider such ideas as extrasensory perception, the above list represents the full range through which man can receive new information. The word new is used here to recognize that a living being has a stock of information received from the past. This stock goes back as far as the inherited traits recorded in his genes. His experience and training have conditioned him over a period of time. The receipt of new information, therefore, forces him to consider what he already knows and how he tends to think. This, of course, makes our problem of information presentation a complicated one indeed.

As with all complicated problems, our choice is to ignore them or to do something about them. If we choose to do something, our only choice is to start a process of elimination and simplification. We eliminate parts of the problem and simplify to a point where we feel competent to handle the remainder with the present state of principles and techniques. To simplify the problem of information presentation, let us concentrate on:

1. Information received through sight;
2. Information that is expressible in words, pictures, or numbers;
3. Information, therefore, that is storable outside of the human mind;
4. Information that can be placed on a flat display surface.

AN INFORMATION FORMAT EXAMPLE

Humans have limits to what they can mentally absorb. Their *span of attention* is limited. The presentation of information should recognize these limitations and, where possible, provide visual arrangements to sustain and extend a manager's span of attention. In this sense, display acts as a memory substitute as well as a place where factors can be seen, sorted, and comparisons made—outside of the human mind. The *hard copy* should reinforce the mental images and strengthen the manager's span of attention. Figure 13–3 represents a situation in the SMART Corporation. The information presented summarizes the status of manpower on a year-to-date basis. The report builds pieces of information from the elements of classes, units, form, and time. It weighs these pieces of information by attaching the quantities produced in the data processing system.

What does this report really tell us, and how well does it do the job? If we were to place this report on the display mock-up shown in Figure 13–2 what sort of analysis could we do?

FIGURE 13–3

INFORMATION FORMAT EXAMPLE

Manpower Status Report

Employee Classification	Jan. 10 Last December		Jan. 10 This December		Percent of Change	
	Number	Per $1,000	Number	Per $1,000	Number	Dollars
Administrative......	100	2,360	110	2,620	+10	+11
Non-exempt Office..	400	3,090	450	3,450	+12.5	+12
Factory............	1,200	7,050	1,240	8,910	+3.3	+26
Total.........	1,700	12,500	1,800	14,980	+5.8	+21

First, we recognize that this is a report in the *people* classification. The units of expression are numbers of people employed in the sub-classes of administration, non-exempt office and factory. We are also interested in the units of dollars paid to these people. The form is in simple counts, or summaries, and we also express the relative changes in numbers and dollars in the form of percentages. Time is identified as the present January 10th, and January 10th one year ago. We are interested in comparing the changes that have taken place during this time period.

The data presented inform us that the wages and salaries, on an overall basis, have increased by 21 percent during the last year. This is a radical change and can imperil our already dangerous profit position. This critical piece of information is shown in the lower right corner of our display. It is the key summary figure of the report. It should be highlighted and it is by its placement, or format, on the report. It is also emphasized by being encircled to catch the eye. All other data lead to this figure and provide the detailed backup. A quick look at the specifics of the report shows that the major rise has taken place in the classification of factory employees. As compared to a rise of some 12 percent in the white-collar salary bill, the dollars spent for factory labor were twice as high, or a 26 percent increase over last year.

The next step would be to ask *why*. The data show that employees increased in the factory by only 3.3 percent, so that it is apparent that either wages increased well beyond this or large amounts of overtime were paid. Management can now ask for additional information to find out just what accounted for this increase. If those who provide the data can anticipate the questions, they should try to be ready with these answers and should present this information in a format that pinpoints the situation and the possible actions which may be appropriate. Attention by analysts at the point where information is formated and displayed can be most effective.

THE ELEMENTS OF FORMAT DESIGN

The dictionary defines format as the parts of a thing that give it its distinctive appearance or shape. It also cites format as distinguished from content. Thus, we can think in terms of the arrangement or shape in which information is presented as a separate consideration.

In Chapter 8 we chose *form* as one of the identifier elements in a "piece of information." In that case we were referring to the results obtained by our choice of *formula,* or statistical measurement technique, by which the data are processed. The following list gives examples of such form-producing techniques.

Simple Counts
Totals, Sums
Ratios, Percentages, Proportions, Fractions
Distributions
Central Values, Average, Median, Mode
Dispersion of Values, Range, Variance, Deviation
Minimum or Maximum Calculations
Correlation Analysis

These examples of form are shown here in order to distinguish the idea of *format* from that of *form*. Whereas form is determined when the data processing method is chosen (e.g., using an average), format depends on the placing of the resultant information on a flat surface. A flat surface has only so many possibilities for the presentation of information:

1. The X and Y placement; where do we put particular pieces of data on the screen or page: at the top, at the bottom, or to the left or right?
2. The sequence which we desire the observer to follow as he reads the data.
3. The amount of space on the surface assigned to particular data; i.e., what are the fields of data and their locations, size, and shape on the surface?
4. The style and size of individual numbers, letters, and lines used.

Note that we have used the word form to refer to an effect on content of messages, whereas format determines the visual appearance of the message.

Books on the preparation of visual aids and on the design of business forms give us some guidance in the formating of information on a surface. Forms design emphasizes the inputs of data into systems, whereas visual aids focus on the output of systems and the input to the human being. With the growing use of high-speed computers both the beginning and the end of the systems cycle are requiring more precision in the actions and reactions of men and systems. In the next chapter we return to this problem of the interplay between action and reaction when we study systems criteria.

The feedback of selected information can be viewed as a quality control process. As in a physical production environment, quality control of data and information requires that we decide what characteristics of quality we want in our components and end products. Value engineering provides techniques in this type of analysis in physical production. These techniques provide for careful selection of maximum (sufficient) quality, as well as minimum (safe) quality.

Inspection, quality control, and reliability analysis blend together in modern manufacturing. Knowing what is going on, controlling the operations, and building confidence in physical outputs is insurance for any type of physical production. A similar form of reasoning is now possible as data and information are formated and displayed for consumption by managers.

A concentration at the point where information is displayed is a particularly important event. This is the point at which the systems outputs are put to the test: Do they satisfy the need to know existing at that moment? Do they produce results that justify the expenses of the design and the human and machine costs of processing the data? In the next chapter we concentrate on these questions under the headings of Feedback and Evaluation of Systems Effectiveness.

The classifications of criteria can provide a powerful context for the feedback and evaluation that is necessary in management information systems. When the criteria classes and their hierarchy relationships are investigated in combination with the classes for describing message contents (see Figure 13–2) we have a comprehensive model for exploration, design, and test.

As noted in this chapter on information display, the feedback of selected information can be treated as a quality control process. The spelling out of criteria for information provides the quality control specifications and, thereby, the basis for information systems design choices.

In Chapter 14 we consider one of the most difficult and most important areas of management systems; that is, the evaluation of the effectiveness of systems as they are tested for the services they should perform for a management. The reading of the next chapter requires a change of pace, for we are moving from the specifics of computer programs and procedures for operating a system back to the necessarily more difficult analysis of problem definitions. This reflects to the typical situation in systems development where we must cycle back through previous phases as we attempt to evaluate how well we have done so far and ask what further improvements should be considered.

Chapter 14

FEEDBACK AND
EVALUATION OF
SYSTEMS EFFECTIVENESS

In Chapter 6 in Figure 6–1 there was described the expansion of documentation throughout the life cycle of a management information system. At the bottom of this figure, the topic of the present chapter was shown with arrows pointing back up through the preceding phases of systems development. This represented the idea that feedback and evaluation take place in and between each phase in the development of a system. They also continue to occur during the actual operation of a system.

Much of what we do and what we learn results from a process of trial and error. We try something and we see what happens. This is *feedback* in the sense of action and reaction. The process of feedback, therefore, involves the whole sequence from the point where an act takes place until we have evaluated the reactions resulting from such actions. The actions and reactions can be simple or complex. Their impact can be insignificant or very important. Feedback as a concept, therefore, can be considered as a synonym for the planning and control cycle in management. The setting of priorities, as discussed in the SMART game and in Chapter 7, emphasized the planning phase. Now we are looking at the control end of the cycle, asking: How well did we do relative to the plan?

FEEDBACK IS DEPENDENT ON THE AVAILABILITY
OF CRITERIA FOR DECISIONS

In specific cases it is important to spell out just what actions will be taken and what the *desired* reactions, or results, will be. This takes us back to the definition of a system; that is, any system has mechanisms or procedures (actions to be taken) to accomplish some purpose. Thus, we can view feedback as the concept that directly relates a system's procedural steps to the end purpose or output stage of the system.

The primary reason why we use feedback is so that we can make comparisons. These comparisons can take place at every level and in every specialty of an organization. The essence of a decision is comparison, and comparison is possible only when alternate choices exist. Choices, in turn, require that some degree of explicitness be available in the criteria or measures upon which decisions will be based. The success of any management information system depends to a large degree on the identification and analysis of the criteria that put explicitness into the feedback process.

Figure 14–1 shows the basic part that criteria play in the feedback process. In the first instance (at *A*) the existing criteria upon which a manager makes his decisions are put to use as he decides, "What should be accomplished?" (at *B*). These decisions are written down as goals and standards (at *C*) and communicated to all concerned parties in the environment of the organization (at *D*).

As the environment changes and events occur the data recording process operates and accomplishment reports are produced (at *E*). These reports are compared to the initial goals and standards as symbolized by the question, "How well did we do?" (at *F*). This leads to a refinement of the manager's decision and associated changes in the criteria and measurement analysis (at *G*).

This involves the manager's choices of working with existing criteria or improving his decision basis (at *H*) by a more thorough analysis of his criteria and measurements.

The arrow at *I* symbolizes the application of the refined criteria into the manager's next cycle of decisions. These criteria are, thus, available as he asks, "What should we accomplish next?" (at *J*). The manager's actual decisions are expressed as adjusted goals and standards (at *K*) and again communicated to the organization (at *L*). The cycle continues as new accomplishment reports are fed back through the system.

This generalized pattern is shown here to demonstrate that improvement in the feedback process depends on an ability to refine criteria as much as it depends on getting the information feedback. In other words, feedback must be fed back to the criteria in the mind of the manager. His decision can be no better than his available criteria. It is for this reason that we concentrate here on management criteria and their use in the evaluation of systems effectiveness.

FIGURE 14–1

MANAGEMENT FEEDBACK ON A TIME SCALE

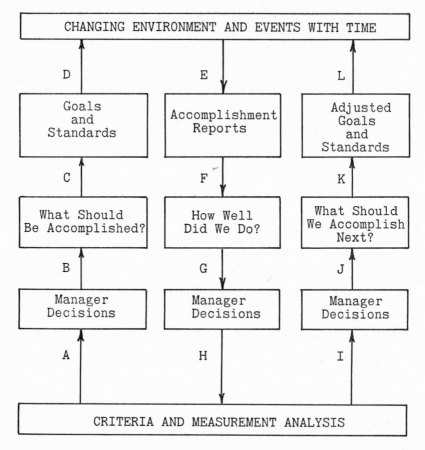

Time ⟶

Here are a few definitions of a criterion as applied to a business situation:

1. A standard of judgment,
2. A standard of measurement,
3. A basis for choosing,
4. A bench mark for guidance.

Criteria represent *selected* bench marks to be used for comparisons. These can vary from terms that require weighting by experienced intuition to terms that are based upon explicit quantitative methods and tests. Criteria can be expressed in generalities or in extreme specifics. The more explicit criteria are those which can be expressed on a numerical scale. For this reason, we are seeing increasing emphasis on quantitative methods. We should not forget, however, that numerical scales can be applied only after a process of identification and classification has been established. As Irwin Bross said, "Numerical measurements involve a very strong ordering of the classes." [1] Thus, any feedback and evaluation phase in the development of information systems should look at the range of both the English words that express classes and the numerical scales which give more explicit structure to the decision situation.

THE IMPORTANCE OF RELATIONS AMONG CRITERIA

Another significant aspect which should be studied is that of the structural relations (hierarchies) among criteria. The dictionary defines a hierarchy as "a series of objects or items divided or classified in ranks or orders." The manner in which criteria are divided or classified in hierarchies can be critical to the level of success in any decision making situation. In effect, a study of criteria in hierarchies can provide a superstructure context in which both organization structures and information structures can be studied and evaluated.

More and more people in both the academic and the business world are seeking to provide better principles and better techniques with which to handle the complexities of criteria choice and utilization. A particularly interesting development is that concerning the treatment of criteria from a hierarchy or structure point of view. It appears that there are enormous areas of opportunity in seeking to improve the criteria upon which business decisions can be made. Professor William Cooper of the Carnegie Institute of Technology, in his presentation before the Sixth International Meeting of the Institute of Management Sciences in Paris, made the following comment:

I would like to note two outstanding areas: (1) uncertainty, and (2) the introduction of hierarchical elements into the class of delegation models. Both are important but it is in the latter area where Professor Charnes and I think the most immediately promising work can be done, especially since there is but little in the way of precedent knowledge in economics, accounting, or related disciplines . . . where one might have supposed that some attention to hierarchical or 'hierarchoid' models might have been examined. In this connection I might also note, for instance, that Dr. Hitch of RAND has himself approached the issues of suboptimization in hierarchical contexts—in his article in the *Review of Economics Studies*—

[1] Irwin D. J. Bross, *Design for Decision* (New York: The Macmillan Company, 1953), p. 199.

and has suggested that such hierarchical arrangements may cast a light on the issues that are often thought to be involved in 'suboptimization.'[2]

In our daily lives we may choose a few simple criteria for our personal decisions, and this may be quite satisfactory. In the modern environment of business decisions, however, it would be quite unusual if such simple criteria were to prove satisfactory. In a business situation, an organization may find itself at a great disadvantage, especially if its competitors are working on their problems at a level of more precise and accurate criteria. The framework, then, for the setting of business criteria is often determined by the pressures of competition and the willingness and ability of a particular management to work with more explicit criteria. More explicit criteria means, of course, that more relationships must appear in the hierarchies.

A VERY ROUGH FRAMEWORK FOR THE STUDY OF MANAGEMENT CRITERIA

Now let us look at one possible set of hierarchies in which management criteria might be studied as guides for systems development and evaluation. This set includes six alternative ways to think about the criteria that can be appropriate in a management situation. We discuss each viewpoint separately and then (in Figure 14–8) bring them together to show interrelations.

The above reference to a "rough framework" should be explained. It is not that we want to discuss criteria in the broad framework shown here. Rather, we are forced to stay this general because very little is known, as yet, regarding formal concepts and techniques for choosing and using management criteria. The following discussion, therefore, is limited to identifying what we believe are worthwhile starting points for the study of management criteria.

1. Concreteness Hierarchy.   Criteria can be ranked by level of abstraction or concreteness. In Figure 14–2 there are shown some examples of this form of hierarchy. The scale from Truth down to Horsepower represents the range of problems with which a management must deal—and for which decisions must be made. The criteria shown in the circle are representative criteria in areas where management systems are now being designed. The chart also symbolizes the problem of getting concrete weights for abstract problems.

Even a simple list of the criteria used for a given management problem can be very helpful—for it shows the vocabulary of worthwhileness and gives at least strong hints as to the resources that might

---

[2] *Proceedings of the Sixth International Meeting of the Institute of Management Sciences* (New York: Pergamon Press, 1960), p. 91.

be justified in the study of such a problem. Also, by looking at the criteria list it is possible to sense where the analysis can be concrete and where qualifications may have to be made because of the relatively abstract level of criteria involved. This can influence the priorities to be given in the systems study.

FIGURE 14–2

HIERARCHY ON A CONCRETE TO ABSTRACT SCALE OF CRITERIA

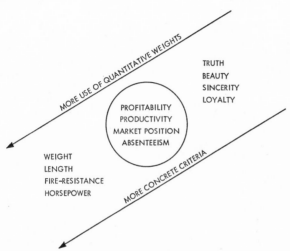

2. Precision Hierarchy (See Figure 14–3). In a practical application a criterion usually has two parts—an English name to give its type or class and a weight to place it on some sort of a scale. Figure 14–3 gives an example of a criterion name and a criterion weight. This example of Inventory Order Point[3] was chosen at a fairly concrete level of the previous hierarchy. This criterion name can be identified at the general level (e.g., Inventory Order Point) or it can (and must for applications) be narrowed by appropriate modifiers as per the list of descriptors shown in the figure. This hierarchy represents the idea of precision in the selection and use of criteria. Explicit information systems require precise criteria. The inverse is also true; that is, to use precise criteria we must have explicit information carried by our systems.

It is possible to think of the number of explicit descriptors that it takes to state the criterion at a given level of concreteness. In the example shown it takes eight separate descriptors to fully define the criterion so that it is usable in a practical situation. The precision with

---

[3] This represents the point to which the quantity of an item in our inventory may fall before we place an order for replenishment stock.

FIGURE 14–3

HIERARCHY BY PRECISION IN THE NAME OF A CRITERION

Criterion Name	*Criterion Weight*
General—Inventory Order Point for:	
Precision	
Detail—Steel	
Sheet	
Coil	
Type C	
⅛″ × 30″	
In stock	3000#s
	Order at this point

which criteria can or should be expressed is a particularly difficult problem in systems design. The notion of a precision hierarchy can at least provide a reminder to check the level of identifiers appropriate to our particular systems requirements. Such checking should be tied directly to the documentation of the system.

FIGURE 14–4

CRITERIA HIERARCHY BY LEVELS OF SYSTEMS ANALYSIS*

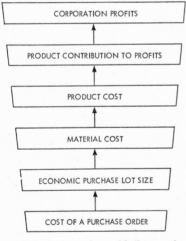

* Each term in a block can be thought of as a measure of effectiveness for which some manager is responsible. Each term can also represent the management information system that backs up the manager in carrying out his responsibility.

3. *Systems Hierarchy.* Figure 14–4 shows how a criterion at one level of management systems fits into the analysis at a higher or more general scope of systems. Only as a management is better able to be explicit in the elements which go into its system at varying levels can it expect to see more clearly the criteria. Quite complicated systems can exist in each of these boxes—but note how the term in the box, when thought of as a criterion, can give the simplified essence of the problem area.

This hierarchy deliberately ignores any of the aspects of how the systems fit into or relate to organization levels or specialties. It is concerned only with the way systems and their criteria fit together. Organization levels and specialties are considered separately in the next two hierarchies.

FIGURE 14–5

CRITERIA HIERARCHY BY LEVELS AND
SPECIALTIES IN AN ORGANIZATION

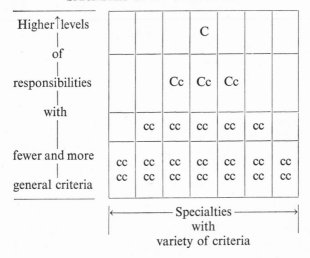

Higher⬆levels				C			
of							
responsibilities			Cc	Cc	Cc		
with		cc	cc	cc	cc	cc	
fewer and more	cc	cc	cc	cc	cc	cc	cc
general criteria	cc	cc	cc	cc	cc	cc	cc

←——————— Specialties ———————→
with
variety of criteria

4. Organization Levels Hierarchy (See Figure 14–5). Criteria can
be treated as a hierarchy of viewpoints associated with a variety of
positions in an organization chart. In such a structure we can study the
changes that take place in the choice and significance of criteria at
different levels of an organization. This type of analysis can be an
extension of the basic approaches of line and staff authorities and
responsibilities. The study of criteria by organization level can be used
to clarify the shift in information requirements between each level of
superior and subordinate.

Dr. Charles Hitch, economist and presently Controller of the Department of Defense, has given us a very important and yet very troublesome principle. He has said, "The criterion for good criteria is consistency with a good criterion at a higher level."[4]

This principle makes great sense because it emphasizes consistency
between the large and the small jobs of any organization. It has a
psychological overtone because it is a reminder that individual criteria
should be considered in the context of group criteria. This, of course, is
the problem of suboptimization that has received so much attention of
late.

The troublesome part comes from our limited abilities to see how
lower level criteria fit into higher level criteria. In the context of

---

[4] J. F. McClosky and F. N. Trifethen (eds.), *Operations Research for Management*
(Baltimore: The Johns Hopkins Press, 1954).

organization levels, we can expect more general criteria to be associated with problems assigned to higher levels of authority and responsibility. The pyramid form of organization structure as shown in Figure 14–5 reflects this notion of larger numbers of more specific criteria operating at the lower levels of the organization and fewer, but broader, criteria operating at the higher levels. There are two primary reasons for this situation. First, there is the positive correlation between higher positions and responsibility for problems that are not susceptible to neat and concrete measurement. Second, the span of attention, and therefore the manager's span of control, is taxed by too large a number of specific criteria. He must, to survive, achieve an ability to work with gross criteria. Perhaps, even more importantly, he must arrange to assure that others at lower levels are using specific criteria for control purposes.

Inventories of criteria associated with the various organization levels can provide a relatively crisp structure of an organization's decision needs. Such criteria can then be used to test for consistency and relevancy in the supporting management systems.

5. Organization Specialties Hierarchy (Also in Figure 14–5). Closely related to the organization levels hierarchy is the one that considers different specialties or functions in the organization. The specialization of responsibilities accounts for many of the disjointed aspects of running an organization. To get the benefits of specialization, the organization sets up groups with separated missions, languages, and loyalties. For specialization to be worthwhile, on the balance, it is then necessary for some overall arrangement to be made in which the separated efforts can be recombined for organization-wide effectiveness. This sets up a need for knowing both the criteria of the separated areas and the criteria of the overall effort. Only with the structuring of both sets of criteria is it possible to evaluate how the pieces contribute to the whole.

Analysis of criteria used by organization specialties is particularly significant when preparing information requirement specifications for systems designs that span more than one specialty. Such concentration on criteria used among specialties can do much to locate areas where common use of data processing output is possible and, conversely, where it is not possible.

6. Time Hierarchy (See Figure 14–6). Selection and weighting of criteria is also influenced by the time structure in which various management decisions are made. Time is a primary problem in most situations in business. Time is particularly significant in the development of business systems. It is our ability (at the start of a study) to scan through time and to come up with at least a general statement of those payoff objectives that provide the broad context for all other analysis in a study. Further, it is our ability to sense when to change our objectives that keeps our study on target even though the target is shifting as time passes.

The selection of the objectives for a specific problem study should identify the time dimension of each criteria that is used to spell out the objectives. The time dimension, in turn, will provide a basis for asking

FIGURE 14-6

CRITERIA HIERARCHIES REFLECTED FROM DIFFERENT TIME FRAMES
AND CHANGING ENVIRONMENT OF THE FIRM

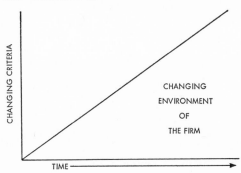

the question, "What values can be operating during both the study period and the period of potential payoff?" These values must be expressed in the form of criteria and related weights. Both the selection of criteria and the related weights will be influenced by the time frame of the study. In different time frames either different criteria may be used or different weights may be applied to the same criteria. The identification of these changes placed on a time scale tells a management when to change its systems.

Despite recent emphasis on real-time systems, much business systems reporting is, and, we predict, will continue to be associated with changes that are expressed in time periods—daily, weekly, monthly, etc. The structures for reporting in various time periods can be tested in the hierarchies of the criteria of such time periods. The result should be much clearer specifications for designing time period reporting into our business systems.

7. *Environment Hierarchy* (Also in Figure 14–6). The environment hierarchy for criteria is probably the most significant structure and the one that is most difficult to analyze. This is the structure of

criteria when there are changes in the opportunities and hazards that go to make up the environment of the organization. In business there is a time for growth and a time to retrench. There is a time for developing new products or services and a time for expanding the market for old products or services.

To attempt to describe the structure of the environment of an organization can be quite a frustrating experience. Yet it is extremely important to determine how the firm is acted upon and how it acts upon its environment. The opportunities and the hazards for the firm can be made explicit only in the descriptions of environmental factors. Statements of objectives of what the firm will do in its unique environment are much more meaningful when they are made specific by the inclusion of the criteria of success. In fact, the very act of doing the work involved in selecting criteria often shows that different objectives should be chosen, or that different weights or priorities should be given to objectives.

The environment hierarchy is made difficult by the very fact that its purpose is to bring out and highlight those factors which will require a management to *make changes* if they are to be successful. In other words, it is much simpler to choose criteria in an environment of stability where the future repeats the past. The setting of criteria in an environment where change is a necessity can be a real test of a management's ability. The management that is demonstrating its ability to be successful in the face of change does so by devoting resources to a very selective surveillance of its environment. Such a management not only looks outward from its base of operation, but it goes out into this environment and gets firsthand knowledge. Such surveillance is usually a team effort. It can be very informal, but more and more organizations are providing formal arrangements for certain aspects of external surveillance. This attention can gradually lead to a consciousness and then a relatively formal description of the criteria which are important and the hierarchy in which they can be related.

Another requirement, of course, is that a parallel consciousness also exists that keeps a management constantly checking to see when the environment calls for changes in criteria in their relationships.

THE STUDY OF CRITERIA AS A PREREQUISITE TO SYSTEMS IMPROVEMENT

Figure 14–7 shows the balancing of the need for stability and the need for change in the criteria hierarchy of a firm. The reasoning is similar to that used in Chapter 5 for the *See-Saw Rule* in classifications. As a firm refines its surveillance approaches, it has the opportunity to adjust the criteria used for decisions. Confusion results, however,

FIGURE 14–7

CRITERIA CHANGES AND
PRESSURES ON MANAGERS

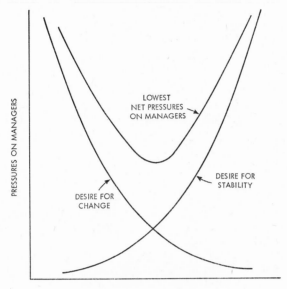

REFINEMENT OF SURVEILLANCE SYSTEMS
AND IMPROVED ABILITY TO REVISE CRITERIA

because managers find it difficult to make decisions when the criteria change so fast.

These opposing forces represent one of the basic problems for a management. Only as the criteria are made more explicit at the level of the environment is it possible to consider the advantages of stability with the advantages of change. This level of analysis is being recognized as fundamental for it is here that the environment criteria framework emerges which, in turn, provides the guidance for the setting of all the other criteria mentioned above.

Figure 14–8 is a visual aid designed to remind us of these criteria structures and to show some of their relationships. The criteria involved in management systems have at least the dimensions derived from the following:

1. The degree of concreteness of the area of investigation;
2. The precision with which a criteria name is chosen;
3. The structure of criteria relationships among systems;
4. The responsibility levels of an organization;
5. The functional specialties of an organization;
6. The variety of time frames used for decisions;

7. The shifts of significance that take place in the environment of the organization.

A management system should provide management with data that are of the most use to them, considering their present and future problems. We are suggesting that the design of a set of criteria hierarchies can provide useful grids in which information needs can be evaluated. More specifically, each of these hierarchies has inherent in it the language of criteria in which management expresses their prob-

FIGURE 14–8

FACTORS INFLUENCING CRITERIA FOR MANAGEMENT SYSTEMS

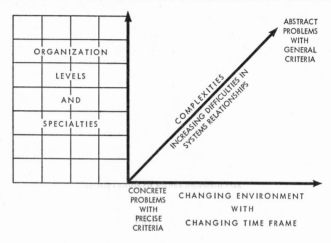

lems. Therefore, an approach that also includes consideration of changes in the criteria can get very close to spelling out the values that should be provided by a management system. The criteria specification for degrees of concreteness, precision, and intersystem relationships can go a long way toward satisfying the information needs of management levels and specialties. At a minimum, their identification and classification should provide us with our best statement of the merits of a particular study.

Some powerful methods of compound analysis are now being developed and applied that incorporate hierarchies of criteria into a wide variety of management situations. The Industrial Dynamics approach of Jay W. Forrester[5] of M. I. T. is being applied to complex problems of policy setting by management. Careful attention is paid to obtaining

_____

[5] Jay W. Forrester, *Industrial Dynamics* (Cambridge, Mass., and New York: M.I.T. Press and John Wiley & Sons, 1961).

the experienced views and insights of practicing managers. These views and insights are incorporated into comprehensive models containing the selected parameters for the particular areas of policy. These models are programmed by a specially devised computer language called Dynamo. When these programs are run on the computer the result is an extended analysis of the study area and the provision of more explicit policy guidance for management. The emphasis is on structure of situations and the types and weights of criteria. The industrial dynamics approach goes well beyond the typical handling of criteria. It includes, for example, criteria that are involved in the psychological, social, and political aspects of policy setting.

Another compound approach is that called the Grid Charting Technique, as developed by Gordon T. Shahin in his research at Ohio State University. The grid charting technique provides a method by which flows of information to management functions can be equated to management information needs. This capability results from the combination of two tabular graphic formats called grid charts and decision logic tables. The grid charts are used to display the flows of information supplied to the various management functions. The decision logic tables are used to display the information requirements or needs of management by relating various conditions to specific management actions within each manager's set of delegated responsibilities. By comparing the grid charts of available information to the specific information needs of management portrayed in decision logic tables the supply of information can be equated to the actual management demands for information. Since grid charts display the production of information and decision logic tables display the customer demands for information, the technique now brings to bear on management information the viewpoints of both production and marketing criteria.

These new developments in management analysis demonstrate the importance of careful attention to criteria selection and especially to the way individual criteria relate to other criteria in a management problem area. Feedback studies can be made on a much more rigorous basis as such criteria hierarchies are developed and tested.

Reflect back on the setting of priorities in the SMART case study in Chapter 4. The variety of possible, alternate assignments carried with it a wide choice of possible criteria and associated weights of significance. When these criteria and weights were not clearly spelled out it became necessary to make forced choices, that is, choices based upon hunch and intuition. The study of criteria is one of seeking gradual improvements that will reduce the dependence on hunch and intuition. With these improvements management can have more confidence in the answers provided to its questions.

Feedback of information through a management information system usually results in answers to two types of questions:

1. Was something done that was supposed to be done? If the answer is Yes, feedback has provided a confidence factor for the manager concerned. If the answer is No, the manager has been warned as soon as possible and can initiate remedial action.
2. What should be done? This is the case where surveillance has been provided and the manager is being fed descriptions of situations, and thus is being given a clearer picture of the problems for which he may make decisions. The feedback can also include descriptions of the alternative courses of action which may be available to him.

The second type of question, of course, is an extension of the first type of question. The first type contains what we called in Chapter 3 the basic and secondary report information, whereas the second type includes recommendations for possible alternative decisions the manager may make.

In either type, the availability of documented statements of the more important criteria will guide the manager as he receives the feedback of his system.

The ultimate test of a management information system lies in the answer to the manager's question, "Has this system helped me to do a better job?" All of the phases of systems development lead to this point, and success is indicated only as the manager answers "Yes" to his own question.

Chapter 15

MANAGEMENT SYSTEMS:
REVIEW AND SUMMARY

As long as people have curiosities, hopes, and aspirations they will organize and work to accomplish their goals. When they can they will "play it by ear" unencumbered by the detail of formal attacks on their problems. When they recognize that informal methods are not sufficient to get results they will build "systems." Systems, in this sense, provide ladders that give us a better chance to reach our more difficult goals.

The structure of an organization gives that organization a strength and resilience to accomplish its selected missions. As missions change it is necessary that adjustments be made in the organization positions, their job specifications, and relationships to other positions. This book has stated that the impact of such changes can be made less severe as the organization develops effective management information systems. Information systems also provide organization strength and resilience. The combination of effective and interrelated structures in organization and systems is worthy of pursuit by all managers.

The methods by which such improvements are made provide the core of the art and the science of management. Since the factors of complexity are admittedly so great in any organization, there is no choice except to emphasize the processes of elimination and selection. This is true when we consider people and their responsibilities or systems and their scope of operation.

THE JOINING OF ORGANIZATION ANALYSIS
AND SYSTEMS ANALYSIS

In this book we have proposed that people in an organization and the systems in an organization be viewed as a set of networks of inter-

199

dependencies. The shape and form of the interdependencies for a particular organization, at a point in time, are functions of (1) the relevant situations, (2) the recognized requirements, and (3) the choices of organization structure and information systems structure. In this book we have concentrated at the point of the interdependencies between organization structure and information structure. If we assume the existence of the typical large mix of well-defined and poorly-defined requirements, we can then narrow to the question of how can these requirements (remembering how they can change) be best satisfied by people-processing and data-(machine) processing.

This problem comes down to what do we need to know to meet our information requirements. "Need to know" must then be satisfied by a balance of the wisdom, knowledge, and skills of people *in combination* with the information produced in the data processing systems. We very much need better rules to help us achieve this "balance." At what point should we inject the logic of human beings into the logic of an information system and thereafter have the machine follow this logic in doing the "work"? What are the relations of the skills of people and the logic of machine processing? When is it premature to place "work" on the machine?

These questions are becoming increasingly important as the computer is applied to questions in the ill-structured areas of management, particularly at the requirements and assumptions level of analysis. Serious questions have been raised recently as to the wisdom of forcing certain questions onto computers before such questions have been carefully prepared. Other doubts have been raised with regard to the quality of data which are being used in machine processing. The fundamental question is, of course, can man give better performance with or without the machine in the ill-structured areas of decision? If this were phrased as a hypothesis, how would it be tested? The point, of course, is that we can answer and improve the answers to these questions only as we are able to gradually reduce complex situations into manageable pieces.

This book has emphasized man-machine relationships or, as stated earlier, the relationships of talents and techniques. Only as the conceptual powers of man are processed into the documentation of systems is it possible to identify and demonstrate real progress in managerial thought and action. The improvement of the practical concepts and techniques is the essence of progress in management. This is a gradual process in which concepts and techniques are being refined and made more realistic. This book has attempted to recognize the critical point where the state of the arts in this field justifies application of resources and promises success. Beyond this point there is a whole universe of problems for which, at present, no satisfactory approaches exist. This universe is the promise of the future that there will be interesting and challenging work to be done for a long time to come.

THE PHASES OF SYSTEMS DEVELOPMENT
AND THE MANAGEMENT OF CHANGE

Those who wish to show results today must work with what exists. This book has presented an inventory of concepts and techniques that can be applied in a cycle that spans the initiation of a system through time to the point where the system is tested and put into operation. This cycle was identified at seven levels, or phases:

I   Problem Definition (Priority Setting),
II   Written Information Requirements,
III   Systems Design,
IV   Programming,
V   Operating,
VI   Format and Display, and
VII   Feedback and Evaluation.

Each of these phases has been looked at in the chapters of this book. The early phases are in direct correspondence with the basic problem of organization planning and control. In these phases, especially, systems development should not appear as a unique and separate organization function. Rather, its success depends, to a large degree, on an arrangement that allows those responsible for systems development to have access to the inner workings—to the overall surveillance operations in the organization. Problem definition will be ineffective, if not impossible, without such an arrangement keyed to top-management planning and control. At this level of organization and in this phase of systems development, organization problems and systems problems are inseparable. The choice of "delegation" from higher levels to a person or to a system requires a clear view of both the man's and the system's capacities. Separation of organization studies and systems studies complicates these decisions.

Putting more men on the job and specializing has always been a tempting means for getting work done. The restraints to such an approach, however, are many. As the economists have told us, diminishing returns can set in as people start to get in one another's way. Especially as specialization accompanies growth of an organization do we see people "getting in one another's way." With a variety of specialized missions, a specialized organization is particularly difficult to change when new requirements call for adjustments.

People-to-people relationships in an organization structure have received and are receiving much attention at both the level of research and the level of application. We propose that work in the areas of conflicts of goals and conflicts of policies be given special encouragement. This is not a recommendation pointed toward the "resolving of conflicts." Rather, the premise is held that conflict is a necessary part of any approach to the handling of organization problems. The very act of any change in an organization injects conflicts into that organization. Differences of opinion as to how certain problems should be solved are natural ingredients of a final and satisfactory solution. Management systems should look at the question of how to insert new requirements into an organization in such a manner that the benefits of differences of opinion (conflict) are obtained within the limits of the capacities of organization personnel to live with the negative aspects of such conflict.

The blending of organization structure analysis with information structure analysis will bring out in the open many heretofore unsuspected problems. To those who have an attitude of "don't make any waves," this approach may make no sense at all. To those who wish to make progress with a minimum of waves, the approach can be most helpful. In an environment where the management of change is a necessity, careful attention to the development of management information systems is steadily becoming more of a necessity.

Typically the manager at any level and in any specialty lives with a large amount of uncertainty as to the actual responsibilities in his job. Certain of his responsibilities can be spelled out in a position description. These are usually generalizations. Other responsibilities are documented in statements of procedures for which the manager is responsible and these tend to be quite detailed and specific. Beyond the position description, and between the position description and the procedures level, there are large areas of job content which remain vague or are ignored. These areas of vagueness can receive a degree of clarification only through the type of analytical study that is provided in a program of management systems development. In such a program careful attention is paid to both the position descriptions of organization personnel and the documentation of the organization's systems.

THE INFORMATION PRODUCTION PROCESS REVIEWED

Figure 15–1 is a visual aid used as a summary of this book's approach to management information systems. It is an extension of the Schematic of the Information Production Process shown in Chapter 3. The numbers shown alongside each box are used to identify the order of presentation in the following summary:

FIGURE 15–1

Summary Diagram for Management Systems

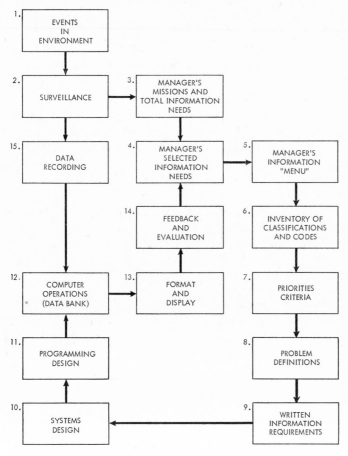

1. Events in Environment.   There is an infinite number of "events" happening every day. To know which events are important and to arrange for recording them is the starting point for management information systems.

2. Surveillance.   This term refers to all those activities by which a better perspective of an organization and its environment is obtained. It is out of the overall surveillance activity that events are initially identified and made susceptible to formal treatment.

3. A Manager's Missions and Total Information Needs.   These are derived from a large number of events happening in *his* environment. His job description should reflect the more significant of these events.

His job specification, in turn, should identify the types of abilities that he needs to work with these particular events. This phase of systems development recognizes the need for developing a consciousness of the possible large scope in any manager's information needs. In particular, we emphasized that the term *total information needs* is an ideal and should be used to demonstrate the impossibility of ever "giving the manager *all* the facts concerning *all* the events." (See Foreword.)

4. A Manager's Selected Information Needs.   These reflect the fact that, typically, it is impossible to collect or use all the possible information that could be presented to him. The care with which job environment events are selected and documented is critical to success in spelling out the key information needs of a manager. We noted the following in Chapter 3.

"An event of significance can happen without anyone knowing about it; and many events occur that are of little real interest to anybody. When an event is recorded as data it means that two basic decisions have been made:

1. Someone decided that this event was important;
2. Arrangements were made to make sure this event would be recognized and recorded when it happened."

This is certainly only the start of the process of selecting a manager's information needs. These selected needs, however, provide the basic justification for all that can follow in the phases of systems development.

5. The Manager's Information "Menu."   This is the organization's documentation of what can be available in existing information systems. Its existence identifies the available set of choices for the manager and guides the system's designers as improvements are sought. The "menu" of information that can be served to managers can be viewed as the documentation of the important systems in the organization. With the information menu available, both the manager and the system's designer have a positive basis for discussing systems requirements.

6. Inventory of Classifications and Codes.   The classification and codes of a business are the fundamental building blocks from which data are processed and information is produced. The process of classification puts the first level of logic into any system; that is, it selects certain pieces and it gives a preliminary set of relationships between the pieces. Coding provides sets of shorthand expressions for classes and, therefore, must reflect the same logic as that built into the classification systems. The identification and analysis of an organization inventory of classification and codes is now being recognized as extremely significant in the design of management systems.

7. *Priorities and Criteria.* Management's most critical decisions are those regarding which and how many resources should be assigned to which problems. Priority setting requires a good knowledge of what types and amounts of resources are available. It also requires careful analysis of the alternative applications of these resources. Criteria are the English words in which measures useful in making choices are expressed. Therefore, there is a close relationship between the selecting of criteria and the setting of priorities. A further consideration is the assigning of relative weights to criteria and then to priorities. An overall framework in which both criteria and priorities can be studied is basic to successful management systems.

8. *Problem Definition.* This subject is certainly not new, but its significance has greatly increased with the appearance of the computer. The speed and expense of using the computer means that priorities must be set more carefully. Priority setting, in turn, requires that each problem be more carefully defined and its ramifications more carefully anticipated. Problem definition, in systems development, specifically means the process of writing down the best statement of management's "needs to know" and what it will take to refine such statements of needs.

9. *Written Information Requirements.* Problem definition is never a one-time proposition. Problems must be refined as better perspective is obtained and as situations change. The same is true of the formal, written information requirements that should result from the careful definition of problems. Chapter 8 covered this phase of information requirements design. Only recently have organizations been willing to assign resources to this careful black and white detailing of the content and form of information requirements.

10. *Systems Design.* Such design presupposes that we have at least a reasonable problem definition and statement of information requirements available before we design the method of producing such information. This does not mean that either the problem definition or information requirements statement will not change. It does mean that we do not let the "how to" aspect outweigh the "why" of the problem area. Systems design for information flow systems requires explicit identification of inputs, processing steps, and the end points of systems output. Because of the needs to see general logic and yet handle large amounts of detail, a progressive charting of content is carried on, going from block diagrams to detailed logic charts.

11. *Programming Design.* This takes over at the point where the computer must be given the word. The word in this case must be in a language that the computer understands. Special languages are available for the human to talk to the machine and also for the machine to talk to itself. Programming design converts the requirements at the level of systems design into these machine languages.

12. Computer Operations (Data Bank). Because there is so much to explain about merely getting systems prepared to go on a computer, we often forget that there are major problems in the running of the system. For this reason, we brought out in Chapter 12 some of the critical problems involved in a computer center and its operation. Data inputs must be monitored. Data inputs must be scheduled and merged with available programming routines. Schedules for computer operations must be carefully set and expedited. Output documents must be produced in required format and distributed to meet customer needs.

13. Format and Display. For those systems whose output goes back to a manager for further analysis and evaluation, it is most important that this output be in the best possible format to facilitate understanding by the manager. The output of a data processing system that provides reports to management should try to recognize what the manager already knows. It should correct any wrong impressions and then add new facts for the manager's evaluation. Today, the formating of information is becoming more significant as we move to extended data communications systems and the automatic display of information.

14. Feedback and Evaluation. Data processing implies a *feed forward* of facts in an organization. *Feedback* concentrates on getting a system's output back to compare what actually happened with what was planned. Feedback also refers to situations where we are trying to improve our operations by a process of trial and error. This may not qualify as formal planning. In either case, feedback is of no use unless a means exists for evaluation of results. It is for this reason that we have emphasized the importance of criteria in feedback and have related feedback to the priorities discussed in number 7 above. Priorities will shift as our feedback informs us of changes in environment and of changes in available resources. Modern techniques of data communications are proving to be major aids to better feedback and evaluation for management decision making.

15. Data Recording. The numbers used above trace the development of the needs for information output. Block 15 emphasizes the inputs of raw data as they are recorded from the surveillance of significant events in the environment of the organization. Data is the *hard copy* of events. Once a selected event is recorded as data it can be moved through a data processing system. The selection of the important events and the ability to recognize when such an event actually takes place are important areas of analysis in the design of a management information system.

Figure 15–1 shows how these 15 topical areas can fit together in the development and operation of management information systems. We have used this framework as a guide in which to demonstrate applications and case study materials.

THE SMART ASSIGNMENTS: BUYERS OF INFORMATION

In chapter 4 the case study of the SMART Corporation was presented to demonstrate certain of the problems in organizing for effective management. In particular, this case study was used to demonstrate the environment in which management information systems can be developed. The ten initial projects provided examples for setting management priorities and assigning resources to studies of selected problems. Problem definitions were shown to be the result of a gradual process of refinement as more information was obtained from the analysts.

The analysts provided reports with facts, reports with conclusions, and finally, reports with specific recommendations. The economics of information production were demonstrated by the budget procedure used to evaluate the success of the Management Systems Department. Costs of study were kept separate from the costs of implementing the systems recommended for installation. The costs of implementing a study were deducted from the estimated savings expected from the improved system. These net savings in the application area were then used in the budget formula to compare with the costs of making the study. This comparison is important to the systems group, for it shows whether or not they have been able to choose and solve problems at a return above cost.

How top management apportions the credit for such project success is an important decision. The overall scheme of incentives should include encouragement for functional managers and those responsible for central systems work. This arrangement is, in itself, a reflection of the way top management sees opportunities for the organization and the way it is willing to assign its resources.

The assignments in the SMART game were deliberately chosen to demonstrate that realism in management includes large areas where the content of the situation is not known. The idea that a manager must pay for getting information to improve his knowledge of a situation is critical to any understanding of what management information systems can do. This game was designed to give examples where the player had to decide what information he wanted and what he was willing to pay for it. The same reasoning should hold for any decision to assign resources to the development of information systems.

MANPOWER PLANNING AND CONTROL VIA PROBLEM DEFINITION

Project 11–0 identified certain of the problems associated with matching the available abilities in an organization with the requirements of new job openings. It is interesting to note that position requirements and systems information requirements depend on the same thing, that is, the careful definition of the manager's problems.

This project (Manpower Planning and Control: Candidate Matching) was carried through the phases of systems development (as shown in the index on p. 170). This index traced the project from its origination at the level of the Executive Committee down to the level of operating detail in the procedures manual. Examples were given of the analysis typical in each phase of the development. The amount of specifics that must be treated in even this relatively small project should give the reader an appreciation of what realism is in the practice of systems development. Both breadth and depth of coverage in a particular system must be carefully chosen by the management team responsible for management information systems design.

THE FIELDS OF OPPORTUNITY

Project 12–0 was used to describe the need for an overall scheme in which to select and weight systems projects. This project emphasized the importance of having a master classification for organizing the surveillance efforts of a firm and for making decisions concerning the selection of priority areas to be studied. An example of such a classification was presented and the ten SMART projects were located in the appropriate section of this classification system. In practice, the ability to keep track of which problems are being given attention and which ones are, at present, not being considered, can be of help to those who must provide overall guidance for management studies. The classification presented here was quite generalized and would have to be form-fitted and made more specific in an actual application.

Once the overall classification is established for the organization, it can be used for many purposes. Projects can be spelled out in appropriate detail for writing out the events and activities that can be, for example, PERT charted. This application, in turn, would provide a means for project planning and control as specific pieces of projects are assigned and scheduled. The problems of feedback and evaluation, as discussed in the last chapter, can also be treated in the context of this overall representation of the organization environment.

The theme of this book is that it is becoming more and more possible to blend the approaches of organization analysis and systems analysis. The common denominator for these two approaches is the problem definition of a manager's responsibilities. When systems and their built-in techniques are viewed as reinforcing the manager and his talents, it is quite logical that an approach be used that includes both. As noted in the introduction to Chapter 1, the state of the arts has now reached the point where management's systems can help to blend both the talents and the techniques of our organizations. The truly smart corporation is the one that seeks a balance of progress between improvements in its talents and in its techniques and brings them together through its studies of management systems.

Appendixes A and B

A. SMART *CORPORATION*
PROGRESS REPORTS

B. *DISCUSSION QUESTIONS*
BY CHAPTER

APPENDIX A*

SUMMARY OF SYSTEMS SURVEY

PROJECT: Product Line Analysis

The significant findings at this time in the survey of Product Line are as follows:

1. The Instrument Industry is growing at an accelerated rate. Our segment of that industry is increasing at a rate of from 10 to 20% per year. Our own sales have increased at but 5% per year. The question here is: What do we have to do to get and hold our "fair share" of the market?
2. The movement of the "full line" or supply of a complete instrument system is a pressure towards some product diversification.

Cost Estimate at End	Savings Estimate at End	Actual Savings to Date
$240,000	$850,000	none

SUMMARY OF SYSTEMS SURVEY

PROJECT: Product Line Analysis

The significant findings at this time in the survey of Product Line are as follows:

1. No recent study has been made of the relationships among end products—either from a design or from a market point-of-view.
2. It would appear that the next step should be to study the present offerings of products in an attempt to see what can be done to eliminate unnecessary variety and immaterial differences.
3. Later, the same problem might be considered from an external or a market view.

Cost Estimate at End	Savings Estimate at End	Actual Savings to Date
$250,000	$900,000	$16,500

Code 1–3

SUMMARY OF SYSTEMS SURVEY

PROJECT: Product Line Analysis

The significant findings at this time in the survey of Product Line are as follows:

1. The Company has had a general policy that every product must stand the test that it carries its share of overhead and makes a profit.
2. However, development budgets have often "underwritten" a product well beyond the point where it should stand or fall by the above test.

Cost Estimate at End	Savings Estimate at End	Actual Savings to Date
$260.000	$850,000	$39,700

SUMMARY OF SYSTEMS SURVEY

PROJECT: Product Line Analysis

The significant findings at this time in the survey of Product Line are as follows:

Although we have attempted to standardize components over the years, it appears that greater emphasis should be placed upon the idea of "unit construction"; i.e., get as much end product differentiation as possible to meet customers' desires, using as few basic components as possible. Our Engineering Department records show that we are now keeping track of 60,000 components and subassemblies.

Cost Estimate at End	Savings Estimate at End	Actual Savings to Date
$260,000	$830,000	$67,200

SUMMARY OF SYSTEMS SURVEY

PROJECT: Product Line Analysis

The significant findings at this time in the survey of Product Line are as follows:

1. At present some 50% of sales dollars are returned from standard catalog "in stock" items. The other 50% of our sales dollars come from sales of "special" or "modified" products.
2. A statistical sampling of standard catalog items gives the following data:

	Percent of Annual Sales
Lowest 10% of items	.3
Second " " "	1.1
Third " " "	1.9
Fourth " " "	2.6
Fifth " " "	3.4
Sixth " " "	4.4
Seventh " " "	5.8
Eighth " " "	8.5
Ninth " " "	16.1
Tenth " " "	55.9

Cost Estimate at End	Savings Estimate at End	Actual Savings to Date
$260,000	$820,000	$104,600

P. 218

SUMMARY OF SYSTEMS SURVEY

PROJECT: Product Line Analysis

The following actions have taken place:

1. An analysis of catalog offerings has resulted in a reduction from 6,500 items to 3,400 items.
2. Some 1,500 of the items now listed in the catalog were formerly handled as special items.
3. Thus, the initial reduction was from 6,400 to 1,900 with 1,500 new items brought in to update the product line.

Cost Estimate at End	Savings Estimate at End	Actual Savings to Date
$270,000	$820,000	$203,900

SUMMARY OF SYSTEMS SURVEY

PROJECT: Product Line Analysis

The following results have been obtained from the Product Line Analysis:

1. Standard stock items inventory (Finished Goods and Work-in-Process) has been reduced by 20%—from $2,500,000 to $2,000,000.
2. Components in stock have been reduced from 60,000 to 40,000, partially through the results of this study. The "scale value"* contribution of this change to the company has been set at $70,000.

Cost Estimate at End	Savings Estimate at End	Actual Savings to Date
$270,000	$840,000	$391,800

* An estimate of what the Company would have been willing to pay (for example, to an outside consultant) to obtain such improvements in the Company.

SUMMARY OF SYSTEMS SURVEY

PROJECT: Product Line Analysis

The following results have been obtained from the Product Line Analysis:

1. "Special" items are now looked at as diversifications of product line and the concentration is on expansion of offerings to provide systems packages.
2. Gradually the company hopes to be in a position to sell these instrument systems packages in the same sense that it now sells individual items from its catalog.

Cost Estimate at End	Savings Estimate at End	Actual Savings to Date
$270,000	$840,000	$592,400

Code 1–9

SUMMARY OF SYSTEMS SURVEY

PROJECT: Product Line Analysis

The following results have been obtained from the Product Line Analysis:

1. Turnover of inventory has improved because of better delivery service to customers.
2. Current asset ratios are now such as to add support to the expansion of plant to take on the "instrument systems packages" development and production.

Cost Estimate at End	Savings Estimate at End	Actual Savings to Date
$270,000	$840,000	$848,300

P. 223

SUMMARY OF SYSTEMS SURVEY

PROJECT: Shipping and Receiving

The significant findings at this time in the survey of Shipping and Receiving problems are as follows:

1. The major complaint about the Receiving Department (excluding some personality conflicts) centers around their failure to notify the using department of the arrival of ordered materials.
2. What the Receiving Department does is send one copy of its Receiving Report to the Production Superintendent. (A second copy goes to the Purchasing Department.) The Production Superintendent notes and routes to the using department.
3. Some of the delay occurs because of this intermediate handling.
4. The Receiving Report may not be issued for upwards of 48 hours— the department supervisor attributes this delay to being "understaffed" and "overcrowded."
5. The second major complaint involves damage to materials from exposure to the elements or improper handling. The department foreman attributes this to "lack of the right equipment."
6. In fairness to the Receiving Department supervisor, it does appear that he accomplishes near miracles in the crowded space allocated to his function.
7. The Department Superintendent has readily agreed to prepare and forward a copy of the Receiving Report directly to the ordering department.
8. He has further agreed to physically isolate each day's receipts which have not had the Receiving Report prepared.
9. The design of the report will be studied for possible simplification.
10. The personnel requirements and job duties will be restudied; layout and material handling equipment will also be scrutinized.

Cost Estimate at End	Savings Estimate at End	Actual Savings to Date
$100,000	$220,000	none

SUMMARY OF SYSTEMS SURVEY

PROJECT: Shipping and Receiving

The significant findings at this time in the survey of Shipping and Receiving problems are as follows:

1. After getting the Production Manager to forgo his copy of the Receiving Report, we directed our attention to the Shipping Department.
2. The Shipping Department's major problem is a breakdown in the release for shipment procedure.
3. The various sales personnel give verbal shipping instructions or none at all.
4. Packaging and routing information is hard to find. The senior shipping clerk makes informal decisions in these areas.
5. Neither the "sales order" nor the "production ticket" is sent to the Shipping Department. They are unable to anticipate their daily work load, nor can they plan their carrier arrangements intelligently.
6. The department foreman greeted us with "open arms." Our suggestions are assured of warm reception (if they don't involve more money).

Cost Estimate at End	Savings Estimate at End	Actual Savings to Date
$100,000	$240,000	$92,400

P. 225

SUMMARY OF SYSTEMS SURVEY

PROJECT: Shipping and Receiving

The following results have been obtained from the Shipping and Receiving study:

1. The Production Planning and Scheduling Department has agreed to supply the Shipping Department with the weekly production schedule.
2. Sales and Engineering have agreed to develop a set of packaging specifications for all catalog items. All variations from these instructions will be charged for and special notice sent to shipping foreman.
3. The Receiving Department study has seen the hiring of an additional employee and the start of a long-range material handling study. The "scale value"* of the improvements to date in the Receiving Department is $10,000 annually.

Cost Estimate at End	Savings Estimate at End	Actual Savings to Date
$100,000	$250,000	$187,700

* An estimate of what the Company would have been willing to pay (for example, to an outside consultant) to obtain such improvements in the Company.

SUMMARY OF SYSTEMS SURVEY

PROJECT: Shipping and Receiving

The following results have been obtained from the Shipping and Receiving study:

1. The Shipping Department reports lower labor costs based on planned work load—also better carrier relations.
2. The packaging study promises long-range probability of savings since it has been enlarged to include styling and cost of containers.
3. For the present the shippers are using their own best judgment—subject to any corrections requested by sales.
4. The "scale value"* of this project in shipping is $20,000 annually. It will, as mentioned, grow with the packaging study.
5. It is suggested that this project be tabled until the packaging report is completed.

Cost Estimate at End	Savings Estimate at End	Actual Savings to Date
$100,000	$260,000	$276,900

* An estimate of what the Company would have been willing to pay (for example, to an outside consultant) to obtain such improvements in the Company.

P. 233

Summary of Systems Survey

Project: Purchasing Department Study

The significant findings at this time in the survey of the Purchasing Department are as follows:

1. Each plant has its own Purchasing Agent who reports to the Plant Superintendent.
2. Basis for issuance of Plant Purchase Order is either a "bill of materials" from engineering department or a "stock requisition" from inventory control. Plant Purchasing Agent verifies authorizing signature then issues Purchase Order.
3. "Approved vendor list" kept separately by each plant.
4. Salesmen may call on any Company personnel, but Purchase Order must originate with Plant Purchasing Agent.

Cost Estimate at End	Savings Estimate at End	Actual Savings to Date
$80,000	$200,000	none

Code 3–2

SUMMARY OF SYSTEMS SURVEY

PROJECT: Purchasing Department Study

The significant findings at this time in the survey of the Purchasing Department are as follows:

1. Reciprocity is strongly urged by several suppliers. No study has been made of the value of the dollar goods purchased from any supplier.
2. Assignment of work within Purchasing Department is according to work load ahead. Each suburban (No. 1 and No. 2) plant has two "buyers" in addition to Plant Purchasing Agent.
3. Prevailing company sentiment is that function is pretty efficient. "We all make mistakes—occasionally."
4. The rate of turnover on major items is roughly two to three times per year.
5. Private purchasing for employees is widely permitted but not encouraged.

Cost Estimate at End	Savings Estimate at End	Actual Savings to Date
$80,000	$200,000	$7,100

SUMMARY OF SYSTEMS SURVEY

PROJECT: Purchasing Department Study

The significant findings at this time in the survey of the Purchasing Department are as follows:

1. Requests for quotations are not uniformly made. In general, items costing more than $1,000 are subject to quote *if* there is sufficient lead time available.
2. Plant Purchasing Agent maintains informal contact with Sales Department concerning adherence to sales estimate.
3. Interviewing hours are 10–12 and 2–3. *No exceptions.*
4. Follow-up involves filing of duplicate copy of Purchase Order one week in advance of requested delivery date. The Purchase Order form is preprinted for each plant with format identical. It contains a perforated acknowledgment section, but little if any attempt is made to secure its execution and return.

Cost Estimate at End	Savings Estimate at End	Actual Savings to Date
$80,000	$200,000	$20,000

SUMMARY OF SYSTEMS SURVEY

PROJECT: Purchasing Department Study

The significant findings at this time in the survey of the Purchasing Department are as follows:

1. Verification of invoices is done by the Receiving Department on its "Receiving Report." This report is compared with the original Purchase Order and approved for payment.
2. Actual inspection of goods is done by the using department. Notification of damage or quality rejects is made on Inspection Report— one copy to Plant Purchasing Agent. On at least one occasion this report arrived after invoice approval and payment.

Cost Estimate at End	Savings Estimate at End	Actual Savings to Date
$80,000	$200,000	$32,200

P. 237

SUMMARY OF SYSTEMS SURVEY

PROJECT: Purchasing Department Study

The significant findings at this time in the survey of the Purchasing Department are as follows:

1. All Purchase Orders are prepared on manual typewriter, using carbon paper for multiple copies.
2. Stock purchase requisitions are typewritten by the inventory control clerk. Bills of material are usually typewritten also.
3. Receiving Reports and Inspection Reports are usually handwritten.
4. The position of Plant Purchasing Agent pays $6,500–$8,500 annually.

Cost Estimate at End	Savings Estimate at End	Actual Savings to Date
$80,000	$200,000	$45,700

Code 3–6

SUMMARY OF SYSTEMS SURVEY

PROJECT: Purchasing Department Study

The following results have been obtained from the Purchasing Department study:

1. Discussion with Plant Purchasing at Plant No. 1 has found a receptive, interested person. Contacts at Plant No. 2 have been largely negative. The Plant Purchasing Agent in the former plant is attending night school at a local college. The Plant Purchasing Agent at the latter plant is a former production supervisor who recently was shifted to purchasing. Plant No. 3 contacts are also negative to date.
2. Plant Purchasing at Plant No. 1 has been reviewed with us and at our suggestion installed an improved "follow-up" procedure which has a "scale value"* of $90,000.

Cost Estimate at End	Savings Estimate at End	Actual Savings to Date
$100,000	$200,000	$90,000

* An estimate of what the Company would have been willing to pay (for example, to an outside consultant) to obtain such improvements in the Company.

Code 3–7

SUMMARY OF SYSTEMS SURVEY

PROJECT: Purchasing Department Study

The following are highlights of a report submitted to the Executive Committee:

1. The purchasing function should be centralized.
2. More attention should be given to securing annual requirements for combined plant needs.
3. Plant Purchasing Agent should assume more responsibility for verification of purchasing needs, specifically—review of the bill of materials in light of on-hand materials and supplies.
4. Incoming inspection should be expedited and invoices not ok'd prior to inspection operation.

(The Executive Board returned the report with this note: "Excellent suggestions—implement with Plant Purchasing Agents and operating management.")

Cost Estimate at End	Savings Estimate at End	Actual Savings to Date
$120,000	$180,000	$90,300

SUMMARY OF SYSTEMS SURVEY

PROJECT: Purchasing Department Study

The following results have been obtained from the Purchasing Department study:

1. The Plant Purchasing Agent of Plant No. 1 has been thoroughly acquainted with proposals and is in the process of selling them to his plant management.
2. Plant Purchasing Agents of Plant No. 2 and Plant No. 3 have stated that their plant managements have "fullest confidence" in the present method of operation—no changes necessary or advisable. However, they have taken proposals "under advisement."

Cost Estimate at End	Savings Estimate at End	Actual Savings to Date
$120,000	$170,000	$105,800

Pp. 241 & 242

Code 3–9

SUMMARY OF SYSTEMS SURVEY

PROJECT: Purchasing Department Study

The following results have been obtained from the Purchasing Department study:

1. Plant Purchasing Agent of Plant No. 1 has secured approval of your suggestions and has instituted changes in procedures along the lines suggested. Estimate of cash savings is $35,000 annually. Savings in form of fewer late deliveries, less equipment downtime, estimated at another $10,000.
2. No action at Plant No. 2 or Plant No. 3.
3. Project to be restudied after year's tryout at Plant No. 1.

Cost Estimate at End	Savings Estimate at End	Actual Savings to Date
$120,000	$170,000	$106,600

SUMMARY OF SYSTEMS SURVEY

PROJECT: Inventory Control—Systems Audit

The significant findings at this time in the survey of Inventory Control are as follows:

1. Approximately twice our working capital is tied up in inventories. This amounts to about $11,700,000.
2. The cost of running the present system of inventory control (not including purchasing or production control activities) is $70,000 per year.
3. The inventory control system is staffed as follows: Each plant has an inventory control supervisor at $5,200 and three clerks at $4,800, totaling $58,800.
4. Inventory Control Supervisor reports to Plant Production Superintendent, who in turn reports to the Plant Manager.
5. Inventory levels are established in conjunction with the Production Superintendent on the basis of personal judgment and past experience.
6. Plant managers have historically resented being blamed for inventory problems such as "out of stock" (averaging 5%) and returns and allowances (averaging 3%).

Cost Estimate at End	Savings Estimate at End	Actual Savings to Date
$80,000	$160,000	none

Code 4–2

SUMMARY OF SYSTEMS SURVEY

PROJECT: Inventory Control—Systems Audit

The significant findings at this time in the survey of Inventory Control are as follows:

1. The Company has historically maintained a strong customer-service policy. One of the various slogans of the Company is 24-hour replacement service anywhere in the United States.
2. There are 6,500 catalog items listed in the catalog. Spare and replacement parts are not shown in catalog. The Engineering Department records are used to service customers' requests for spare and replacement parts. Their 3 x 5 card records cover 60,000 components and subassemblies.
3. Inventory items are designated by original sales order number plus consecutive number appearing on Bill of Materials. Example: Recording paper, Code 3006–12.
4. Each plant purchases separately.
5. Buyers in purchasing departments are assigned by job orders, not by class of item.
6. Purchase specifications are prepared by Engineering departments and are not subject to revision by the purchasing function.
7. Less than 20% of items purchased are procured on an annual contract basis.

Cost Estimate at End	Savings Estimate at End	Actual Savings to Date
$85,000	$180,000	$18,300

Code 4–3

SUMMARY OF SYSTEMS SURVEY

PROJECT: Inventory Control—Systems Audit

The significant findings at this time in the survey of Inventory Control are as follows:

1. The survey shows that some 85% of the items in inventory represent only 15% of our dollar sales.
2. Items taking up 10% of our warehouse space have not moved in the last three years. Book value involved is about $500,000. These items should be studied for scrap and salvage value.
3. Inventory Control reports to the Controller and to the Purchasing Agent are both too late and not informative enough to allow appropriate financial and purchasing decisions.

Cost Estimate at End	Savings Estimate at End	Actual Savings to Date
$75,000	$185,000	$40,600

P. 246

SUMMARY OF SYSTEMS SURVEY

PROJECT: Inventory Control—Systems Audit

The significant findings at this time in the survey of Inventory Control are as follows:

1. A monthly inventory report is taken off the inventory record cards. Report is issued to the Plant Manager with a carbon copy to the Financial Officer.
2. This report is issued approximately ten days after the end of the month.
3. Inventory Control reports show the following information:
   a) Amount on hand end of last period.
   b) Amount purchased this period.
   c) Amount issued this period.
   d) Amount allocated but not issued this period.
   e) Amounts on hand at end of this period.
   f) Dollar value of ending inventory (LIFO).

Cost Estimate at End	Savings Estimate at End	Actual Savings to Date
$75,000	$185,000	$77,100

SUMMARY OF SYSTEMS SURVEY

PROJECT: Inventory Control—Systems Audit

The significant findings at this time in the survey of Inventory Control are as follows:

1. Both suburban plants manufacture roughly 50% (sales volume) to stock and 50% special order.
2. Yearly sales forecasts are for total Company, not by plants. Production control allocates orders on basis of available machine time.
3. Vendors are complaining that Company has tendency to order on a rush basis.

Cost Estimate at End	Savings Estimate at End	Actual Savings to Date
$75,000	$185,000	$110,500

P. 248

Code 4–6

Summary of Systems Survey

PROJECT: Inventory Control—Systems Audit

The following recommendations have been made to the Executive Committee:

1. There should be established a centralized Material Control Department reporting to the Director of Finance.
2. Inventory Control groups in plants should continue to report directly to Plant Production Superintendent—but would be under functional control of Material Control Department for methods and procedures to be followed.
3. Sales forecasting should be given attention as a separate study.
4. There should be immediate attention to having available sales forecasts once every three months rather than the present yearly forecast.

Cost Estimate at End	Savings Estimate at End	Actual Savings to Date
$75,000	$185,000	$152,200

SUMMARY OF SYSTEMS SURVEY

PROJECT: Inventory Control—Systems Audit

The following recommendations have been made to the Executive Committee:

1. The Systems Department, working with Sales, Engineering, and Purchasing should study the following:
   a) Standardization of component parts.
   b) Development of new classification and coding system for all materials.
   c) Vendor Relations.

Cost Estimate at End	Savings Estimate at End	Actual Savings to Date
$105,000	$190,000	$168,400

P. 250

Code 4–8

SUMMARY OF SYSTEMS SURVEY

PROJECT: Inventory Control—Systems Audit

The following actions have been taken:

1. The Executive Committee has agreed to establish a centralized Materials Control Department under the Director of Finance.
2. The Director of Marketing has been given an additional appropriation of $10,000 a year for the next three years for improving sales forecast performance.

Cost Estimate at End	Savings Estimate at End	Actual Savings to Date
$130,000	$290,000	$170,300

Code 4–9

SUMMARY OF SYSTEMS SURVEY

PROJECT: Inventory Control—Systems Audit

The following acts have been taken:

1. Obsolete materials have been removed from inventory with a scrap and salvage recovery of $50,000.
2. The Purchasing Department has made these improvements.
   a) Min-Max analysis has improved the out-of-stock situation with estimated savings in production downtime of $20,000 per year.
   b) Vendor relations have improved. It is noted that certain vendors are now willing to anticipate our orders and actually are carrying in their inventories materials formerly in ours. It is estimated that this change in attitude is worth some $40,000 per year to us.

Cost Estimate at End	Savings Estimate at End	Actual Savings to Date
$130,000	$340,000	$254,700

Code 4–10

SUMMARY OF SYSTEMS SURVEY

PROJECT: Inventory Control—Systems Audit

The following results have been obtained from the Inventory Control–Systems Audit study:

1. General coordination among departments has improved.
2. More attention to the importance of inventory costs has been reflected in associated areas such as:
   a) Space utilization.
   b) Engineering design.
   c) In-process spoilage.

Cost Estimate at End	*Savings Estimate at End*	*Actual Savings to Date*
$130,000	*$340,000*	*$350,800*

Code 5–1

SUMMARY OF SYSTEMS SURVEY

PROJECT: Typing Pool

The significant findings at this time regarding the Typing Pool problem are:

1. The meeting referred to was held January 11, 12 and 13 in New York City. It was a workshop entitled "Office Overhead—How to Keep the Roof from Falling in."
2. The typing and steno pool reports were made by two companies, neither in our industry; both with clerical employment at least twice ours.
3. Be this as it may, both the speakers and the current literature support the idea that savings are probable at our level of employment.
4. Further investigation seems advisable.

Cost Estimate at End	Savings Estimate at End	Actual Savings to Date
$100,000	$300,000	none

P. 254

SUMMARY OF SYSTEMS SURVEY

PROJECT: Typing Pool

The significant findings at this time regarding the Typing Pool problem are:

1. It now develops that the Advertising and Public Relations Departments have been using a typing and stenographic pool for approximately two years. Their results have been very satisfactory.
2. The problems have not been technical. In fact, with the active assistance of equipment manufacturers, such problems as dictating capacity were quickly dissolved. The Industrial Engineering Department has provided each with a very flexible and attractive stenographic pool layout.
3. Personnel problems dominated the early days. Central were those involving reassignment of personnel with apparent loss of status or position.
4. The "girls" were sold on a "trial basis for six months." The presentation emphasized the more even distribution of work and the possibility for more and varied work assignment.
5. The administrative problems of pick up and distribution of work were easily worked out. These have been written up in considerable detail.
6. Other department managers have expressed growing interest in this technique.

Cost Estimate at End	Savings Estimate at End	Actual Savings to Date
$100,000	$250,000	$3,000

Summary of Systems Survey

Project: Typing Pool

The following results have been obtained from the Typing Pool study:

1. A complete write-up on the Company experience with typing pools has been prepared; it incorporates the trials and successes of the Advertising and Public Relations Departments.
2. This write-up has been circulated to major clerical area managers.

Cost Estimate at End	Savings Estimate at End	Actual Savings to Date
$100,000	$200,000	$121,800

Code 5–4

SUMMARY OF SYSTEMS SURVEY

PROJECT: Typing Pool

The following results have been obtained from the Typing Pool study:

1. Merger of department pools should receive study at a later date.
2. No further activity is required at this time.

Cost Estimate at End	Savings Estimate at End	Actual Savings to Date
$100,000	$200,000	$141,900

SUMMARY OF SYSTEMS SURVEY

PROJECT: Policy Formulation and Compliance

The significant findings at this time in the survey of Policy problems are as follows:

1. A policy manual is used in our factory operations to guide foremen and factory management in carrying out Company policies with relation to factory employees. This manual covers, among other things, the proper administration of our agreements with the union.
2. In Sales and Finance Divisions there is a written manual which is used by the branch sales offices. The manual instructs branch personnel how to carry out their various functions.

Cost Estimate at End	Savings Estimate at End	Actual Savings to Date
$150,000	$400,000	none

P. 264

Code 6–2

S<small>UMMARY OF</small> S<small>YSTEMS</small> S<small>URVEY</small>

P<small>ROJECT</small>: Policy Formulation and Compliance

The significant findings at this time in the survey of Policy problems are as follows:

1. In the other divisions of the Company some policies are written, but distribution is limited.
2. It would appear that there is a high degree of informality in determining and implementing policy in the Corporation. This often causes trouble in carrying out system study recommendations.

Cost Estimate at End	Savings Estimate at End	Actual Savings to Date
$200,000	$450,000	$9,800

SUMMARY OF SYSTEMS SURVEY

PROJECT: Policy Formulation and Compliance

The significant findings at this time in the survey of Policy problems are as follows:

1. The organization change that led to the formation of the Executive Committee was based upon the recognition of need for improved development of policy in the Corporation.
2. The committee through its assignment of this problem to the Systems Department is asking for a rather comprehensive analysis into policy concepts.

Cost Estimate at End	Savings Estimate at End	Actual Savings to Date
$200,000	$450,000	$14,300

Code 6–4

SUMMARY OF SYSTEMS SURVEY

PROJECT: Policy Formulation and Compliance

The following actions have taken place with regard to the Policy study:

1. A survey has been made to collect, sort and classify that which now exists in the area of written policy.
2. The attached sheet, covering 48 management problem classifications, has been developed as a framework for separating policies.

Cost Estimate at End	Savings Estimate at End	Actual Savings to Date
$250,000	$650,000	$42,700

INDUSTRIAL MANAGEMENT POLICY AREAS
Classifications for Information Requirements Analysis

1. History of Management
2. Top Management Executives Research Approaches
3. Economics of American Industry (Industry Characteristics and Statistics)
4. Executive Planning and Control
5. Organization Concepts, Methods, and Procedures
6. Controllership
7. Finance
8. Pricing and Estimating
9. Accounting
10. Travel and Expense Accounts
11. Systems and Procedures (Industrial Engineering–Office)
12. Business Operations
13. Legal Service
14. Mathematical Tools for Management
15. Product Design and Development Engineering
16. Design (Technical Service to Line Departments); Also Closely Related to Research
17. Design of Machinery
18. Operative Planning and Control (Industrial Engineering–Shop)
19. Plant Location
20. Facilities Utilization
21. Property Management and Control
22. Labor Law
23. Personnel—Industrial Relations and Labor Relations
24. Employment Stabilization
25. Selection, Placement and Promotion, Discharge, Retirement, and Training
26. Collective Bargaining Employee Representation
27. Wage and Salary Administration
28. Fringe Benefits
29. Employee Stock Ownership and Profit Sharing
30. Employee Morale and Group Opinion—Leadership
31. Supervisors of Direct Workers—Supervisory Training
32. Grievance Procedure—Discipline

33. Working Conditions	41. Warehousing and Stores
34. Personnel Records	42. Production Control
35. Employees' Programs	43. Production Execution
36. Safety	44. Quality Control
37. Supply	45. Distribution
38. Purchasing	46. Sales Operation and Management
39. Traffic	47. Delivery of Product to Purchasers
40. Receiving	48. Collection and Credit Work

P. 268

Summary of Systems Survey

Project: Policy Formulation and Compliance

The following actions have taken place:

1. A presentation has been made to the Executive Committee using the attached diagram (Configuration of Scope of Cycle of Policy Formulation and Compliance) to highlight the elements felt to be significant for further study.
2. The Executive Committee feels the study is progressing well and would like it to continue.

Cost Estimate at End	Savings Estimate at End	Actual Savings to Date
$270,000	$680,000	$78,900

Code 6–5 (cont.)

CONFIGURATION OF SCOPE OF CYCLE OF POLICY FORMULATION AND
COMPLIANCE

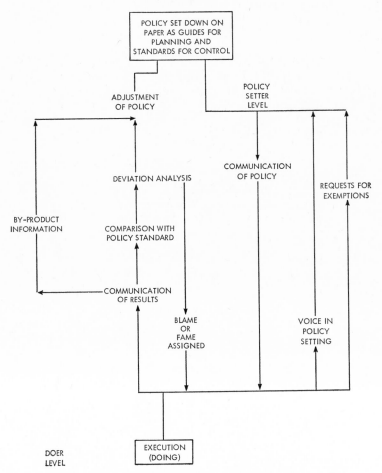

P. 270

SUMMARY OF SYSTEMS SURVEY

PROJECT: Policy Formulation and Compliance

The following actions have taken place:

1. The Executive Committee asked for a basic statement that it could use to acquaint all levels of management with the importance of well-thought-out policies.
2. The following statement was presented to and accepted by the Executive Committee:

   A well-developed policy framework often determines the success or failure of a company. Explicit policies communicated and followed up provide consistency and continuity of action among the members of the management team. This Company is building its policy framework on the following concept:

   For every policy set in this Company there is an associated value received and an associated cost incurred. A good policy must stand the test of value above cost.

Cost Estimate at End	Savings Estimate at End	Actual Savings to Date
$270,000	$700,000	$121,100

SUMMARY OF SYSTEMS SURVEY

PROJECT: Policy Formulation and Compliance

The following actions have taken place:

A procedure has been set up for the Executive Committee meetings:

1. Problems are collected and arranged in agenda for meetings according to priority ranking.
2. Appropriate information is brought to the meetings to match the problems being discussed.
3. Minutes of the meetings are analyzed, sorting out policies, procedures, and responsibilities assigned in the organization.
4. These policies, procedures, and responsibilities are kept up-to-date in a central information center supervised by the Secretary of the Executive Committee.

Cost Estimate at End	Savings Estimate at End	Actual Savings to Date
$230,000	$700,000	$213,200

P. 272

Code 6–8

SUMMARY OF SYSTEMS SURVEY

PROJECT: Policy Formulation and Compliance

The following results have been obtained from the Policy Study:

1. There exists a feeling of greater confidence in management throughout the Company.
2. There has been a reduction of interdepartmental frictions.
3. Systems study recommendations are being received and put into
   practice more readily.

The Executive Committee estimates that the new approach to policy
setting has a "scale value" * of $800,000 to the Company.

Cost Estimate at End	Savings Estimate at End	Actual Savings to Date
$230,000	$800,000	$800,000

* An estimate of what the Company would have been willing to pay (for
example, to an outside consultant) to obtain such improvements in the Company.

P. 273

Code 7–1

SUMMARY OF SYSTEMS SURVEY

PROJECT: Automatic Factory Study

The significant findings at this time in the survey of the Automatic Factory are as follows:

Systems personnel have been assembling literature on the "Automatic Factory." Several copies of Goode and Machol's book on Control Systems Engineering have been ordered.

Cost Estimate at End	Savings Estimate at End	Actual Savings to Date
?	?	none

SUMMARY OF SYSTEMS SURVEY

PROJECT: Automatic Factory Study

The significant findings at this time in the survey of the Automatic Factory are as follows:

Two basic approaches appear to have been used in the automatic factory developments:
1. Automatic-component-assembly.
   Used primarily to handle and position accurately small components for assembly. Equipment is operated by card or tape instruction.
2. Modular design.
   Components are manufactured during assembly. Equipment is mechanized to form, cut, trim, and assemble—gradually building up modules from subassemblies and components.
   Both systems focus on printed circuits and the use of dip soldering.

Cost Estimate at End	Savings Estimate at End	Actual Savings to Date
$250,000	$750,000	$3,500

SUMMARY OF SYSTEMS SURVEY

PROJECT: Automatic Factory Study

The significant findings at this time in the survey of the Automatic Factory are as follows:

Several meetings have been held with the Engineering Department. These meetings have been of the seminar format—with discussion of what various companies have done so far in the development of "automatic factories."

Cost Estimate at End	Savings Estimate at End	Actual Savings to Date
$250,000	$750,000	$5,300

P. 276

Code 7–4

SUMMARY OF SYSTEMS SURVEY

PROJECT: Automatic Factory Study

The significant findings at this time in the survey of the Automatic Factory are as follows:

Meetings continuing.

Cost Estimate at End	Savings Estimate at End	Actual Savings to Date
$250,000	$750,000	$7,100

SUMMARY OF SYSTEMS SURVEY

PROJECT: Automatic Factory Study

The significant findings at this time in the survey of the Automatic Factory are as follows:

Meetings continuing.

Cost Estimate at End	Savings Estimate at End	Actual Savings to Date
$250,000	$750,000	$8,000

P. 278

SUMMARY OF SYSTEMS SURVEY

PROJECT: Automatic Factory Study

The significant findings at this time in the survey of the Automatic Factory are as follows:

Meetings continuing.

Cost Estimate at End	Savings Estimate at End	Actual Savings to Date
$250,000	$750,000	$9,200

Summary of Systems Survey

Project: Automatic Factory Study

The significant findings at this time in the survey of the Automatic Factory are as follows:

1. Meetings continuing.
2. Analysis of component modular assembly being carried on by Engineering Department.

Cost Estimate at End	Savings Estimate at End	Actual Savings to Date
$250,000	$750,000	$12,800

SUMMARY OF SYSTEMS SURVEY

PROJECT: Automatic Factory Study

The significant findings at this time in the survey of the Automatic Factory are as follows:

1. Instrument housings and enclosures now being studied for standardization possibilities.
2. Similar study being made of electrical connectors.

Cost Estimate at End	Savings Estimate at End	Actual Savings to Date
$250,000	$750,000	$15,700

Code 7–9

SUMMARY OF SYSTEMS SURVEY

PROJECT: Automatic Factory Study

The following results have been obtained from the Automatic Factory study:

1. Several instrument prototypes have been made using ideas developed during the Automatic Factory study.
2. The Sales Department is exploring possibilities for marketing of these equipments.
3. Production Control and Purchasing are preparing reports on the impact that automatic factory operations would have in their areas of responsibility.

Cost Estimate at End	Savings Estimate at End	Actual Savings to Date
$250,000	$750,000	$17,900

P. 282

SUMMARY OF SYSTEMS SURVEY

PROJECT: Automatic Factory Study

The following results have been obtained from the Automatic Factory study:

1. A government agency has approved a "standby" arrangement to underwrite the installation of a complete assembly facility using the ideas developed during the Automatic Factory Study.
2. This arrangement (plus the confidence of the Executive Committee in the future of these new approaches to product development) has been the basis of the "scale value" * of $840,000 assigned to this study.

Cost Estimate at End	Savings Estimate at End	Actual Savings to Date
$25,000	$840,000	$842,100

* An estimate of what the Company would have been willing to pay (for example, to an outside consultant) to obtain such improvements in the Company.

SUMMARY OF SYSTEMS SURVEY

PROJECT: Executive Information Display Center

The project team has made several visitations to organizations who are using visual displays of information. The two most interesting trips were to the Much-Merged City Bank and the Fly-by-Night Airlines.

Bank personnel were very enthusiastic about the use of closed-circuit TV displays as used by the bank tellers for verifying customers' accounts. Fly-by-Night Airlines uses visual displays for information retrieval in their reservations system. They also have an impressive arrangement that displays, on a large screen, a complete set of information showing the flight schedules and relevant situations for all routes. This includes weather conditions, passenger loads, and time until next maintenance is required.

Cost Estimate at End	Savings Estimate at End	Actual Savings to Date
?	$600,000	none

Code 8–2

SUMMARY OF SYSTEMS SURVEY

PROJECT: Executive Information Display System

It appears that the Executive Conference Room is the most appropriate location for the Executive Information Display System. The small stockroom adjoining the conference room can be used to locate projection equipment for "back-projecting" data to show in the Conference Room.

Plant Engineering has estimated that they could make the necessary alterations in these two rooms for under $5,000. We are checking to see how much it will cost to hook-up this conference room display with our computer center located three miles away at our No. 2 Plant. We have also asked the At-Your-Elbow Computer Company to prepare a preliminary estimate of what a standard installation will cost.

Cost Estimate at End	Savings Estimate at End	Actual Savings to Date
$70,000	$600,000	$5,000

SUMMARY OF SYSTEMS SURVEY

PROJECT: Executive Information Display System

The Telephone Company has asked us to estimate the traffic we can expect on the tie-line between the conference room and the No. 2 Plant Computer Center.

The Computer Company has asked us to provide a set of specifications for the volume and variety of information that will be displayed.

We are now going to our executives and asking them to tell us the answers to these questions.

Cost Estimate at End	Savings Estimate at End	Actual Savings to Date
$100,000	$800,000	$7,000

P. 286

SUMMARY OF SYSTEMS SURVEY

PROJECT: Executive Information Display System

The Management Systems Department Manager was asked to report on progress on this project at the Quarterly Review Meeting on the Board of Directors. After several discussions with the Executive Vice President, it was agreed that such a briefing would be premature and it was postponed until the next Review Meeting.

Cost Estimate at End	Savings Estimate at End	Actual Savings to Date
$150,000	$600,000	$8,000

To: Systems Department Manager

FROM: Chairman, Executive Committee

SUBJECT: Executive Information Display System

Due to the pressures of other priority work, none of the members of the Executive Committee have been able to prepare statements of their information needs. This project will be inactivated until further notice.

Cost Estimate at End	Savings Estimate at End	Actual Savings to Date
$150,000	$200,000	$10,000

P. 293

Code 9–1

Summary of Systems Survey

Project: Clerical Work Measurement

The significant findings at this time in the survey of Clerical Work Measurement are as follows:

1. Consultant's "price tag" is $50,000 for installation of their system (called M.C.T.—measured clerical time). Price includes training of two SMART employees in application of their data.
2. Number of clerical employees has risen 300% in last 10 years—up to 10% mark in last year.
3. No Company clerical operations are measured.
4. Approximately 20% of factory operations are on "measured day work" but none on incentive.
5. Factory standards are administered by the Industrial Engineering Department. But there has not been any widening of coverage during past 3–5 years.
6. No work method or work measurement has been done in the clerical area.

Cost Estimate at End	Savings Estimate at End	Actual Savings to Date
$100,000	$300,000	$52,600

SUMMARY OF SYSTEMS SURVEY

PROJECT: Clerical Work Measurement

The significant findings at this time in the survey of Clerical Work Measurement are as follows:

1. Local wages and salary survey shows that SMART Company earnings for typical clerical position are 10% higher than area average, but actual base rates are in line. This is interpreted to mean that "overtime" is pushing up actual earnings.
2. Survey is an annual affair based on written job descriptions—no on-the-job verification of duties.
3. There are no clerical labor unions in the city, nor have any organizing attempts been made.
4. Approximately 30% of the "non-exempt" weekly employees are "SMART Vets"; i.e., have in excess of 10 years with Company.
5. Personnel Department reports indicate low turnover and absenteeism among clerical employees.
6. There is no discernible dissatisfaction with major clerical operations, such as accounting and billing.
7. The Company has fostered a "security of employment" sentiment. There are few discharges and no layoffs of clerical workers.

Cost Estimate at End	Savings Estimate at End	Actual Savings to Date
$100,000	$300,000	$101,900

Pp. 295 to 302

Code 9–3

SUMMARY OF SYSTEMS SURVEY

PROJECT: Clerical Work Measurement

The significant findings at this time in the survey of Clerical Work Measurement are as follows:

1. The following report was submitted to management:
   In response to your request we submit the following answers:
   a) The prediction of the consulting firm is probably conservative. This source has tremendous savings potential.
   b) The present Company personnel is not qualified to undertake such an installation without further training of staff industrial engineers. Development of reliable Company data could run well in excess of $50,000.
   c) It is suggested that this type of study be postponed because:
      1) There is little, if any, management interest or enthusiasm for this project.
      2) The effect of employee morale would be significant.
      3) Wider coverage of production jobs would probably give better results because of the numbers of employees involved and the existing talents of the Industrial Engineering Department.

It is recommended that the offer of the consultant be declined.

Cost Estimate at End	Savings Estimate at End	Actual Savings to Date
$70,000	$150,000	$107,600

SUMMARY OF SYSTEMS SURVEY

PROJECT: Self-Service Stockroom

The significant findings at this time regarding the Self-Service Stockroom problem are:

1. The self-service type stockroom was introduced by General Electric and Bell Telephone Labs just prior to World War II. It was designed after the supermarket self-service idea, with the first thought being to provide the best service to the customer.
2. These companies found that this type of stocking operation was best suited to the Research and Development phase of an organization.
3. It is quite possible that our present engineering and experimental stockrooms could be set up on a self-service basis.

Cost Estimate at End	Savings Estimate at End	Actual Savings to Date
$90,000	$220,000	$11,200

P. 304

Code 10–2

SMALL CAPS Summary of Systems Survey

Project: Self-Service Stockroom

The significant findings at this time regarding the Self-Service Stockroom problem are:

1. A survey has shown that there is much dormant inventory in the various engineering projects.
2. A plan has been designed to have Self-Service Stockrooms set up in each plant.
3. It is estimated that $25,000 is the total valuation of inventory needed in each of the three self-service stockrooms to support the particular plant's engineering group.

Cost Estimate at End	Savings Estimate at End	Actual Savings to Date
$90,000	$220,000	$29,900

SUMMARY OF SYSTEMS SURVEY

PROJECT: Self-Service Stockroom

The significant findings at this time regarding the Self-Service Stockroom problem are:

1. Present book value of engineering materials is shown as $20,000 per plant.
2. Physical inventories in each of the stockrooms of the three plants show inventories as follows:

Plant No. 1: $25,000
Plant No. 2:   27,000
Plant No. 3:   23,000
         ——————
         $75,000   Total Engineering
                   Materials Inventory

Cost Estimate at End	Savings Estimate at End	Actual Savings to Date
$90,000	$220,000	$51,500

P. 306

Summary of Systems Survey

Project: Self-Service Stockroom

The significant findings at this time regarding the Self-Service Stockroom problem are:

1. Further study shows that the major part of engineering material stock is not kept in the stockrooms—but rather is spread out over testroom shelves and in the desks and cabinets of engineers.

Cost Estimate at End	Savings Estimate at End	Actual Savings to Date
$90,000	$220,000	$76,400

Code 10–5

SUMMARY OF SYSTEMS SURVEY

PROJECT: Self-Service Stockroom

The significant findings at this time regarding the Self-Service Stock-room problem are:

1. An estimate of engineering materials not kept in stockrooms is $120,000 overall for the company.

Cost Estimate at End	Savings Estimate at End	Actual Savings to Date
$90,000	$220,000	$104,100

Code 10–6

SUMMARY OF SYSTEMS SURVEY

PROJECT: Self-Service Stockroom

The significant findings at this time regarding the Self-Service Stock-room problem are:

The Engineering Department has explained the situation of high engineering materials inventory as follows:

The ultimate goal of having engineering materials is to give the best possible service to support engineers in profit-making design. Engineers need to have components for experimental models and prototypes. Ideas are generated by having components readily available. Thus, a natural reason exists for the engineer to accumulate an "inventory." We agree there must be controls—at the same time, we ask that the controls over engineering materials do not go to the point of making the engineer "guess" what the parts look like.

Cost Estimate at End	Savings Estimate at End	Actual Savings to Date
$90,000	$220,000	$148,300

Code 10–7

SUMMARY OF SYSTEMS SURVEY

PROJECT: Self-Service Stockroom

The following actions have taken place:

1. The self-service stockrooms are now guided by a committee representing Engineering, Accounting, Purchasing, and Systems Departments.
2. This Committee has developed a core of items to be kept in the self-service stockrooms by analyzing withdrawals over a period.
3. Displays have been installed in these rooms for the purpose of showing new items to engineers for possible use.
4. "Can you use this in your design?" placards are being placed on non-moving items for a period, and then these items are considered for salvage or scrap.

Cost Estimate at End	Savings Estimate at End	Actual Savings to Date
$90,000	$220,000	$175,800

SUMMARY OF SYSTEMS SURVEY

PROJECT: Self-Service Stockroom

The following results have been obtained from the Self-Service Stockroom:

1. Engineering Materials Inventory has been reduced from $195,000 to $75,000.
2. Engineers, though not satisfied, have been much more cooperative in reducing their "private stores."
3. Engineers have found the displays to be very helpful in acquainting them with new materials and associated ideas.

Cost Estimate at End	Savings Estimate at End	Actual Savings to Date
$90,000	*$280,000*	*$268,700*

APPENDIX B

QUESTIONS FOR CHAPTER 1 (SCOPE OF MANAGEMENT SYSTEMS)

1. Why is the proportion of white-collar jobs increasing in the labor force? What impact does this have on the processing of information?
2. How do white-collar jobs differ basically from jobs involving physical labor? Relate your answer to the recent growth of mechanization or automation in the office.
3. As mechanization and automation increase in an office, what new problems may have to be considered?
4. Why is it so difficult to define "a system"?
5. Does a system have to work effectively to be a system?
6. What forces are at work which encourage the search for more effective systems in business management?
7. What are some of the limitations to the integration of business systems?
8. Why must good systems design be a prime responsibility of *all* management?

QUESTIONS FOR CHAPTER 2 (CHARACTERISTICS OF AN ORGANIZATION/INFORMATION STRUCTURE)

1. What are the key relations of organization analysis and systems analysis?
2. How can information systems help to provide flexibility and adjustment to changes in an organization?
3. What is involved in the meshing of authority and information in an organization? Do information systems conflict with authority systems? Explain.
4. The design of an information system is generally relegated to staff personnel. What problems are likely to arise from this and why? What suggestions can you make for an approach to overcome these problems?
5. Distinguish between "paper work" and a management decision. How are these two connected?
6. If we had a perfect information system, would we still need managers? Explain.

7. Why should a variety of people be involved in a systems study? Can there be basic changes in a data processing system without there being created a need to make changes in the organization structure? Explain.

8. Coordination as a requisite for effective management is now being extended to include coordinating of both people and the systems with which they work. How does an organization coordinate among its systems?

QUESTIONS FOR CHAPTER 3 (THE INFORMATION PRODUCTION APPROACH)

1. Mass production of physical products has been a source of pride to American industry. Do you believe that the mass production of business information can also be a source of pride to American industry? Explain.

2. What considerations favor the use of an end-product-oriented systems approach to information?

3. What is management planning and control information? How does it differ from data used to process such things as pay checks and purchase requisitions?

4. What is meant by the "production of information"? How large is the market for this production?

5. Explain why it is advantageous to get data in a form suitable for processing as a by-product of another operation.

6. Do you believe that a problem which is well-defined is half-solved? How does this reasoning influence the setting of the objectives for a systems study?

7. Can the same data that are used for day-to-day operations of a business also be used for management planning and control? Explain.

8. How does data that go into management reports differ from those which go into operating systems?

QUESTIONS FOR CHAPTER 4 (CASE STUDY: THE SMART CORPORATION)

1. How would you design this game so that individual differences of analysts' abilities could be identified and considered in assigning manpower to projects?

2. In the SMART Corporation Case you were asked to assign priorities to various projects by means of the dollars you were willing to assign to salaries on these projects. What were you getting for these salaries? How could you determine whether or not you had set good priorities?

3. What is meant by the statement, "A good system is always a compromise"?

4. Was money your only criterion in selection of projects? What other criteria could you have used?

5. In the design of this game, projects were not interacting; i.e., each was studied separately. In practice, which of the SMART projects do you think would have influence on other projects?

6. Why did you work on the Executive Information Display System? Or, why did you not work on this project?

7. Under what circumstances would it be appropriate for management to use a budget formula that includes a factor that is *three* or *four* times the costs of salaries?

8. Is it true that in an actual organization you would have had very little difficulty in getting the facts for your priority selection of projects? Explain.

QUESTIONS FOR CHAPTER 5 (CLASSIFICATION AND CODING APPROACHES)

1. Why are classifications so important to systems designers?

2. Who should be responsible for the classifications which are used in an organization?

3. How does an analyst determine the breadth of coverage that should be in a classification system?

4. Why do useful classifications emphasize both similarities and differences?

5. What are the limitations to the refining of classifications, i.e., the degree of detail in the system?

6. Codes provide for the compression of data. Why is this important in the design of systems?

7. How do codes relate to classifications?

8. What "price is paid" for the advantages of using codes?

QUESTIONS FOR CHAPTER 6 (INTRODUCTION TO DOCUMENTATION)

1. Why is evidence important in a court of law?

2. Why is evidence important in the development of a management information system?

3. All business information should be keyed to the kinds of problems with which a particular business must cope. Explain how you would go about making an analysis to survey and provide a continuing record of the most important problems of a business.

4. In which phases of systems development is it more difficult to provide documented evidence?

5. Why does documentation expand as a study moves through the phases of systems development?

6. What are the problems of keeping a systems documentation up-to-date?
7. What can be done to improve the quality of an organization's documentation of systems?
8. What are the merits of a Documentation Manual?
9. Is documentation useful as evidence only after the system is designed? Explain.

QUESTIONS FOR CHAPTER 7 (SETTING SYSTEMS PRIORITIES)

1. Define a management priority.
2. Why are priorities necessary in the design of management information systems?
3. How are management priorities expressed?
4. It has been remarked that management is a "guessing game." Under what circumstances can it be? What can management information systems do to reduce the amount of guessing?
5. Evaluate the following statement: "It is worthwhile to treat problem definition as a continuing activity during a study."
6. Why are both criteria and weights required in the use of priorities?
7. What are the relationships between the following pairs of terms?
   a) Classification and Priorities
   b) Documentation and Problem Definitions
8. What part do people in authority play in the setting of priorities for the study of management information systems?

QUESTIONS FOR CHAPTER 8 (INFORMATION REQUIREMENTS DESIGN)

1. Why is Information Requirements Design called Extended Problem Definition?
2. Why not collect all the information that management can use?
3. What requirements are placed on higher level management as they decide to improve their management information systems?
4. How would you go about determining a particular manager's information needs?
5. Why is it so difficult to decide precisely which data to gather and to store for use in the future? To repeat, what is meant by the statement that "a good system is always a compromise"?
6. Discuss the following quotation: "I know of no case where getting information faster can be justified on the grounds of cost savings."
7. What is meant by the statement that information informs only when there is a recognized need to know?

8. If you were asked to improve the Key Information Content Classifications, what classes would you add or substitute?
9. Why do information-need classifications expand so fast as we try to get to the specific requirements of a manager?

QUESTIONS FOR CHAPTER 9 (SYSTEMS DESIGN)

1. Describe the primary factors in making a systems analysis.
2. Why is the flow charting technique so widely used in the phase of systems design?
3. Why do we use flow charts with varying degrees of detail in them?
4. What are the advantages of standardized flow chart symbols? Are there any disadvantages?
5. What do we mean when we say a flow chart is a picture of a system? What does such a picture show? What are its limitations?
6. Explain how flow charts relate to organization charts.
7. Why is the study of relationships important in the design of business systems? What types of relationships are important?
8. Evaluate the following statement: "With more of a dependence upon computer-based information reporting, executives will seek to control or 'own' the more significant parts of the data-storage scheme. Each will attempt to build data input, data assembly, and information output in the image of his responsibility." What does this mean to the designer?

QUESTIONS FOR CHAPTER 10 (PROGRAMMING DESIGN BACKGROUND)

1. What is a computer worth? What does a computer cost? How would you go about finding out?
2. "A computer is simply a substitute for clerical workers and not a very good one." Agree or disagree, but defend your position.
3. How does one "stay ahead of the machine" in a management job? Under what circumstances can a computer "replace" a manager?
4. Describe the major components of a digital computer. What contribution does each of these make to the processing of data?
5. What determines the type of input-output equipment that is selected in a particular installation?
6. Can only large organizations make use of computers? Explain.
7. What is more important—speed of a computer or accuracy of a computer? Under what circumstances?
8. Why do computers have such large memories? Discuss how a computer memory might differ from a human memory.

QUESTIONS FOR CHAPTER 11 (PROGRAMMING DESIGN APPLICATION)

1. Why treat a computer as a problem in languages?
2. What is meant by a "character" of data? How is this term used to describe capacity of computer equipment?
3. Can decisions of a computer be shown in a flow chart? Can a machine make a decision? Explain.
4. Explain why measures of work loads are important in systems analysis.
5. Why must the manager, the systems designer, and the programmer work closely together?
6. In the candidate matching systems design, what was meant by the "logic of the system"?
7. Why does the file maintenance routine appear in so many management information systems?
8. How does the designer determine what he will program as "exceptions" in his system?

QUESTIONS FOR CHAPTER 12 (SYSTEMS OPERATIONS: DAY-TO-DAY PRODUCTION)

1. What does it take to go from a systems flow chart to an operating computer system?
2. Why should a manager worry about the incompatibility of data from one piece of equipment to another?
3. What information should be in the management information system that is used to manage a computer center?
4. How should performance be measured in a computer center?
5. To what degree is the planning and control for day-to-day-operations of an information system similar to the planning and control in manufacturing physical products? To what degree are they different?
6. What does Quality Control mean in a computer center?
7. Does a systems designer have any responsibility for the operating phase of systems?
8. Why is documentation so important in the day-to-day computer operations?

QUESTIONS FOR CHAPTER 13 (OUTPUT FORMAT AND DISPLAY)

1. How does information display relate to the problems of management priorities and criteria selection?
2. "The computer forced management to clean up its data inputs; the

information display console will force management to clean up its information outputs." Discuss.

3. Knowledge has been defined as a structure made of elements in certain relationships and assembled with certain weights. What is the importance of weights in knowledge?

4. How do quantities enter into a piece of information? How do quantities differ from other identifier elements that go to make up a piece of information?

5. Why is it so difficult to decide precisely which data to gather and to store for use in the future?

6. With computers, does the need for the following management tools increase or decrease? Explain.
    a) Work Measurement
    b) Work Simplification
    c) Forms Design
    d) Record Retention Analysis

7. Define the following terms and discuss how they *relate to* office mechanization and automation:
    a) Transfer of data between various types of equipment
    b) Quality of input data
    c) Quantity of input data

8a. What is meant by the concept of centralization and decentralization of authority?

8b. How are management information systems involved in the determination of appropriate degrees of centralization and decentralization?

QUESTIONS FOR CHAPTER 14 (FEEDBACK AND EVALUATION OF SYSTEMS EFFECTIVENESS)

1. There are no inexpensive computers. On what possible bases might a computer installation be justified? Explain.

2. Why do we talk about the goals of a business in the plural? What is the significance of this in the design of management information systems?

3. Who should set the criteria for the design of a management information system? Explain.

4. What part do criteria play in the design of a management information system—especially, what do criteria have to do with systems values and measurement?

5. How are "feedback" and "exception reporting" related? How should "exceptions" be determined for a management information system?

6. Describe the changes that take place in the kinds of problems for which a manager is responsible as he is promoted up through the ranks of an organization. How do these changes influence the characteristics of the

criteria that a manager will use in his decision making? What is the relationship of criteria to the information needs of a manager at any level of the organization?

7. In practice, how would you go about selecting the criteria that should be used in designing the output of a particular management system? How would you test to see if these were good criteria?

8. Evaluate the following statement: "The more abstract and dynamic the problems an organization absorbs, the greater part autocratic decision must play." What problems does this statement suggest to the systems designer?

9. How are business criteria influenced by:
   a) organization level?
   b) the time span of decision for a manager?
   c) uncertainty in the manager's problems?

QUESTIONS FOR CHAPTER 15 (MANAGEMENT SYSTEMS: REVIEW AND SUMMARY)

1. Present an abstract of one of the chapters of this book. Indicate why you believe there is more "information" in your abstract than in the original reading.

2. How do management information systems give an organization "a strength and resilience to accomplish its selected missions"?

3. Are people not more important than systems? Do not some systems take over the work of people? Then how do we justify the expanding use of systems?

4. How should a management make decisions regarding the rate at which it should improve its management information systems?

5. What limitations presently exist with regard to the types of problems that can be handled with computer-based systems?

6. Are we running out of questions because the computer is now giving us all the answers? In the SMART case did you have more, or fewer, questions at the end of the third play?

7. How do talents and techniques blend together in the design and operation of management information systems?

8. "A technique is the documentation of talent." Explain.

9. Can technique get far ahead of talent? Under what circumstances? Can talent be limited by lack of technique? Under what circumstances?

INDEX

321

This book has been set on the Linotype in 11 and 10 point Times Roman, leaded 1 point. Chapter numbers and titles are in 18 point Bodoni #375 italics. The size of the type page is 27 by 45 picas.